WILD
WASATCH
FRONT

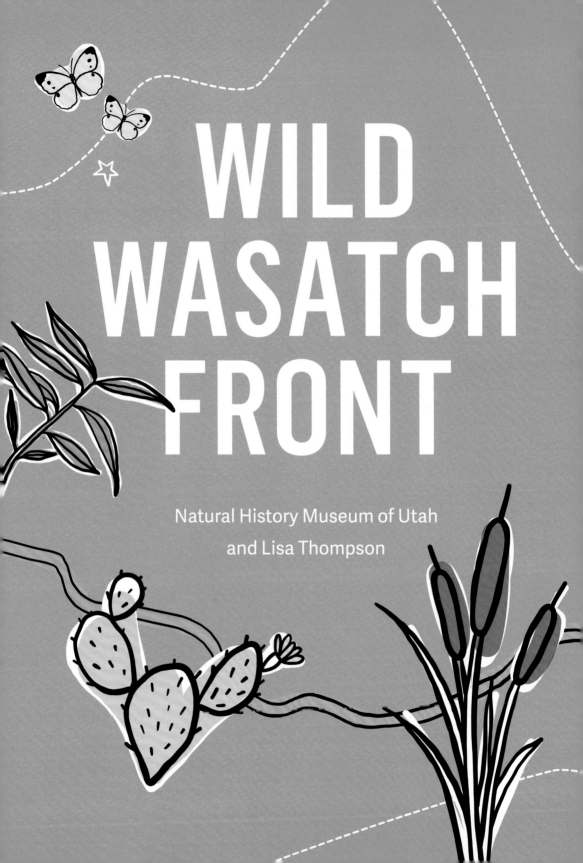

WILD WASATCH FRONT

Natural History Museum of Utah

and Lisa Thompson

EXPLORE THE AMAZING NATURE
IN AND AROUND
SALT LAKE CITY

TIMBER PRESS
PORTLAND, OR

Dedicated to all the wild plants and animals
that are part of our communities
and to the people who take the time
to get to know their wild neighbors

Published in 2024 by Timber Press, Inc.,
a subsidiary of Workman Publishing Co., Inc.,
a subsidiary of Hachette Book Group, Inc.
1290 Avenue of the Americas
New York, New York 10104

timberpress.com

Printed in China on responsibly sourced paper
Text and cover design by Leigh Thomas,
based on a series design by Anna Eshelman
Cover illustration by Casey Clifford

The publisher is not responsible for websites
(or their content) that are not owned by the publisher.

The Hachette Speakers Bureau provides a wide range of
authors for speaking events. To find out more, go to
hachettespeakersbureau.com or email HachetteSpeakers@hbgusa.com.

ISBN 978-1-64326-080-8
A catalog record for this book is available from the Library of Congress.

CONTENTS

FOREWORD

We are immersed in nature. It's all around us. Utah, with its tremendous ecological diversity, offers fantastic opportunities to explore nature in major biomes ranging from deserts to wetlands and along elevational gradients from mid-elevation forests to high-elevation alpine zones. The specialized flora and fauna of these varied ecosystems inspire discovery in the wild places of our state. We tend to consider the nature around us every day—the nature where we live—less often. Most of Utah's human populations live in urban centers, but even in developed landscapes, nature is there—often in surprising ways.

The Natural History Museum of Utah illuminates the natural world and the place of humans within it. We recognize that not only are we immersed in nature, but we are part of it. We find beauty in Utah's natural environments—in the brightly colored spring blooms of a desert plant, the camouflaging white winter coat of a forest-dwelling ermine, and the agile flight of a patrolling wetlands dragonfly. But we also find wonder in the state's built and managed environments—the unassuming land snails in our gardens, the industrious squirrels in our city parks, and the inquisitive magpies just about everywhere.

With this urban nature guide, inspired by the "Nature All Around Us" exhibit developed at the museum, we hope to nurture your curiosity about our natural world and stimulate exploration and discovery of life in all its forms and all its places. Focusing on the habitats and biodiversity found in Utah's urban environments, this guide offers helpful biological information about many of the plant and animal species often encountered in cities and towns along the Wasatch Front—how to identify these species and where and when they are likely to be seen. Within each species account are stories that we hope will help illustrate the plant's or animal's connection to humans and illuminate our place within the natural world.

The Natural History Museum of Utah is all about science. Many of the species included in this guide are also represented in the museum's natural history research collections—preserved specimens that document where and when these species occurred in Utah. With the museum's emphasis on investigating and sustaining biodiversity, our researchers—often and increasingly with help from citizen scientists—study how plant and animal species have moved from place to place and how their populations have

▼ There's no line where nature stops and cities begin. Whether hiking a trail in the foothills or strolling down your street, you can meet dozens of species of wild plants and animals in cities along the Wasatch Front.

changed through time. These investigations yield important insight into how environmental change affects biodiversity and may help predict the effects of future change.

So get out there! Explore, observe, and discover the nature that's around you every day. There are mysteries awaiting you in your own backyard, and each species you see has a captivatingly unique story of adaptation and survival.

Jason R. Cryan, PhD
Executive Director, Natural History Museum of Utah

INTRODUCTION

It may seem counterintuitive to think of nature as being a part of a city, but we share the places we live with an abundance of wild plants and animals. This book is a guide to the nature thriving right under our noses in cities and suburbs along the Wasatch Front. If you know how to look, you can discover an astonishing number and variety of wild plants and animals living in your neighborhood. With each wild neighbor you meet, your neighborhood will become a little richer.

► Nature and cities are intimately intertwined. You can often find nature thriving and providing valuable services even in unexpected places.

A few years ago, we asked visitors at the Natural History Museum of Utah where they experienced nature in their lives. We were starting work on an exhibit called "Nature All Around Us"—the inspiration for this book—and wanted to know how people in our community thought about nature. Not surprisingly, the vast majority of those we talked with mentioned canyons, mountains, and national parks—the traditional places that spring to mind when we think of nature. Along the Wasatch Front, canyons and mountains are a short drive—or even a short walk—from home for many people, so it's easy to understand how we can overlook the nature that's all around us every day where we live, work, and play.

Some people said that, by definition, nature and cities cannot coexist. This book, however, presents a different way to think about the relationship between cities and nature—not as separate, but as inseparable parts of an interconnected system. The exciting thing about this perspective is that it can help you connect with nature in your everyday life. It means you don't have to travel far from home to spend time in nature.

Another idea we heard is that nature in cities isn't "real" nature, because it's influenced by humans. The nature you'll encounter in Wasatch Front neighborhoods is a rambunctious mix of species—some that have lived here for a long time and many newcomers—interacting with humans and the places we shape. As plants and animals from around the globe meet and adapt to the challenges and opportunities of city life, experiments in ecology and evolution are unfolding all around us. And isn't that what nature is all about?

All ecosystems are constantly changing, but ecosystems in and around cities are particularly dynamic. In an era of rapid global environmental change, these ecosystems may hold important lessons about how we can help nature adapt to change and allow it to thrive—in cities and many other places. Throughout this book, you'll find references to citizen science projects across the Wasatch Front that could use your help. Gathering data will help us better understand the ecosystems in and around cities, manage our role in them, and plan for our changing future.

The book begins with nine short essays written by local professionals and thoughtful writers whose work involves understanding the relationship between humans and nature. The essays explore how nature and cities shape each other and how we might welcome more nature and the many

▲ Once you start looking, you may find hundreds of wild plants and animals, like this adorable jumping spider, hanging out in your neighborhood.

▼ Perfectly at home in cities, pigeons are among the surprising number of animals and plants that thrive alongside humans.

vital services it provides to our cities. You'll find Utah stories about novel ecosystems, backyard habitats, creatures that thrive in cities, the power of trees, our relationship with water, and the power of community.

The middle section of the book is a field guide featuring 127 species you're likely to encounter in your neighborhood or on a visit to a nearby park or open space. You've probably seen many of them, but you may not have had a proper introduction. The field guide will help you get to know the wild plants, animals, fungi, and street trees in your community, with tips for identifying them, descriptions of their amazing adaptions, and examples of our interconnected stories.

The final section of the book is a guide to twenty-one field trips for exploring nature in or on the edge of Wasatch Front cities and suburbs. Some of these sites offer opportunities to glimpse unusual species or tremendous biodiversity. Some are great places to explore the connections between human and natural history. All of them will enable you to practice your naturalist skills and meet more of the species featured in this book. At least one of these field trip locations between Ogden and Provo will be close to most Wasatch Front readers. Of course, the field trips represent just a fraction of the options available for nearby nature adventures—our list of potential field trips was more than double what we could include in this book.

This book would not have been possible without contributions of time and expertise from dozens of people—museum staff, expert naturalists, scientists working at a variety of organizations, local land managers, historians, graduate students, photographers, and more. Like the "Nature All Around Us" exhibit that inspired it, the book reflects the knowledge and generosity of our community. You can read more about the people who contributed near the back of the book. Our deepest thanks to them all.

Hidden worlds await discovery outside your door. Just one street, yard, or planter box can yield new wonders that change with the cycles of the day and the seasons. Be curious, look closely, and get to know your wild neighbors.

► Playing in nature is vital for children's physical and emotional development. Cities can provide places where kids can discover nature.

► A great horned owl roosting on a power pole in Utah County may seem like a strange juxtaposition, but the abundance of rodents scurrying across open lawns in cities are easy pickings for adaptable owls.

► The Galena Soo'nkahni Preserve on the Jordan River is one of dozens of open spaces in or near cities along the Wasatch Front where you can explore nearby nature.

What's in a Name?

Scientists in different fields use different standards for capitalizing the common names for the species they study. To be consistent and make the book more conversational, we lowercase common names, except when they include place names and proper nouns—for example, house finch, California gull, and Woodhouse's scrub-jay.

Some species have many English common names. In most cases, we use the common name listed on the iNaturalist app. This free app is a great tool for identifying plants, animals, and fungi—you might want to use it as you develop or hone your skills as a neighborhood naturalist.

Scientific names in the book follow the usual rules: they are italicized, with the genus capitalized and the species name lowercase. The scientific name of the California gull, for example, is *Larus californicus*.

THE NATURE
OF CITIES

Embracing New Nature

Emma Marris

I step out my back door, coffee in hand, and my bird feeder explodes.

Three Eurasian collared-doves (*Streptopelia decaocto*) had been breakfasting on my platform feeder, and I have flushed them. They take off with their usual dramatic ruckus of furious wingbeats and cries—a loud, raspy "hwaah! hwaah!"—practically making me spill my coffee. They fly a few feet away, and I sit down to enjoy the moment, knowing that in no time, they'll likely start their constant song—a mournful, owly "koo-KOO-kook." It is one of the most distinctive motifs in my backyard soundtrack.

Eurasian collared-doves are loud and obvious. They'll happily eat all your birdseed. They look like slimmer, creamier pigeons wearing black necklaces. And as their name suggests, they aren't native to the United States. Once found only in India, Sri Lanka, and Myanmar, they have spread across Europe and North America. For all these reasons, many people dislike them, but I can't help but admire them.

As goofy and loud as they are, they have been incredibly successful as a species. After being introduced to the Bahamas as pets in the 1970s, some of the birds got loose and hopped over to Florida in the 1980s. They were first seen in Utah in Orem in 1997. Today, they are common all along the Wasatch Front.

Researchers believe bird feeders like mine have helped Eurasian collared-doves spread. They really are a feature of humanized landscapes. So are these doves simply a kind of outdoor pet, kept collectively by all the people with bird feeders, or do they interact with other species in a more ecological way?

One study in Spain provides some clues. Introduced Eurasian collared-doves are a significant prey item for northern goshawks (*Accipiter gentilis*), which are native to

▼ Eurasian collared-doves are part of the novel ecosystems composed of plants and animals from around the globe that humans have helped create in cities and suburbs along the Wasatch Front.

▲ Recently arrived species and longtime resident species mingle in the Wasatch foothills.

Spain. The doves help make it possible for the raptors to thrive in a mixture of farmland and nonnative plantation forests of eucalyptus from Australia. The hawks nest in the Australian trees, but they hunt in the Spanish farmland areas where the doves chow down on grain.

A Changing World

Such mixed up ecologies are increasingly common in our changing world. Researchers in the Spanish study helpfully define these "novel ecosystems" as "ecosystems created deliberately or inadvertently by human activity that show a species composition and abundance previously unknown in that area . . . [that] do not depend on continued human intervention for their maintenance."

A tidy garden isn't quite a novel ecosystem because a human plants, weeds, and manages it. But an overgrown alley or empty lot might be one. Many novel ecosystems are old farm fields or plantation forests—like the eucalyptus forests in Spain. Their two key characteristics are that they have a new mix of species and they are at least semi-wild. Scientists estimate that some 36 percent of Earth's surface is covered in land that is not used directly by people but is embedded within a zone of human use, such as a city or an agricultural area. These places include abandoned farmlands, unmanaged timber plantations, and steep, rocky, or boggy areas that are difficult for humans to use. Many of them could be defined as novel ecosystems.

Novel ecosystems include both native species and introduced species. Many of us have learned to be pretty negative about introduced species, especially those deemed "invasive." Introduced species can be significant agricultural and timberland pests. It is also true that some nonnative animals—particularly predators such as rats and domestic cats—can cause big, unwanted changes, especially on islands. If you dig into the data on invasive species, nonnative animal predators on islands are by far the most

likely to cause an extinction of a native species. Nevertheless, these animals, which are sometimes culled by conservationists to protect vulnerable native species, should not be blamed for the environmental disruption they cause. They should always be treated as humanely as possible. After all, it is usually humans who relocate them.

Plants and animals introduced to continents have caused very few species extinctions. A search of the International Union to Conserve Nature's Red List of Threatened Species for 2022 shows that 265 species have gone extinct in recorded memory in the United States. Of these, 132 species were in Hawaii—demonstrating the very different dynamics and the much greater extinction risk on islands. Of the mainland extinctions, the Red List indicates that thirteen of these extinctions have been affected by invasive species, but it shows introduced species as the primary cause of just a single extinction. The other twelve species faced a variety of additional threats as well, including habitat loss and pollution.

Introduced species are definitely very abundant in specific places, and they can absolutely cause local declines in native species, either through predation or competition. It's easy to understand why the manager of a specific park or reserve would want to control or eradicate very successful introduced species, especially if the goal is to showcase the area's native flora and fauna.

On larger landscape scales, the initial population boom of a new introduced species often settles down after a century or two and the plant or animal becomes less abundant. Other species learn to hunt or eat it. It becomes woven into the ecosystem—naturalized, in botanist's parlance. For example, you may recall hearing about hordes of fire ants invading the southern United States. Newspapers wrote exciting stories when these insects arrived in large numbers, but no one bothered to update the story years later, when the fire ant population numbers fell to a tenth of their initial estimates and native ant populations bounced back.

Even though Eurasian collared-doves have spread across the country quickly and have become very common, little evidence suggests that they are causing any environmental havoc. The Centre for Agriculture and Bioscience International, which maintains a compendium of invasive species, does classify the Eurasian collared-dove as an invasive species but says that, although some believe that they may be competing with other bird species, such as the European turtle dove (Streptopelia turtur) and native North American doves such as the mourning dove (Zenaida macroura), negative effects have yet to be explicitly demonstrated. Like many native species, Eurasian collared-doves carry West Nile virus and the disease-causing parasite Trichomonas gallinae. But I cannot find any evidence that this bird is a serious existential threat to any native species.

Learning to Love the New

I feel free to enjoy these noisy feeder hogs as they flap around and sing their melancholy song. I remind myself that they have no idea they are "invasive." From their perspective, my backyard is home.

When professional restoration ecologists use the term "novel ecosystem," it usually also implies that the changes to the affected area are significant enough that there's no realistic prospect of restoring it to its "native" state. Perhaps the climate is warmer now, or the nutrient profile of the soil has changed, or some of the introduced species are so firmly ensconced that it would be impossible to remove them. In cities, this sort of situation is pretty common. The urban heat island effect, for example, can magnify anthropogenic (human-caused) climate change, making places significantly hotter than they were before a city was built around them. Development can also change the soil. Many urban ecosystems are growing in construction rubble or fill soil brought in from outside the city. Often this soil is heavily compacted by runoff from adjacent pavement or by vehicle and foot traffic. Road salt used to melt snow and ice can even change the pH of the soil. These factors, along with the constant influx of nonnative seeds and animals, mean that maintaining a purely native restoration project inside a city is going to be hard work.

Botanist Peter Del Tredici studies urban novel ecosystems. He calculated that 9.5 percent of Somerville, Massachusetts, a relatively dense East Coast city, is covered in "spontaneous vegetation" that no one planted. And in Detroit, the figure is as high as 20 percent. These plants may be considered weeds, but they do a lot for us. They absorb heat, sequester carbon, and sop

◄◄ Puncturevine is notorious for its sharp seed capsules that pop bicycle tires and hurt puppy paws. This introduced species has been targeted for removal along urban trails in the Wasatch Front.

▼ The common pill woodlouse is one of the many introduced species that have settled into new habitats without causing disruptions.

◄ Fire ants are following a common pattern for species introduced to new habitats. Populations grew rapidly when they first arrived in the southern United States before declining sharply.

◄ Species that thrive in cities are adapted to rapidly changing environments. Their resiliency may be key to providing ecosystem services cities depend on, such as cooling, retaining water, and preventing erosion.

up toxic chemicals and excess fertilizer from home gardens. They create oxygen, control erosion, and serve as homes and food for wild animals. In some cases, they can even create habitats for endangered species.

On the other hand, novel ecosystems are often dominated by common hardy generalist species, such as dandelions, dock, alfalfa, ailanthus (also known as tree of heaven), sparrows, and the Eurasian collared-dove. These are flexible, tough species that can survive well in the human world. Some of the same species are found in cities all over the world. Novel ecosystems feature fewer rare and unique specialist species.

So are novel ecosystems good or bad? The first thing to realize is that this is not really a scientific question. Ecologists can tell us how ecosystems are changing or how the parts of a novel ecosystem interact, but they can't tell us whether or how much to value such an ecosystem. In the end, we must make these decisions as individuals and as a community. Should we spray the foothills around our neighborhoods with expensive and toxic herbicides to remove "weeds" that have become well-established? Or should we use those resources for other projects, such as building trails or protecting key wildlife corridors?

Naturalized Nature

For me, novel ecosystems are a sign of nature's resilience. Yes, they are different from what was there before, and they don't have a very long evolutionary history in the areas they populate. But they are often surprisingly diverse and vibrant—even beautiful. They show that life is adaptable and tough. Especially in cities, where expecting all the plants and animals to be strictly native seems less important than it might be in a national park or other protected area, novel ecosystems seem to me to be something to celebrate.

I really enjoy exploring urban novel ecosystems and reveling in the mix of native species, horticultural escapees, common "weeds" and "pests," game

▲ Over the last century, eastern fox squirrels have become common in many cities in the West. They both add to the biodiversity of those cities and make their ecosystems more similar to those of other cities.

◀ When native Cooper's hawks along the Wasatch Front dine on introduced Eurasian collared-doves, both species are connected in a novel ecosystem.

species and agricultural plants, and other plants and animals that have figured out how to thrive in the margins of the human world. Just last week, I followed an urban stream that ran through several culvert pipes and empty lots until I found an unexpected mini-grove of willows surrounded by introduced grasses where California quail and northern flickers were foraging. What a pleasure to hear their wild noises in a scrubby field I had walked by a hundred times without even noticing!

Collared-doves are knit into novel ecosystems like that empty lot by becoming food for other species. In Poland, they are eaten by rooks and jackdaws; in the United Kingdom, domestic cats, foxes, stoats, and raptors prey on them. In Utah, Cooper's hawks, peregrine falcons, prairie falcons, and merlins all chow down on Eurasian collared-doves, according to the experts at HawkWatch International in Salt Lake City. Interestingly, Cooper's hawks that consumed the introduced doves were contracting avian trichomoniasis from their prey, and some died as a result. Very quickly, however, the Cooper's hawks became resistant to the parasite in yet another example of a species quickly adapting to another's presence.

Looking at it from an ecological perspective, Eurasian collared-doves are fueling up on energy from my feeder, eating grain grown by human farmers, and they'll likely one day become food for a raptor or coyote—and then also for beetles, worms, fungi, and bacteria. Their energy will flow into the soil, where it might nourish my garden roses or the native rubber rabbitbrush in the hills behind my house. In a strange way, I might be helping those hardy desert plants produce their bright yellow flowers next September. In the beauty of their blooms, the doves will truly become "naturalized."

Emma Marris writes about human relationships with the nonhuman from Oregon. She is the author of *Rambunctious Garden: Saving Nature in a Post-Wild World* and *Wild Souls: Freedom and Flourishing in the Non-Human World.*

At Home with Humans

Riley Black

What does a city look like to a mule deer?

The groomed flower beds and square city blocks around Salt Lake City might not look like what we consider "wildlands," but deer don't know the difference. It's not unusual to see their hoofprints along sidewalks below the foothills after rainstorms while walking your dog, or even to stumble accidentally upon a small group of them grazing on someone's lawn.

At first glance, spotting deer among the driveways and urban alleys of the Wasatch Front may seem a little strange. It's certainly not the image that most of us conjure up when we consider these large mammals. Do a basic Internet search on mule deer, and the photos that come up will show them standing in some open space, often looking elegant in their fluffy winter coats. What we don't see are the deer that live among our urban neighborhoods and cemeteries—deer that know the streets about as well as we do. Taking that thought a step further, what if this behavior isn't something strange, but part of a relationship we've created and maintained with these animals? Considering that possibility takes us into the world of synanthropes, the creatures that are learning to live with us.

What Is a Synanthrope?

Let's break down the word into its constituent parts: The Greek word *syn* means "together with," and the word "anthrope" is short for *anthropos*, Greek for "man." These are the organisms that, whether we like it or not, live together with us by benefitting from the habitats and resources we create.

Take a walk through downtown Salt Lake City, past the offices, hotels, and shops, and you can readily go synanthrope-spotting—a game that stretches your mind as well as your legs. If you stroll during the spring, you may see small clusters of people with binoculars standing outside the historic Lion House, looking up to catch a glimpse of peregrine falcons nesting

▶ Mule deer have adapted to living with people along the Wasatch Front as we've built developments in their winter range in the foothills.

▲ Peregrine falcons nearly went extinct in North America in the 1960s until a revival program based in cities saved them.

among the buildings on the other side of the street. Of course, the entire reason that the area around Temple Square is so attractive to falcons is because of all the plump pigeons that coo and waddle around the sidewalks, as well as house sparrows that pick up bread crusts and other tidbits that people leave behind. You may even spot a constant human companion, a brown rat, as it rushes under a shrub as you pass by. And I can speak from experience that house mice are certainly happy to inhabit soft, cozy places in my basement. Neighborhoods along the Wasatch Front are wilder than we often give them credit for.

Room to Grow

And let's not forget plants. Animals are the most obvious synanthropes—a raccoon rummaging through your table scraps in the garbage bin is a pretty clear example—but plants also benefit from the ways we use and modify the landscape. The ornamental plant myrtle spurge (*Euphorbia myrsinites*), for example, was once recommended as a waterwise species that Utah homeowners could plant to spruce up their gardens. Gardeners found that the nonnative species was so at home in our conditions that it quickly

◄ Common sunflowers flourish in challenging habitats with lots of regular disturbance—even in a crack in the pavement on a busy street.

escaped the confines of their yards. This plant seems to prefer areas that have been disturbed by humans, and it grows along sidewalks and in corners near where it initially escaped. Around the lower Avenues near downtown Salt Lake City, you can readily spot these scaly plants growing up from the curbside, where they are now a part of the local ecology.

Although myrtle spurge has generated plenty of controversy—and even disdain—many of us are perfectly at home with other synanthropes. The common sunflower (*Helianthus annuus*), for example, is beloved by many. In late summer, sunflowers are bright and welcome sights along many Wasatch Front roadsides. Along Interstate 15, the plants' bright yellow flowers form beautiful ranks along the highway as red-tailed hawks and other birds of prey perch on roadside fence posts.

Although the common sunflower already has a long history with us—America's Indigenous peoples were cultivating the plant more than 4000 years ago—the inherent biology of sunflowers enables them to thrive in human-disturbed habitats. That's because these synanthropes grow fast, produce lots of seeds, and don't live very long. In harsh spots, such as a roadside, sunflowers are able to withstand conditions that other plants cannot, and they take full advantage of the extra elbow room. In fact, roadside sunflowers seem to grow faster and are more prolific than sunflowers that grow in what appears to be untouched grassland.

Amazing Adaptation

Whether it's a sunflower or a pigeon, an organism's ability to make the most of our rapidly changing world is an essential and inherent part of nature. Some organisms may have a relatively narrow set of parameters that suit them, with less human disturbance being preferable. Then again, some

► Cities may be making raccoons smarter—scientists think these intelligent, adaptable, and curious animals are learning to be better problem-solvers as a result of navigating human-made obstacles.

species are more flexible in their needs or just happen to have characteristics that fit well with places modified by human handiwork. Consider raccoons. These masked omnivores are active at night, dine on just about anything they can swallow, and use their dexterous hands to probe and pry. Raccoons didn't need to change very much to live with us. Their inherent behaviors enable them to take advantage of all the riches we leave outside—or inside, if the windows aren't shut tight—during a time when we're usually sleeping.

Not all city- or suburban-dwelling species are synanthropes, however. Mountain lions, for example, have ventured farther into neighborhoods along the Wasatch Front, but biologists are not yet certain if these cats are truly benefitting from human presence or merely finding ways to work around human development. The difference between a true synanthrope and a species that coexists with us despite our presence can sometimes be difficult to determine. The key is that the organism noticeably benefits from human activity, often by being more numerous, leaving more offspring, or demonstrating some other measurable factor. That can make it somewhat difficult to define which species are synanthropes and which are not. A garden tomato, for example, may meet these criteria, but it is not a synanthrope. It was planted in the garden, grown and tended to, and it may have even been intentionally modified to survive and produce larger fruit.

What about coyotes? Coyotes are a conundrum for ecologists, who are just beginning to study synanthropes and their roles in our lives. Coyotes are certainly present in the neighborhoods of the Wasatch Front, but, as in other cities, it's unclear just how comfortable they are living beside us. A five-square-mile patch of city can support a few more coyotes than the same amount of wild space, and urban coyote pups are five times more likely to survive than those in less disturbed habitats, but coyotes still seem to avoid people whenever possible and act much like their country relatives. Whether coyotes remain on the outskirts or are on their way to becoming full-fledged synanthropes is something that can be understood only with time.

Sussing out synanthropes is more than just a numbers game. Naturally, we want to know why some species thrive among us. Sometimes it's a matter of inherent biology, like roadside plants that can tolerate high amounts of oil and other road runoff. Other times, the animals adjust their behaviors

◄ Coyotes are cautious city dwellers. They like the resources cities offer, but not the people.

according to what we do. A bird's nest partly made with candy wrappers and cigarette butts may look like a tragic commentary on ecology to some, but for the bird, the hodgepodge home reflects the inventiveness and resilience of a synanthrope in a place where a variety of materials are available for nest building.

In fact, some of our human-made products may prove a benefit. In sparrow and finch nests, for example, the nicotine in discarded cigarette butts woven into the nests acts as a pesticide that helps protect adults and nestlings from parasitic ticks, while the dense filter material within the butts acts as an insulator. Birds will make the most of what is available (but that's no excuse to throw a spent cigarette on the ground). And birds like ever-inventive crows and ravens have been known to take even greater advantage of human-modified landscapes—for instance, by dropping hard-to-crack nuts on roads where cars regularly pass to let the machinery do all the hard work.

Redefining Nature

Ecologists are just beginning to understand what makes a synanthrope and how they keep us connected to ecological webs that we might otherwise be blind to. That's why synanthropes are critical to our twenty-first-century conversation with nature. Nature is often framed as a phenomenon that is *out there*, away from people, in unspoiled places. This view of nature is like a patchwork quilt that we desperately want to keep intact. Although the world is going through a real biodiversity crisis, nature is not something inert that is simply torn apart by the changes we impose. Instead, nature encompasses us, even as we reweave it from the inside out. Synanthropes are powerful reminders that even the most developed city, even the newest cul-de-sac development, is still a part of nature and offers an altered landscape that will affect who survives and who is pushed to the margins.

For as long as humans have inhabited Earth, some of the species we share the planet with have suffered for our whims while others have benefitted. Organisms—from rats to earthworms—have spread around the world along with humans, changing the nature of the places we call home.

▶ All the pigeons living in cities today are descendants of escaped domesticated pigeons—they're quite at home with humans.

▲ House sparrows have evolved with humans for thousands of years and now never live far from human development.

How could we change our world so fundamentally and not expect nature to respond just as it has through past mass extinctions, glaciations, climate change, and more? Every life on our planet is tied together as a result of millions of years of change. What makes us different is that we can see this biological tapestry, a key realization that frames today and will shape tomorrow. What future will we make, with nature so eager to meet us?

Riley Black is the author of *The Last Days of the Dinosaurs: An Asteroid, Extinction, and the Beginning of Our World* and other books about fossils. Her byline has appeared in *National Geographic*, *Slate*, *Scientific American*, and many other publications. She lives in Salt Lake City.

Backyard Habitats

Amy Sibul

When you hear the word "wildlife," what do you think of? What about the words "wildlife habitat"? The majority of us probably picture a large mammal, such as a bighorn sheep, somewhere far away from a city, on a mountain surrounded by forest. Most of us don't picture a backyard, a city park, or an apartment balcony. But these human-created environments can provide habitats for wild plants and animals just as surely as a high mountain forest.

Anywhere you see a wild organism, you're looking at its habitat. You can think of habitat as all the components of a place that provide an organism with the water, food, and protection it needs to survive. Urban and suburban habitats support a surprising diversity of wild plants, animals, and fungi that collectively make up the ecosystems in which we spend the most time.

What an organism needs from its habitat can change over time on a daily, seasonal, or annual basis. What a bird needs as it builds a nest is different from what it needs as it prepares to migrate, which is again different from what it needs as it tries to stay alive during a blizzard or a heat wave. What a plant needs in order to germinate can be very different from what it needs during flowering. The variability of habitat required by a plant or animal actually allows for a diversity of options for creating wildlife habitats in our yards.

What Makes a Yard a Wildlife Habitat?

Wildlife habitats in cities and suburbs come in many sizes—from as small as an apartment balcony or a few planter boxes to as large as a vacant lot or city park. Almost any space can be a habitat if it offers four resources all animals need: food, water, cover, and places to raise young. Providing habitat is easier than you might think.

FOOD: Include a variety of plants in your yard to provide food for wildlife all year long—flowers to provide pollen and nectar, leafy plants to host

▶ Colorful hanging baskets of flowers or potted plants, a bird feeder or two, and a shallow dish of water on a balcony or porch can provide habitat for birds and pollinators.

▲ You don't have to build a pond to provide water for wildlife—a birdbath, water container garden, or simply a shallow dish of water will do the trick.

insects, and shrubs and trees to provide seeds or berries. Add a bird feeder or two to supplement birds' natural diets.

WATER: All animals need clean drinking water to survive. In addition, birds need water for bathing to keep their feathers clean and free of parasites and to cool down in hot weather. Other species, including amphibians, actually live in water. You can provide water for wildlife in a variety of ways, from a birdbath or shallow dish of water to a water container garden or pond.

COVER: Wildlife need places to hide to feel safe from people, predators, and inclement weather. You can help provide cover by not keeping your yard too tidy. Shrubs, thickets, brush piles, and rocks are great hiding places for animals, and tiny creatures can find refuge in a layer of leaves on the ground.

PLACES TO RAISE YOUNG: The long-term survival of wildlife in your community depends on their ability to reproduce and raise their young successfully. Many places that offer cover can double as a safe nursery. Add a

bee nest box or a birdhouse to enrich your habitat and provide places for these cavity nesters to raise their young.

Let's take a closer look at how you can support two of the most common types of wildlife in neighborhood habitats: birds and bees. Making your yard welcoming to these creatures will support many other animals too.

Planting for the Birds

In our backyards, we tend to see birds more often than wild mammals, reptiles, and amphibians, especially in our dry climate. Birds draw our attention by being active during the day, singing beautiful songs, and often sporting bright colors. Surprisingly, suburbs often support more bird species than nearby wilder lands. Suburbs offer a variety of habitats and plants where diverse birds can find food and shelter. Plus, there are feeders full of birdseed.

If you hope to attract birds to your yard, first make sure your yard is safe for them. Two big sources of danger encountered by birds in our neighborhoods are windows and house cats. Window collisions and cats kill more than three billion birds in North America every year. You can use screens, film, window paints, or hangings to reduce the reflective surface of your windows. If you own a cat, try to keep your little hunter indoors as much as possible. Pesticides are another major source of harm to birds—anything that poisons the food they eat, whether insects or plants, can be toxic to the birds too.

The key to creating habitat for birds is providing a variety of plants that offer food and shelter. A lawn composed of a single species of grass is a food desert for most birds and other organisms. And lawns don't provide shelter for birds looking to roost for the night, take cover during a storm, or rest during migrations. Planting flowers, shrubs, and trees that provide vertical structure and cover will attract a surprising array of birds to your yard. These plants will also draw insects, which insect-eating birds will thank you for.

▶ Plants that provide nectar, seeds, or berries will draw a variety of birds to your backyard habitat, like cedar waxwings that gobble juniper berries in winter.

Because different birds eat different types of food, try incorporating an assortment of flowering plants to support nectar feeders, berry eaters, and seed eaters. Avoid deadheading (removing spent flowers from) your plants so that seed eaters can enjoy a meal. In the fall, leave some small, shallow pockets of leaves or even a small brush pile where overwintering insects can take shelter. They'll provide insect-eating birds a snack on a cold winter day.

Choosing plants that provide multiple habitat needs for birds is a great idea, especially for small yards. Chokecherry trees *(Prunus virginiana)*, for instance, offer abundant pollen and nectar in the spring for bees and birds and then provide juicy berries for birds to munch in the summer. They also create a place for birds to nest, roost, and take shelter.

Bird feeders, whether for seed-eating goldfinches or nectar-sipping hummingbirds, are legitimate additions to any backyard habitat. Not everyone has the space for a lot of plants, but just about all of us can put up a feeder. Keep your bird guests safe by cleaning your feeders often, offering healthy food, and siting feeders a safe distance from windows. A bird feeder is also a great way to participate in citizen science—from November to April, the Cornell Lab of Ornithology supports the Project FeederWatch citizen science effort to count the birds that visit feeders across the United States.

"Bee" the Change

We know about western honeybees *(Apis mellifera)*: they make honey, live in large social hives, and might sting you if you accidentally get too close or try to harvest their honey. Honeybees are excellent pollinators, but they are a single species among 20,000 other species of bees that pollinate the world's plants, including those in our backyard gardens.

You may have heard that bees are in decline. Honeybee populations are experiencing large annual mortality rates, in part because of inhospitable conditions in our agricultural landscapes, including crop monocultures,

◄ A mason bee cleans out a tube in a nest box before laying her eggs inside.

pesticides, herbicides, and overcrowding from commercial pollination practices. Even more detrimental to biodiversity are the declines being documented in wild bee populations, including bumblebees and mason bees. Yards and parks can provide important habitats for these vital pollinators, sustaining them while our agricultural landscapes do not.

Bees need two main types of habitat: nesting and foraging. About 75 percent of the approximately 4000 North American bee species nest in the ground. Just a few square feet of bare soil with no mulch or woodchips can attract many species of solitary, ground-nesting bees. Since they don't produce honey or have huge concentrations of babies in one location, solitary wild bees are quite docile and tend to ignore humans. These bees haven't evolved powerful venom like honeybees, so attracting them to your yard won't lead to bee stings.

The other 25 percent of wild bees nest in cavities, including hollow plant stems or leftover beetle burrows in wood. You can create habitat for these bees by allowing hollow-stemmed plants to remain in your garden during the fall and winter and by adding a bee nest box to your yard. Buy a nest box or make your own from a container full of hollow reed stems or a wooden block drilled with holes. Each cavity opening should be about one-eighth to one-half inch in diameter and at least five inches deep. Place the nest box at least a few feet off the ground and attached to a tree or post that won't shake in the wind. It should also be protected from hot afternoon sun.

Bees eat pollen and nectar and feed both of these floral products to their young. Foraging habitat for bees consists of flowers that bloom in spring, summer, and fall—a landscape that both humans and bees enjoy. Many of our most beautiful perennials are popular with bees, including sunflowers, penstemon, prairie coneflowers, and flowering sage. Bees also love members of the mint family that we love to cook with, such as rosemary, oregano, peppermint, and thyme. Incorporating these lovely and edible flowering plants into a planter box or a garden supports bees and a wide diversity of wildlife neighbors.

▲ Providing a bee nest box and including a variety of flowers in your habitat will help support declining wild bee populations.

◀ Several nearby neighbors with wildlife-friendly yards make a bigger impact by creating a larger patch of habitat. A sign in your yard may inspire others.

For more information on bee habitat, check out the Xerces Society's website. This national nonprofit organization focuses on invertebrate conservation and offers a wealth of information about providing insect habitat in your yard.

Small Habitats Make a Big Difference

Private, residential yards typically account for about a third of the green space in urban areas, and each individual yard that offers wildlife habitat is important. The multiplier effect of many adjacent wildlife-friendly yards is huge. Together, these yards can create large patches of habitat for small creatures as well as corridors that connect open spaces to enable bigger creatures to travel safely through our neighborhoods.

Consider working with neighbors and community partners to enhance your neighborhood's wildlife-friendly habitat at a larger scale. Building wildlife habitat as a community can create a sense of belonging for both humans and the wildlife we hope to attract. If people in your neighborhood committed to taking a few simple steps to incorporate habitat components into their landscaping, it could add up to a substantial impact on wildlife abundance and diversity. In fact, wildlife biologists have studied the impact of bird-friendly city landscaping on bird diversity and found that neighborhoods with consistently wildlife-friendly landscaping support almost twice as many bird species as neighborhoods with less wildlife-friendly landscaping.

One fantastic example of a collective community effort to promote backyard wildlife habitats comes from Nibley, Utah. Members of this northern Utah town formed the Cache Valley Wildlife Association, a local grassroots collective that pursued and successfully attained certification for Nibley as a National Wildlife Federation (NWF) Community Wildlife Habitat in 2016.

Individual homeowners can apply to become a Certified Wildlife Habitat through the NWF after providing sources of food, water, cover, and breeding habitat in their yards while employing sustainable landscaping practices. The Nibley community effort to earn certification was remarkable, involving a partnership of private homeowners, businesses, schools, and parks that agreed to protect, restore, and build wildlife habitat throughout the town

while also providing wildlife education and outreach events. In all, eighty-seven Nibley homeowners, five schools, and sixteen parks and businesses worked together to achieve this prestigious certification, the first in the state of Utah.

Whether you want to start with a window planter box or are ready to organize your neighborhood habitat effort, lots of organizations can provide helpful guidance. Check out resources from the Audubon Society, the Xerces Society, and the National Wildlife Federation. Look for programs offered by your local government. For example, Salt Lake City's Pesticide Free SLC program offers resources for a less toxic approach to yard care that promotes the health of humans and our wild neighbors. If you take the pledge to go pesticide-free, you get a sign for your yard that helps raise awareness of safe urban habitat practices.

Imagine what our cities and suburbs would look, sound, and smell like if every property owner created a bit of quality wildlife habitat. Imagine the new neighbors we could welcome to our communities.

▲ This backyard in Nibley contributes to the town's Community Wildlife Habitat certification, offering layers of vegetation, from ground covers to treetops, where birds and insects can find food and shelter.

Amy Sibul is currently an administrator at the University of Oregon, but was a biologist and community engagement specialist at the University of Utah for 12 years. Her expertise is in conservation biology, community engagement, and bee biodiversity. She's passionate about helping folks have experiences that foster respect for and curiosity about diverse peoples, communities, and organisms.

Nature
Nurtures
Our Cities

Lewis Kogan

My friend Reileen lives on the west side of the Salt Lake Valley, in a house not far from the Jordan River Parkway trail. Almost every morning, Reileen carries her hard-sided kayak to the top of the riverbank, climbs in, and expertly slides down the embankment like a muskrat, slipping almost soundlessly into the glassy water. The droplets falling from her paddle making the only sound in the chill morning air, she glides under leafy tunnels formed by tree trunks and limbs extending from the riverbank and dipping down almost into the water. As she passes under each, she lets the rustling of the foliage and gurgle of water under her boat envelop her.

▶ Flowing through the center of the densely populated Salt Lake Valley, the Jordan River offers city dwellers a chance to connect with nature within a few minutes of home.

Only several yards from the roads and homes of the adjoining neighborhood, in the heart of Utah's capital city, the impositions of the bustling metropolis feel entirely absent here. Gliding under another leafy tree-arch, Reileen feels a sense of awe and reverence that seems to grow and expand with each morning that she spends on the river. In this world, there is only water, leaves and sky, the sound of birdsong, and the occasional plop of a river turtle slipping under the surface. The stillness and the beauty rouse her spirit and fill her with a wonderment that stays with her all day long.

When I first met Reileen, I had recently moved to Salt Lake City from rural Montana, and, to me, the Salt Lake Valley seemed a bewildering metropolis. I thrived on time spent ambling through fields and forests back home, and I expected to miss those experiences sorely. Reileen took me on my first paddle on the Jordan River, which quickly put my misgivings to rest. As we drifted past bank beaver lodges and under cliff swallow dwellings and the curious dangling nests of Bullock's orioles, the sights and sounds of the city were almost entirely absent.

Despite the occasional submerged shopping cart, broken concrete slab, or island of floating plastic, this seemed a space given over to wildness and the rhythms of nature. Although we were floating through the heart of a valley packed wall-to-wall with well over a million residents, bobbing along on the river felt undeniably refreshing, restorative, and peaceful.

Restoring Mind and Soul

After spending a few years working for one of the Salt Lake Valley's municipal parks and recreation departments, I came to appreciate intimately what I always intuitively understood: parks and natural areas are good for us. And for those of us who live in cities and whose daily lives are generally confined primarily to indoor spaces, parks and natural areas are a necessity.

I sometimes joke that without our public green spaces, city dwellers would quickly descend into madness, chaos, and infirmity. That jest isn't quite accurate, but it isn't entirely off-base. An increasing body of research demonstrates that accessible green spaces are indeed necessary for our physical health, our mental health, and even our social and environmental health. In short, parks and natural areas make our cities livable.

A few months after moving here, I stumbled upon a particularly sublime little treasure while on an exploratory late-winter stroll. On top of a windswept knoll in a grassy open space preserve, jutting out just above the upper limits of a residential neighborhood, I spotted a couple of old metal mailboxes tucked into a rocky cleft. Inside the mailboxes were dozens of notebooks and journals, where thousands of visitors had penned astonishingly personal notes, prayers, confessions, and musings. I sat on the little promontory for hours reading the inscriptions. Darkness finally forced me to stop and descend back to the street below, but I couldn't stop thinking about what I had read.

There were messages to deceased friends and family members, love poems, narratives of personal struggle and hardship, and resolutions to

▶ The thousands of messages inscribed within these journals on a ridge just above Salt Lake City reflect the restorative power of being in nature.

◀ A study conducted by University of Utah researchers showed that even a thirty-minute walk in nature calmed participants' brains and helped them think more clearly.

seize the moment and to live with newfound purpose. And in nearly every message was a common thread: the beauty of nature—the peaceful union of earth and sky, rock and flower—provided perspective on life. These simple things were a healing balm for deep emotional wounds. They gave inspiration and clarity that many had been seeking for years.

At the time, these summit "confessionals" seemed strange, but they shouldn't have. Research from cities around the world continues to provide an ever-clearer picture that humans derive significant mental health benefits from natural areas, parks, and other green spaces in their communities. According to numerous studies, city residents who live within walking distance of a park or natural area—especially one that is large or has pleasing natural features such as mature trees, flowing water, or birdlife—are significantly less likely to suffer from depression, anxiety, and stress.

In fact, studies show that the more frequently we visit green spaces, the less stress we experience. It appears that in many ways, simply spending time in outdoor spaces and interacting (even passively) with nature arms us with tools to process—and let go of—the negative emotional baggage in our lives. And this surprising, sublime process was unintentionally being

◄ Research shows that exercise in green spaces has even greater physical and mental health benefits than exercise indoors or in nongreen outdoor places.

captured in the little summit register I had stumbled across, in the words of thousands of people who visited this space and were experiencing the benefits of time in nature firsthand.

Healthy Parks, Healthy People

An even larger body of research connects access to urban parks and natural areas with improved physical activity and physical health, including a healthier body weight, a decreased risk of chronic illness, and a significantly longer lifespan. Exercise in parks and open spaces has been shown to have greater benefits to our physical and mental health than exercise indoors or in nongreen areas, such as running along a street. And even greener streetscapes can provide measurable physical health benefits: research from one large North American city published in 2015 suggested that living in a neighborhood with a high density of street trees improved people's health outcomes in ways that were comparable to their being seven years younger.

Urban parks and natural areas are particularly important for kids growing up in cities without easy access to places like national parks and forest lands. According to data compiled by the National Recreation and Park Association, children living within walking distance of a park are five times more likely to be a healthy weight. Time spent outdoors and in nature can measurably reduce children's stress, anger, and aggression, and it results in better relationship skills, enhanced academic performance, and positive behavioral impacts.

On the flipside, too much time spent indoors, combined with sedentary lifestyles and overexposure to electronic media, also has real and measurable impacts on a child's development, including higher rates of physical and emotional illness, learning difficulties, and impaired social skills. This has become such a potent problem in American childhood that it is now often referred to as "nature-deficit disorder," a term coined by writer Richard Louv in his book *Last Child in the Woods*.

▶ Spending unstructured time exploring, playing, and imagining in nature is key for children's physical and emotional development.

Access to Urban Nature Isn't a Given

It seems like the answer is easy: build parks in every neighborhood, and cities will be full of happy kids, right? Well, it turns out it's not always that simple. Physical access is extremely important, and organizations such as The Trust for Public Land have made huge strides working with cities to ensure that there is a park within a ten-minute walk of every home. But access to wild natural areas and spaces for creative free-play, as contrasted with traditional sports fields and plastic playground equipment, is important for combatting nature-deficit disorder in urban kids. The geography of natural open spaces is not equitably distributed, especially in historically marginalized or disadvantaged communities. Low-income, under-resourced neighborhoods are usually also the areas with the least access to scenic natural and recreational assets.

The Salt Lake Valley is no exception to this rule. Natural areas here are more commonly located in wealthier, whiter neighborhoods near the foothills of the Wasatch or Oquirrh ranges or the creeks that flow out of them. In the center of the valley, where more of the ethnically and economically diverse communities tend to be, wild scenic open spaces are in short supply.

For planners and land managers looking to address these inequities in access to natural areas and recreational assets, the Jordan River corridor is especially critical. Though this urban river has a 150-year history of abuse and neglect, it offers the most significant opportunity for restoring equitable access to large natural open spaces through the center of the Salt Lake Valley. More than half of the entire state's population lives within a ten-minute drive of the Jordan River, making it a green-space resource of vital importance to city managers, planners, and advocates working to combat nature-deficit disorder and connect people—especially kids—to nature within their cities.

◄ A ribbon of city parks and natural open spaces lines the Jordan River as it runs through three counties and thirteen cities in the Salt Lake Valley.

▶ A mentor can help kids feel comfortable, safe, and welcome in the outdoors.

Kids Need Nature Mentors

It may be difficult to fathom, but many urban kids will grow up without ever observing a starry night sky, listening to birdsong, or splashing their feet in a stream. That's because physical proximity to natural open spaces is not the only barrier that prevents urban kids from connecting to nature and spending time outdoors. Many kids who haven't spent much time in outdoor settings may feel scared or uncomfortable and may not be sure about what to do in natural open spaces. So without mentorship and guidance on how to enjoy the outdoors, their proximity to a natural area may not matter.

To support children in developing a relationship with nature, a growing number of cities, counties, and states across the country are adopting some form of a "children's outdoor bill of rights." Although these efforts differ from place to place, the purpose is the same: identify the inalienable rights that every child should have to access fundamental outdoor experiences.

In 2019, Salt Lake City and the State of Utah each created a children's outdoor bill of rights to identify outdoor experiences every child should have access to. These efforts also include mobilizing resources to help urban kids develop familiarity with nearby natural areas, provide them with guidance

▶ "Catching a bug" is one of the thirteen experiences in the Salt Lake City Children's Outdoor Bill of Rights.

and mentorship as they learn how to explore and experience the outdoor world, and ultimately support children and their families, friends, and communities in finding sustainable ways to access and enjoy nature.

The Wasatch Front is full of nature, as the pages of this book clearly show. Even in our busiest cities, nature is all around us. Take time to explore some of the wild places our valleys and foothills offer. And if you already visit one or two of them regularly, challenge yourself to explore somewhere new. It's certain to be good for you. Next time you go, consider taking a friend, relative, coworker, or neighbor. Time outdoors is often better shared, and if we all reminded one another to make time for nature—and provided a little mentorship or a helping hand now and then—we would all be the better for it.

Lewis Kogan has worked at the intersection of people and nature for two decades as a ranger, trail builder, environmental specialist, and park manager. He lives in Salt Lake City.

Salt Lake City Children's Outdoor Bill of Rights

We believe that every child has the right to:

- Catch a bug
- Follow a foothill trail
- Listen to the sounds of nature
- Observe a starry sky
- Play in the snow
- Splash in a stream
- Identify a wild plant
- Spot and identify a wild animal
- Visit a mountaintop
- See Great Salt Lake
- Climb a rock
- Paddle a boat
- Explore a cave

To learn more, visit the Salt Lake City Children's Outdoor Bill of Rights website.

The Health of Urban Nature Is Our Own

Julia Corbett

When the COVID-19 pandemic sent us home in 2020, we went outdoors. Neighbors conversed across lawns and sidewalks, and city parks and trails filled with people. My friend Natalie ate most every meal in her little backyard, wondering, "Why didn't I do this before?" It made perfect sense: feeling confined indoors made us yearn for outdoor spaces without walls and ceilings that were peaceful and rich with life. In rediscovering outdoor places all around us, we learned how much we cherished them—needed them. Daypacks, bikes, binoculars, and kayaks flew off the shelves.

It's strange to think of reconnecting with nature as a silver lining in a pandemic that created such suffering. But against a backdrop of uncertainty was deep comfort in the constancy of nature in our everyday lives— knowing that the sun would rise every morning and make its way across the city, and knowing that trees would respire and cast shade, birds would call, and the sky would convey its moods with wind and clouds. In hard times as well as regular ones, nature is key to our physical, mental, and emotional health.

COVID-19 understandably elevated the importance of health and shifted how we perceive it. Health isn't just about being disease-free; it's a broad sense of well-being, an equilibrium in how we move through

the world—which depends upon the health of that world. Some scientists and doctors have moved beyond traditional biomedical conceptions of human health to focus instead on planetary health. In simple terms, our health and nature's health are one and the same: healthy natural systems support human health, and unhealthy natural systems harm human health. COVID-19 itself is an example of this mutual relationship, borne by animals stressed and squeezed by environmental degradation and pushed closer to humans, upon whom they shed their virus.

Wendell Berry expressed this mutualism in an essay in *The Long-Legged House*: "We have lived our lives by the assumption that what was good for us would be good for the world. We have been wrong. We must change our lives so that it will be possible to live by the contrary assumption: what is good for the world will be good for us. And that requires that we make the effort to know the world and learn what is good for it."

The challenges posed by the urban environment are shared by all who call this place home. It's mutually beneficial to make life healthier for all—for your family and for the families of bees, flowers, mammals, birds, and trees, along with the water, air, and soil on which all our families depend. In a significant way, the health of urban nature is a barometer for the health of its citizens, wild and domestic.

Let's consider some important components of health for humans and wilder nature: dark skies, quiet spaces, clean air, and cool places.

Dark Skies

◄ People went outdoors to yards, parks, and trails during the COVID-19 pandemic, seeking comfort in the beauty and constancy of nature.

► The glow of artificial lights in cities blocks out the stars and negatively impacts our health, but the good news is that fairly straightforward light pollution solutions are available and can save energy.

A photograph of the United States taken at night from space shows a country illuminated by lights that delineate coastlines and mark population centers. Humans have lit up the planet and the space beyond to such a degree that 80 percent of people who live in the developed world cannot see the

◄ Citizen scientists are working with Tracy Aviary to document bird collisions with buildings in downtown Salt Lake City in an effort to make the city safer for birds.

Milky Way in the night sky. If all my curtains are open, I can walk through my house at night without turning on a light, because the urban "skyglow" leaks in from every direction. It's not dark, and that's not healthy.

Animal bodies and plants operate on circadian rhythms of daylight and darkness that artificial lighting subverts. We've all evolved to sync our bodies and brains—blood pressure and temperature, when to eat and sleep—to natural light–dark patterns. LED lights, such as those from some streetlights and cell phones, emit a large amount of blue light, which suppresses sleep-important melatonin and interferes with our night vision. Light pollution also impacts nocturnal animals such as bats and owls, as well as toads and certain insects and butterflies. Some frogs won't sing their mating calls under the glare of artificial light (or when it's too noisy). Light pollution exposes animals most active at dawn and dusk to predators and reduces the time they have to find food and shelter and successfully reproduce.

Artificial light can also disrupt the reproductive cycles of birds and impact their migration. Accustomed to relying on stars to navigate at night, birds can be confused by city lights. Some scientists say that nocturnal flight calls help birds collectively make decisions about how to navigate through a blaze of city lights; yet despite these vocalizations, a major cause of death (especially during migration) is from birds crashing into lighted buildings. Hundreds of millions die each year in these collisions. Tracy Aviary is documenting bird collisions in downtown Salt Lake City through the work of citizen scientists. Each morning, teams collect the birds that died the night before during their spring and fall migrations.

Utah has designated a record nine parks as Dark Sky Parks, but it needs to darken its urban areas too. For starters, cities can replace old street lights that send light up into the night sky with lights that shield and direct warmer light tones downward where it's needed. Ordinances could support motion-sensor lights in vast parking areas and minimized nighttime lighting in office buildings. And homeowners could make their homes and

▲ White-crowned sparrows sing shorter, simpler songs at higher frequencies in cities because traffic and construction noises mask the low notes in their songs.

◄ The thrum of traffic is the largest component of noise pollution in cities.

neighborhoods darker by updating outdoor lighting to be "dark-sky friendly" and by turning off all outdoor lights before going to bed. If city residents lobbied their workplaces and the businesses they patronize to reduce light pollution, we would all live healthier.

Quiet Spaces

During the initial COVID-19 lockdowns, people reported that they heard more birds. In one study, ornithologists discovered that when humans stayed home, white-crowned sparrows (*Zonotrichia leucophrys*) doubled their communication distance with quieter songs that were much more intricate and attractive to females. When it was quiet outside, people could hear many more of these dapper birds at twice the distance. In a noisy soundscape, these sparrows are essentially yelling, said one ornithologist, and they are forced to simplify their songs in the same way you may shout out a greatly simplified story in a noisy restaurant.

All creatures with ears suffer in a mangled soundscape. When it's too loud, it's difficult to communicate and the noise is a source of chronic stress. A study of tree swallows, for example, found that nestlings exposed to more human-generated noise were smaller and slower to fledge and develop than those reared in quieter places. All creatures that use their ears to alert to danger, locate and catch food, and find and attract a mate are less successful when they live in noisy places.

As the Wasatch Front population grows and grows, noise pollution becomes more serious. The source of that noise is primarily electromechanical, generated by all our machines. I live a couple of miles from the interstate, but I can hear the ever-present traffic there as a loud and constant hum. (I enjoy imagining how thousands of electric vehicles would bring a welcome quieting of this city.)

It's hard to escape noise pollution's effects, because our brains process sound all the time, even when we're asleep. Because our ears are on duty 24/7, we are hard-wired to react to noise, and that's not healthy. Exposure to loud and/or constant noise ramps up humans' heart rates and multiplies

◀ Poor air quality shortens the average Utahn's lifespan by two years and also harms wildlife.

stress hormones, which can lead to increased blood pressure and heart disease. One study of noise concluded that the average resident of a large city loses more than three healthy life-years as a result of the din, which contributes to hearing loss, obesity, diabetes, and cognitive impairment in children.

Clean Air

For many of us, life seems pretty focused on Earth's crust, to which gravity binds us. But we live within an atmosphere that reaches six miles above our heads and is made and moved by all of us. Each of us breathes 23,000 breaths a day; in an essential way, we are what we breathe.

The pandemic taught us a lot about air—how air from our breaths transports the virus to others and also what happens to air when human activity slows down (in what some scholars call an anthropause). Air, of course, is the invisible transporter of sound, light, and pollutants. During the COVID-19 shutdowns, less human activity created a perfect environment for a natural experiment to observe how profoundly we alter the air. The air in thousands of cities changed from brown to blue. Residents of Jalandhar, India, could see the Dhauladhar mountain range in the Himalayas for the first time in thirty years. Millions of us personally experienced that the living world could be different and healthier for everyone: you cannot unsee a mountain range or unbreathe a clean breath.

When I moved to Salt Lake City more than twenty-five years ago, most people thought air pollution occurred only during winter inversions, when a dense layer of cool air swaps places with warmer air, trapping pollutants in the valley. Now we know that unhealthy air can occur year-round. Clear links have been made between air pollution exposure and asthma, respiratory and heart problems, problems in pregnancy, numerous kinds of cancers, and even autism. Like noise exposure, exposure to air pollution can shave one to three (or more) years off a person's life.

Animals also suffer from air pollution. A study of bird abundance and air quality over a fifteen-year period determined that air quality regulations that reduced smog in thousands of counties resulted in 1.5 billion fewer bird deaths. Ozone pollution is especially harmful to small migratory songbirds such as warblers and finches, because it damages their respiratory systems, compromises the health of plants they eat, and reduces insect numbers. Long-term exposure to air pollution can poison wildlife by disrupting endocrine function, causing organ damage and increasing vulnerability to disease and stress, and harming habitat and food sources.

Generating electricity with clean, renewable energy and putting thousands of electric vehicles on our streets would go a long way toward clearing pollutants from our air. We could all take deep, healthy breaths.

Cool Places

Since the 1970s, Utah has warmed three degrees Fahrenheit as a result of climate change—well above the global average, making us the fifth fastest warming state in the nation. And the last six years have been the hottest ever recorded, creating serious consequences for the nation's second-driest state. In a hotter climate, water evaporates more quickly and thirsty animals and plants require more. Less precipitation falls as snow, which means less water is available for summer use as it melts.

For much of the year, there is a clear green line between the watered city and the unwatered land surrounding it. Although (some) humans are able to turn on their air conditioners and sprinklers, other creatures lack such options. Warming temperatures increase animal mortality, whether from heat stress, lack of water, or desiccated forage. Researchers warn that heat stress—particularly from extreme temperatures—could become a major factor in future species extinctions. Birds suffer more than other animals because they are largely active during the day.

Heat waves with extreme temperatures are the deadly consequences of the worsening climate crisis, and their frequency, intensity, and duration are expected to increase, resulting in the deaths of humans and other animals. Cities along the Wasatch Front are more vulnerable to extreme heat because of the urban heat island effect. A city's buildings and roads absorb more of

► This thermal image taken on a hot summer day in downtown Salt Lake City shows the cooling power of trees. The shaded grass (shown in blue and green) is forty degrees cooler than the exposed pavement (shown in yellow and red).

◄ The light-colored roof over the Natural History Museum of Utah reflects light and helps keep the building cooler, while solar panels provide a source of renewable energy.

the sun's heat than vegetated landscapes do and then release it at night, resulting in much higher daytime and nighttime temperatures. The impacts of the heat island effect include increased energy consumption, increased air pollutants, and compromised human health—plus, of course, decreased comfort. These impacts are experienced disproportionately by people of color and by those who live in low-income, under-resourced urban neighborhoods that lack the trees and greenery present in wealthier neighborhoods.

Cooling the landscape of the urban Wasatch Front is important for our health and the health of urban nature. More trees and greenery—especially low-water plants—would provide shade and reduce temperatures. Light-colored, reflective roadways and roofs would also help dramatically. Because a black roof can be as much as forty degrees hotter than a white one, various cities in the United States are undertaking campaigns to replace black roofs with white ones.

The population of the Wasatch Front is expected to grow significantly in the next decade, putting increasing pressure on our health as well as the health of the urban nature we love. The pandemic brought many people outdoors, which helped them connect with cherished, constant nature. An important step is to give back. Learn about urban nature, enjoy it, drink it in, and consider what it needs from you in return—dark, cool, quiet spaces and clean air. Urban nature needs your fascination, love, and protection.

Julia Corbett explores human relationships with the living world and how culture affects our perception and valuation of all that keeps us alive. A professor emerita of communication and author of four books, she now splits her time between Oregon and a Wyoming mountain cabin.

We All Need Trees

Tony Gliot

Cities and forests grew together in the valleys of the Wasatch Front. When European-American settlers arrived in 1847, expanses of tall grasses and sagebrush filled the valleys. Cottonwoods, box elders, and a handful of other tree species grew mainly along the banks of streams and rivers. The valleys certainly weren't desolate deserts, but they weren't forests either. The vast majority of trees that form a green canopy across the valleys today were planted and nurtured by people.

Utah settlers went to great lengths to plant trees that reminded them of the homes they left behind and that provided shelter, shade, and sustenance in their new cities. In 1851, Salt Lake City passed an ordinance requiring every lot owner "to set out in front of their lots such trees for shade . . . [that

► Sagebrush, not trees, dominated the view across the Salt Lake Valley in 1869.

would] be the best calculated to adorn and improve the city." Initially, just a handful of species were available—black locust, Siberian elm, Lombardy poplar, and fruit trees.

Garden clubs and horticultural societies soon began experimenting with any tree they could get their hands on to see what species would flourish in Utah. In the early twentieth century, when many growing American cities were removing trees to make way for roads and buildings, residents of the Wasatch Front continued planting. The Salt Lake Valley went from supporting just a few tree species prior to 1847 to more than 290 different species today. Salt Lake City's urban forest alone includes more than 88,000 public trees—a figure that doesn't include all the trees in yards and other private spaces.

The urban forests of the Wasatch Front are examples of biodiversity created by humans. They are ecosystems shaped by both biological and social forces in an amazing collaboration between trees and people. The fact that huge organisms such as trees survive in cities seems rather miraculous when you stop to think about it. With pollution, compacted soils, poor drainage, road salt, heat, vibrations, and new diseases, city life is often hard on trees. Urban trees not only survive, but they share gifts that make our cities livable for people and many other creatures.

▼ The vast majority of trees that create a cover of green in the valleys along the Wasatch Front were planted and nurtured by people.

▲ Utahns made planting trees in their new cities a priority. This 1911 Arbor Day Ceremony celebrated a tree planting in Salt Lake City's Liberty Park.

Trees Make Cities Livable

The number of trees, especially large trees, in our neighborhoods has a big impact on the number and kinds of animals that live in our communities. You can think of each tree as a bustling community of its own. Animals find food and shelter in every part of a tree—among its branches and leaves, beneath its bark, and between its roots. Collectively, the trees in an urban forest create a network that birds, squirrels, and bats travel through and call home. Filled with life—from the more obvious mammals and birds, to tiny invertebrates and mysterious fungi—urban forests are dynamic places full of energy and wonder.

Humans also depend on urban forests for a wide range of ecosystem services that improve city life in myriad ways. You've undoubtedly experienced one of the most important services urban trees provide—their cooling power. Just as the shade of one tree can help keep you cool on a hot day, the shade of many trees helps lower temperatures in a city. Buildings and pavement absorb heat from the sun during the day and release heat at night, preventing an urban area from cooling overnight—a phenomena known as the urban heat island effect. Trees combat this by shading heat-trapping surfaces. Shaded surfaces can be up to forty-five degrees cooler than surfaces in the full sun. Trees also act like natural swamp coolers, cooling the daytime air as the water they release from their leaves evaporates.

A 2015 study by the University of Georgia of fifty cities in the United States ranked Salt Lake City among the top three most impacted by the

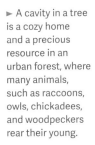

► A cavity in a tree is a cozy home and a precious resource in an urban forest, where many animals, such as raccoons, owls, chickadees, and woodpeckers rear their young.

▲ These two 1998 satellite images of Salt Lake City show the cooling effects of trees and water: the hot yellow and red areas in the infrared thermal image on the right are mostly roads and buildings, while the cool green and blue areas represent trees, other plants, and water.

◄ Trees lining a street provide a wide range of ecosystem services that improve city life and help create a sense of place.

urban heat island effect. Tapping into the cooling power of trees in more neighborhoods of all kinds—residential, commercial, and industrial—will be key to coping with a changing climate as the average summer temperatures along the Wasatch Front continue to rise.

Cooling is just the tip of the tree-benefits iceberg. Strategically placed trees can reduce energy consumption by blocking summer sun and winter winds, can increase property values, and can dampen harmful urban noise and light pollution. We are learning more about how, in the right context, trees can filter pollutants from our air as well as absorb and store carbon, all while producing oxygen that we breathe.

Trees also play an important role in how our communities manage scarce water resources. Though trees consume water themselves, the shade they provide can actually reduce the amount of water our lawns and other planted landscapes require. Tree canopies can also reduce the burden on our stormwater systems by intercepting rain, so that the soil has more of a chance to absorb water rather than losing it as it quickly flows into storm drains. This leads to healthier urban streams with better water quality.

Deep-Rooted Connections

Our connections to urban forests, however, go much deeper than these important ecosystem services. A wave of research beginning in the 1980s has demonstrated that trees have a profoundly positive impact on our social, mental, and physical health. A now-famous study showed that patients healing from surgery spent fewer days in the hospital if their windows offered views of trees. We've since learned that trees can be just what the doctor ordered to help us destress and recharge as we venture outdoors to exercise or meet new friends.

Our relationship with trees in the urban forest is often deeply personal. Many of us have a special connection with a particular tree—perhaps it's a

► Many people experience a personal connection to a tree that plays a special role in their life.

How to Meet a Tree

In springtime, find a flowering tree. Observe how the tree in full bloom stands out in the landscape. Try to imagine how the tree might appear to other animals. Are the flowers fragrant? See if you can spot any bees or other pollinators at work. Are any birds getting an early start on building nests?

On a hot summer afternoon, force yourself to endure a few moments of unobstructed sun before seeking respite in the shade of a tree. Stay a while and enjoy the tree's microclimate. Allow your preoccupations to drift away until only the present moment remains. Trees are great at helping us calm our minds.

In autumn, spend some time close to a tree whose leaves have changed color and are beginning to fall. Watch the squirrels frantically work to store food. Can you spot crows and jays adding to their food caches? The beauty and urgency of autumn in the urban forest is exhilarating.

Don't mistake leafless for lifeless in the winter. Though the urban forest's deciduous trees may be sleeping, many creatures that rely on trees are still quite active. See if you can spot animal tracks leading up to a tree or crumbs of food that have fallen from an animal feasting in the tree canopy above. Want to get out of the chilly wind? Pine and spruce trees can create wind breaks in the winter, and they smell great too!

◄ This tree, along with thousands of others, was wrenched from the soil during a 2020 windstorm in Salt Lake City.

tree we planted, played in as a child, admired for its beauty, or found solace under. Trees' longevity makes them steady companions and witnesses to our lives. We often turn to trees to help us commemorate important events or people. We may plant a tree in our yard to celebrate a birth or memorialize a relative. At public memorials, such as the International Peace Gardens at Jordan Park, Memory Grove Park, and along the Ogden River Parkway, trees preserve a community's memories.

When our favorite trees suffer, we grieve. In September 2020, hurricane-force winds toppled or damaged more than 4500 public trees in Salt Lake City and many more trees on private property. Towering giants lay helpless on the ground, often with portions of their roots wrenched from the soil. The media used the metaphor of a battlefield strewn with corpses to describe the damage. Many people experienced a visceral reaction to the destruction of so many trees all at once. There was an outpouring of grief among stunned neighbors who wandered the streets and posted on social media, mourning the loss of trees as companions, symbols, refuges, and landmarks. The windstorm was also a reminder that all ecosystems are dynamic and that, in an urban forest, people can play a key role in helping the forest recover and be resilient in the face of future disturbances.

Enduring Forests

Today, the biggest threat faced by the urban forests of the Wasatch Front is drought, but the source of the problem is probably not what you think. Given our arid climate, the vast majority of our trees need supplemental water to survive and thrive. Past generations seem to have understood this need, but now many trees are dying of thirst because people are unintentionally underwatering them. In fact, 75 percent of the public trees that die in urban forests along the Wasatch Front are victims of underwatering.

Because different species and sizes of trees require different amounts of water, there is no one-size-fits-all watering advice for trees, but sprinklers

► A Salt Lake City arborist prunes and shapes a large public tree to help it withstand high winds and heavy snows.

and other irrigation systems designed for lawns definitely don't provide sufficient water to sustain trees. A lawn or garden needs frequent, shallow watering, while a tree requires a deep drink less frequently. (You can learn more about how to water trees properly on the Salt Lake City Urban Forestry website.)

Another way community members can support healthy trees is to make sure they stay in shape. As trees grow, they benefit greatly from pruning to promote strong, healthy branches and an overall shape that can withstand wind and snow. Shaping can also remove branches that are likely to interfere with cars, pedestrians, and buildings. It's best for the tree—and for us—if we prune branches that will not be a part of the tree's permanent structure while they are still small. Cities' urban forestry divisions often take care of trimming public trees, and a tree professional can provide guidance for shaping trees on private property. (The Utah Community Forest Council is a great resource for tree care.)

We can do more to ensure that the gifts of the urban forest are distributed equitably throughout our communities and to maximize their benefits for community health and resiliency. Cities are collaborating with residents to close gaps in the urban forest canopy in neighborhoods with sparse tree cover. City orchards tended by residents could become sources of local, healthy food. The wood pruned from urban forests could be reused in countless ways—to produce mulch and biochar (a charcoal-like substance made by burning forestry waste and used as a soil additive), lumber for sign posts, materials for trails, furnishings for public facilities, or creative projects by artists and schools.

Considering the amazing benefits of trees, it might be easy to think that if we plant enough of them we could solve lots of the world's environmental problems. In some respects, this may be true, but if we focus only on tree planting at a global scale—or even on a large-city scale—we might overlook the value and needs of the individual trees that currently surround us. We may overlook the power we have as individuals to help ensure that the trees closest to us thrive. Individual acts of care make a big difference.

Residents of the Wasatch Front have been nurturing urban forests for more than 170 years. Even after 170 years, this forest is still young. The future holds opportunities for growth and refinement as we learn more about and invest in collaborating with trees. The urban forest will undoubtedly face setbacks and challenges from insects, disease, weather, urban growth, and climate change. But people need trees, so the forest will endure, and that's a pretty comforting thought.

....

You can get to know a variety of trees in several arboretums along the Wasatch Front that are free to visit.

- Bertrand F. Harrison Arboretum on the Brigham Young University campus, Provo
- Murray City Park Arboretum, 296 East Murray Park Lane, Murray
- Ogden Botanical Gardens, 1750 Monroe Boulevard, Ogden
- Mark Smith Memorial Arboretum at the Salt Lake City Cemetery, 200 N Street, Salt Lake City
- State Arboretum of Utah on the University of Utah campus, Salt Lake City
- Utah State University Botanical Center, 920 South 50 West, Kaysville

Tony Gliot is the lucky person with the job of growing and managing trees for the benefit of people who live in Salt Lake City. Officially, he's the Salt Lake City Forester and director of the city's Urban Forestry Division.

It Starts with Water

Brian Tonetti

Water is sacred to many, necessary for all. Along the Wasatch Front, streams burst into valleys from the canyons carved into the towering Wasatch and Oquirrh mountain ranges. These tendrils of life cutting through the broad, high-desert valleys once formed meandering green veins. Some combined and others evaporated. Eventually, they flowed into what is now Great Salt Lake, where water molecules evaporated in the dry air, leaving behind the mineral salts they carried. Then the cycle began anew.

For thousands of years, Indigenous peoples fished in the streams, foraged from vegetation growing along their banks, hunted wildlife grazing nearby, and traveled and traded along their corridors. With deep cultural connections to their life-sustaining waters, they stewarded the health of the streams and built communities near their shores. When European-American settlers arrived in the Salt Lake Valley in 1847, they quickly began to change the flow of water through the valley. In fact, within two days after arriving, the first settlers had planted five acres of potatoes and dammed City Creek to irrigate the land. Thus began a century of taming streams to serve the needs of burgeoning cities.

A Century of Taming

Rivers and streams were truly the lifeblood of growing cities in Utah's dry climate, as they provided the water that made building communities possible. Rivers became a vital part of many communities' infrastructures, but they were often taxed to their limits by demands for irrigation, industrial power, and drinking water. Increasing diversions left some old stream channels devoid of water.

Problems with flooding, steeply eroded banks, and water quality led many people to see these urban waterways as nuisances or threats. Because spring often brought floods that damaged fields and houses along the

◄ By 1909, the banks of City Creek had eroded as a result of efforts to control its flow.

▶ The City Creek Aqueduct, a large underground pipe, was under construction east of State Street in 1910.

stream banks, settlers channelized waterways, straightening their previously meandering flows to control flooding. This caused the stream banks to erode, and the resulting steep gullies became safety concerns. Streams also doubled as early sewer systems, an "out of sight, out of mind" way to eliminate waste that led to polluted waters. In an attempt to address these challenges, Salt Lake City began to divert portions of its streams into underground pipes in the early twentieth century. Gray replaced green as creeks were traded for bricks and mortar, concrete, and asphalt.

Some Salt Lake City residents lamented the loss of their sustaining streams. The author of a 1921 *Deseret News* article opined, "To hide

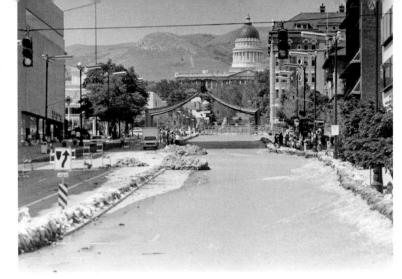

► City Creek flowed down State Street in 1983, prompting some to rethink the Wasatch Front's relationship with urban streams.

completely the flowing water [of City Creek] within a conduit and to make of [North Temple] a stretch of ordinary pavement would be to throw away an opportunity for which many cities would gladly pay a million dollars."

Impervious surfaces in growing cities created another problem. Hard surfaces, such as roads, buildings, and parking lots, prevent rainwater from soaking into the ground. Cities built stormwater systems to channel rainwater running off these surfaces into storm drains, which dumped directly into waterways. These smooth, concrete pipes and straightened, deepened streams sped up the water's velocity. As a result, during big storms, torrents of water came crashing through storm drains in flash floods that damaged streams and neighborhoods.

In 1983, a paradigm-shifting catastrophe opened the door for a new relationship with our urban waterways. The combination of a large winter snowpack and rapid spring melt caused many streams to swell along the Wasatch Front. Floods in Provo Canyon shut down the highway, Utah Lake threatened to flood Provo, and mudslides were common. Most famously, City Creek overtopped its banks at a culvert in Memory Grove Park when flood debris restricted its flow. The resulting "State Street River"—created by lining State Street with thousands of sandbags—caught headlines as people kayaked and fished in downtown Salt Lake City. After fourteen days, the flooding subsided, wooden pedestrian bridges were dismantled, and thousands of sandbags were removed. Damage in Salt Lake County was estimated at $34 million; statewide, the total was $200 million.

In 1995, Salt Lake City began to reconsider the last century of urban water management, realizing its inadequacy as a long-term solution. One of the first glimmers of change was the transformation of a parking lot into City Creek Park, where a section of the creek reemerged from a buried pipe to flow above ground once again—gray to green. Now, benches, trees, and a stone-lined creek create an oasis in the heart of downtown Salt Lake City.

◄ Cultural daylighting draws attention to underground waterways through art projects or signage—in this case, a section of Red Butte Creek, which was diverted underground in the early 1900s.

▶ You'd never know that Red Butte, Emigration, and Parleys Creeks entered the Jordan River here through two concrete pipes beneath the pavement.

Envisioning a Century of Repair

In 2014, I gathered with twenty other students in the bowels of the University of Utah's College of Architecture and Planning. We were tasked with creating a new vision for the Salt Lake Valley's urban waters—shifting from a century of taming to a century of repair and revitalization. Our hundred-year plan proposed "daylighting" the valley's underground streams—bringing them back to the surface.

Daylighting involves restoring a diverted underground stream back to a naturally functioning aboveground waterway and riparian (streamside) ecosystem—or restoring it to the most natural state possible given factors upstream, surrounding land use, and available space. Daylighting can also be architectural or cultural in nature. Architectural daylighting brings an underground stream to the surface through an engineered channel with a concrete streambed and banks, like City Creek in City Creek Park. Cultural daylighting celebrates a buried stream through markers or public art to showcase its historic path.

Starting with City Creek, we traced each of Salt Lake County's seven major creeks from their headwaters to their confluence with the Jordan River. Each class started with a new canyon and creek to explore. We noticed that three of the creeks—Red Butte, Emigration, and Parleys—spilled into the Jordan River at the same location, 1300 South and 900 West in Salt Lake City. Our initial visit to the site revealed a neglected lot sandwiched between an auto shop and a half-burnt home. A fisherman who sat in a makeshift captain's (computer) chair explained that he'd been fishing here for forty years, rattling off an impressive list of catches.

Back in the classroom, we explored the location's rich potential and conceived a plan for the Three Creeks Confluence—the demonstration project of our century-long plan to uncover and restore the creeks in the Salt Lake Valley. To ensure that the plan could live beyond our classroom walls, we formed the Seven Canyons Trust, a nonprofit dedicated to uncovering and restoring the buried and impaired creeks in the valley.

▼ The Three Creeks Confluence project uncovered 200 feet of waterway and created a new community gathering space with a fishing pier, boat access, and a bridge to the Jordan River Parkway.

With support from Salt Lake City, the Seven Canyons Trust raised more than $3 million for the construction of the Three Creeks Confluence. We uncovered 200 feet of the combined streams and constructed a Jordan River Trail connection, fishing bridge, and plaza space. We created a space for the community to connect with nature and the waters that sustain us. And this was just the beginning.

In partnership with Salt Lake County and all eight streamside municipalities, the Seven Canyons Trust envisioned the "Seven Greenways Vision Plan"

that highlighted opportunities for creating greenways on each of the seven creeks flowing into the Salt Lake Valley. A greenway is a corridor along a stream and adjacent land that can serve many purposes, including enhancing bicycle and pedestrian access, generating economic activity, increasing resilience to flooding, and providing valuable habitat for wildlife. The plan inspires a common vision over the next century to revitalize our waterways and connect people in the Salt Lake Valley through greenways.

Investing in Rivers to Build Community

Despite the many challenges urban rivers face, they offer some of the most valued natural spaces in our neighborhoods. Increasingly, city planners and residents realize investing in the health of urban rivers creates better places to live for people and wildlife. This transformation is happening all along the Wasatch Front. Where abandoned cars once lined the banks of the Ogden River, boardwalks and trails now meander through new riparian habitats and wetlands intended to clean stormwater before it flows into the river. Where 2500 tires, 200 batteries, and 15,000 tons of debris were fished out of the river, kayakers now surf wave trains and anglers catch trout in restored riffles, runs, and pools.

With investment from the many communities through which it flows, the abused and neglected Jordan River has now become a regional open space and recreation gem. Bikers, runners, walkers, and the occasional equestrian flock to the fifty-mile trail that connects Utah Lake to Great Salt Lake. Canoeists and kayakers float among restored cottonwoods and willows. Kingfishers and kestrels perch in trees, while deer, beavers, and foxes browse, build, and hunt below. Riparian restoration sites dot the corridor,

◄ The Ogden River was of little value to people or wildlife until tons of garbage and abandoned cars were removed from its banks and channel during renovation.

► Improvements to fish habitat along the revitalized Ogden River earned sections of the river Utah Blue Ribbon fishery designations.

and the surrounding community is increasingly supportive of the Jordan River's rehabilitation and protection.

The restoration at the delta of the Provo River and Utah Lake created habitat for the endangered June sucker (*Chasmistes liorus*). The dynamic delta ecosystem disappeared as the river was channelized and the area drained and cleared for farming, roads, and an airport. New braided channels and wetlands re-create critical spawning habitat as the Provo River meanders toward the extended Utah Lake shoreline. New trails, river access, fishing platforms, and a viewing tower provide recreation opportunities near Provo neighborhoods.

These are only a few of the river revitalization projects undertaken by communities along the Wasatch Front. They demonstrate the many benefits of restoring urban waterways: increasing visual attraction, creating a sense of place, and masking the sounds and sights of the urban environment. Residents gain restored access to nature, critical for the development of children and the mental and physical well-being of adults. These places also provide gathering spaces for picnics, events, and festivals, and become living laboratories for nearby schools. Streamside pathways and commuter trails create active transportation and recreation connections. In fact, a 120-mile trail now winds along the Provo River, Murdock Canal, Jordan River, Great Salt Lake, and Ogden River, connecting communities and their adjacent ecosystems.

Restoration and daylighting can also increase property values and business revenues. Along the Ogden River, property values almost doubled post-restoration between 2000 and 2018. The population along the river corridor has increased by 37 percent, compared to an increase of 21 percent throughout Ogden. People want to live, work, and play near our waterways.

Restoring and daylighting urban waterways also offers many ecological benefits for our communities. These projects can reduce flood risk by removing choke points created by culverts and slowing water velocity with new meanders and vegetated banks. Streams increase groundwater infiltration and storage, especially with the inclusion of a floodplain. Groundwater can become an increasingly important source of drinking water as climate change creates uncertainty and a growing population taxes our water systems.

An estimated 80 percent of Utah's wild species rely on riparian ecosystems, though these habitats represent less than 2 percent of the Wasatch Front's total land area. Birds offer a prime example of the key role of our riparian habitats. The Wasatch Front is a critical stopping point for neotropical migratory birds, where riparian vegetation supports the nesting and breeding of these world travelers. More than 7.5 million birds—three times the number of their human neighbors—and 250 different avian species depend on the riparian ecosystems along the Wasatch Front. By creating new and healthy riparian habitats, we can support Utah's biodiversity, decrease habitat fragmentation, form wildlife corridors, and improve fish passage.

Work to revitalize our streams also revitalizes our communities and our connection to nature—the place that sustains and nurtures us. The next time you pass a stream, don't forget to thank its waters. Maybe wave, though it's not a "goodbye"—rather, a "see you later." See you later as the snow in the mountains. See you later as drops falling from a trout on a line. See you later as a stream from which a dog drinks. See you later as the sound that soothes. See you later as the saline waters nurturing millions of winged migrants. See you later as clouds that pass by the window in the classroom or office, in the backyard, in the forest, or in the wilderness of the Wasatch. It all starts with water.

Brian Tonetti is a founder and the executive director of the Seven Canyons Trust, a nonprofit working to uncover and restore the buried and impaired creeks in the Salt Lake Valley. His passion for waterways developed out of a love for skiing (a frozen watersport).

Cities that Work with Nature

Sarah Jack Hinners

Psychologist Eric Fromm coined the term "biophilia" (literally, "love for life") to describe the connection humans feel to other living things. Later, ecologist E. O. Wilson developed the "biophilia hypothesis," proposing that biophilia is innate to humans: we all feel a desire, or even a deep need, to connect not just with other humans but with nonhuman life. Our expressions of biophilia may be close to home as we place a bouquet of flowers on a table or enjoy the companionship of a pet, or they may take us into the wilderness to hike or camp.

In cities and towns, however, we often leave little room for nonhuman nature in our daily environments, and when we do, it is almost always an afterthought. We eliminate the "nature" to build our buildings and homes and roads and parking lots, and then we add "nature" back in the form of landscaping. But nature fills the spaces we leave for it and also finds the spaces we didn't intend for it to occupy. It thrives in private spaces such as yards, gardens, and commercial landscapes; in the public realm in parks and open spaces; and in forgotten and unclaimed places like vacant lots and abandoned railway corridors. It creeps into sidewalk cracks and gutters and puddles after a rainstorm. We spend a lot of time and effort fighting elements of urban nature we deem unwanted and just as much time encouraging the elements we deem desirable.

As an urban ecologist, I think constantly that there must be better, less effortful ways to live a biophilic life in the city. Because connection to nature is so important to humans, how can we do a better job of purposefully nurturing it in the spaces we inhabit? How can we create biophilic cities that provide close and daily contact with nature for residents?

Consider, for example, the fascinating American cultural and ecological phenomenon of the front lawn, an idealized emblem of desirable urban nature. Neighbors compete (overtly or subtly) to have the most perfect, emerald-green, weed-free, inch-and-a-half-high turf on the block. But in reality, urban nature is a mixture of the intentional and the unintentional. For every tree or rosebush or lawn that we plant and carefully nurture, there are multitudes of other plants and animals that grow and thrive uninvited and unnurtured by us, such as ubiquitous dandelions, sunflowers, trees of heaven, birds, squirrels, and raccoons.

▲ Lovely and uninvited, violets materialize in lawns across the Wasatch Front each spring.

My front lawn, for example, contains many species of grass, along with a carpet of violets that bloom in shades from white to dark purple in the spring and pretty much any other spreading and low-lying plant species that has adapted to regular mowing. These plants that cover the ground while staying green during the hot summer provide textural complexity to my lawn. They include clover, yarrow, and late-summer purple asters, which spread laterally after mowing and create a September carpet of mauve stars. I'm sure that the lawn traditionalists in my neighborhood are horrified, but these spring and fall displays of uninvited, unintentional flowers are beautiful and bring me—and the bees—much joy.

Let Nature Do Its Thing

The key to a more biophilic city, I believe, is to provide more opportunities for nature to come in and do its own thing. Green infrastructure is one approach to doing just that, by incorporating biophilia into the planning and design of our urban areas. It is based on the idea that nature and natural systems are and should be as essential to the functioning of a city as roads and sewer pipes. To perceive urban nature through a green infrastructure lens, we can start by asking several questions: What benefit or service does this (tree, park, yard, parking strip, vacant lot) provide to the city? Does it offer shade, erosion control, or habitat for wild creatures? Is it filtering pollutants or providing a respite for humans?

After we've asked and answered those questions, we can ask follow-up questions: What green infrastructure is possible here? Where could we invite nature to come in and do good things? These lines of thinking are biophilic. The first group of questions enables us to consider and value each element of urban nature—for example, before we cut down a tree or pull up a plant, we can stop and consider what services it is providing. The follow-up questions lead us to look for opportunities: Where can we create a place where something can grow?

Water Unwise

In July 1847, when Brigham Young famously stood at the mouth of Emigration Canyon looking out over the Salt Lake Valley, he probably saw a landscape familiar to anyone who has lived in the Great Basin—grasslands with scattered sagebrush. The grasses would have already faded to pale gold. Dark green ribbons and patches of trees would have delineated the waterways of creeks and the Jordan River and places where springs or a high water table provided moisture. In Utah, the color green is inextricably linked to water, and, like water in this dry place, green is precious and rare.

What limits our potential for biophilic cities in Utah is available water. The average annual rainfall along the Wasatch Front is about fifteen inches, which creates an environment that is considered semi-arid, though not true desert. Inconveniently, most of that precipitation arrives during the colder months, when plants are dormant and unable to utilize it fully. The proximity of the Wasatch Mountains is a tremendous advantage, as the water from melting snowpack sustains us throughout the hot, dry summer. However, we use our precious water unwisely here. We have designed our cities to regard rainfall as something so abundant as to constitute a nuisance that must be gotten out of the way as quickly as possible, while simultaneously using inordinate amounts of potable water.

The older residential neighborhoods along the Wasatch Front, consisting of single-family homes with green lawns on tree-lined streets, are the perfect places to observe the irony of our approach to water. The sycamores, lindens, maples, locusts, catalpas, and horse-chestnuts that line our streets are not native to Utah, but they can survive here if they receive enough water. And the shade they provide in the intense summer heat is increasingly critical to livability as the climate warms.

▼ This constructed wetland is an example of green infrastructure. It was built to enable trash to settle out of stormwater before it enters the Jordan River but also created habitat for wildlife.

A large percentage of these street trees grow in park strips, the vegetated strip between the street and the sidewalk that's usually about four to eight feet wide. Much of the underground root area of the tree is under the street and sidewalk. That leaves only the narrow park strip and nearby yard to capture rainwater and enable it to infiltrate into the soil, where the roots can access it. When it rains, most of the water runs off impervious surfaces—streets, sidewalks, and roofs—and travels along the gutter at the edge of the street until it reaches a storm drain, which carries it as quickly as possible into the nearest stream.

Meanwhile, the thirsty tree roots lie within inches of that precious flow and have no access to it at all. To keep trees alive, we use our potable water supply, which is derived from snowmelt captured in reservoirs high in the mountains and treated for drinking, to water our trees and grass.

In the predevelopment landscape, most of the rainwater soaked into the ground, where it made its way to streams slowly via groundwater, filtered along the way through soil and plant roots. In most developed urban areas, the runoff moving through storm drains includes a host of pollutants that are carried from urban yards and surfaces, including trash, fertilizers, oils and grease, and even heavy metals—all of which are detrimental to the receiving stream. In addition, in heavy rains, water from runoff flows so quickly that resulting flash floods erode the stream banks. The stream degradation caused by urban runoff is so ubiquitous worldwide that the scientific community has a name for it: urban stream syndrome.

This standard approach to managing water in urban areas was developed in wetter climates to minimize flooding. Indeed, we see flooding sporadically in Salt Lake City after an intense storm drops water too fast for the storm sewers to carry it away. However, the conventional approach to managing stormwater is counter to supporting biophilia, because it treats our scarce natural precipitation—the source and support of all our beloved greenness—exclusively as a hazard and fails to perceive it as a resource.

◄ Many of the trees in our urban forests grow in park strips surrounded by compacted soils and impervious surfaces, which keep rainwater from seeping into the soil and make it inaccessible to tree roots.

► This trash was carried by neighborhood runoff into storm drains leading to streams that feed the Jordan River.

▲ Impervious surfaces in the urban landscape, such as roads and sidewalks, prevent rainwater from soaking into the soil.

A New Relationship with Water

On the University of Utah campus, next to the Architecture Building where I work, we once had a flooding problem that was associated with very conventional urban design. A wide sidewalk extended down a slope toward the building, and between the sidewalk and the building was a lawn that also sloped downward. During heavy rains, water would rush across the sidewalk, down the grassy slope, and into the building's ground floor—it was lots of water that did plenty of harm and no good.

When the university replaced some pipes under that grassy slope, students and faculty worked with the university grounds team to redesign the sloping area to capture rainwater runoff and redirect it into a sand-filled, rock-lined channel bordered with plants—a bioswale. A bioswale is an example of a green infrastructure approach that values water as a resource. The rocks slow the speed of the water as it runs off the sidewalk and keep it from eroding the soil. The water then percolates quickly into the sand, replenishing groundwater supplies. Throughout the area, we planted a pollinator garden, with a path for wandering and flat rocks for sitting.

◄ This pollinator garden at the University of Utah grows in a bioswale that was designed to slow rainwater and enable it to soak into the soil.

Although the plants in the garden are watered by a drip irrigation system, they use less water than the lawn did. Their roots will have access to the rainwater stored deep in the soil, and they may even filter out some of the pollutants in the water, leaving it cleaner as it soaks deeper into the ground. Because of the bioswale, the building no longer floods and the campus community now has a beautiful garden to enjoy.

As a side note, even this carefully designed pollinator garden includes a mix of intentional and unintentional species. As they do all over the West, sunflowers spontaneously germinated here, as did a sprawling native datura plant, its huge, white, trumpet-shaped flowers opening in the evening to attract moth pollinators. We remove other uninvited arrivals, such as bindweed, because they are "weedy" and we need to keep up appearances, but each uninvited guest is at least given consideration for its value to the garden community. Over time, the plants in this garden have successfully reproduced and spread, filling in some of the bare gaps. And, of course, the garden party has attracted a wide variety of pollinator guests, including bees, hummingbirds, and butterflies.

Another great local example of green infrastructure is the reconstructed section of Grant Avenue in Ogden, which is now a "green street." Instead of channeling rainwater through a typical curb-and-gutter system, runoff is channeled into a planted strip via curb cuts. This rainwater planting strip serves to beautify the street, protect the Ogden River from pollutants and flash floods, and increase safety by separating the bike lane from vehicle traffic.

Here in Utah, changing our relationship with water may be our best shot at encouraging nature in our urban world. Many homeowners believe that to use water sustainably, they need to do away with all the greenery in their yards. Certainly, this reduces water use and doesn't require mowing or weeding, but it is not biophilic. It provides neither beauty nor joy, nor the sound of a breeze passing through leaves, the buzz of bees, or cool shade in the heat of summer. Instead of avoiding greenery, one of the easiest low-effort green infrastructure practices for homeowners is to direct the downspouts from roof gutters into small depressions in the landscape. The increased moisture in the deeper layers of the soil can support a lush plant community—a rain garden—and where the plants thrive, so do more birds, insects, and other wildlife.

Rather than give up our urban nature in the name of water sustainability, we need to be strategic about managing and directing the water we do have; protecting our creeks, rivers, lakes, and wetlands and making them accessible; and learning to see and appreciate the uninvited guests. If something is thriving, we should appreciate its ability to thrive where many tender things cannot and look for the beauty there—like a lawn with spring violets and autumn asters.

Sarah Jack Hinners, PhD, is an urban ecologist at the University of Utah. She grew up in the country, miles from the nearest paved surface, and is passionate about connecting urban dwellers with nonhuman nature in everyday life.

► Curb cuts, such as these on Grant Avenue in Ogden, enable rainwater to flow into vegetated areas instead of past them.

◄ Use the rain that falls on your roof to water your yard by directing downspouts toward thirsty grass and other plants that can absorb it.

The Power of Community

Ellen Eiriksson

"This is the best class ever!" a soaking wet student shouted as he emerged from Salt Lake City's Jordan River. Lorie Millward and her class of middle-school students were on a daily walk, exploring a trail near school, when Ernesto noticed something at the river's edge. After donning a pair of waders, he carefully descended the gently sloping bank, where he promptly slipped into the slow-moving river. The experience jump-started a new interest in nature for Ernesto. As Lorie recalls, "He became an energetic explorer after baptizing himself [in the river] completely."

Going with the flow of student interest and exploration was a cornerstone of Lorie's vision for her 2008 Museum Studies class at the Salt Lake Center for Science Education. For the school year, the students embarked on a journey to create their own in-school museum. To gather inspiration, students spent time in the school's backyard, equipped with tools to collect specimens, explore, and inquire. They didn't know it yet, but by embracing exploration, Ernesto and his class were close to making an exciting discovery with national implications.

Anyone Can Be a Scientist

Every day, people around the world are making contributions to the field of science. Citizen science involves collaboration between members of the public—people not formally trained in a scientific discipline—and scientists. Citizen scientists ask questions, make observations, submit input, look through data, and even help to analyze and publish new scientific ideas. Because it can involve anyone, anywhere, the term "community science" has emerged as another way to describe this holistic practice.

In the weeks following Ernesto's river dip, Lorie's students came across a bright red insect on a tree trunk that resembled the common eastern box elder bug (Boisea trivittata) they were accustomed to seeing in the neighborhood,

► The first sightings of European firebugs in the Western Hemisphere were in Salt Lake City around 2008.

but this bug had different markings. This curious new insect turned out to be a European firebug *(Pyrrhocoris apterus)*, which is not a native of Utah or even of North America. Though they had been previously spotted in the state, there was no formal record of the European firebug in Utah.

Lorie seized the opportunity for learning and contacted the U.S. Department of Agriculture (USDA) to report the insect. Because the species was not known to be established anywhere in North America at the time, the USDA asked that the class collect specimens and data to help the agency learn more. Students also took multiple field trips to the Natural History Museum of Utah (NHMU) to explore the collections and talk with scientists about developing research skills.

The class proceeded to gather hundreds of insect specimens, take photographs, write field notes on behaviors, and eventually submit a report to the USDA. Using this student-collected data, the agency formally announced that European firebugs had established in North America in a New Pest Advisory Group notice published in 2009. This declaration of establishment was a direct result of students finding, reporting, and collecting data on the European firebug population around the school. This is the heart of citizen science: a group of observant and excited individuals who are not formally trained in science but are participating in science nonetheless.

Recording Urban Biodiversity with iNaturalist

Many species of plants and animals are living alongside us in cities and suburbs. NHMU citizen science volunteer Rebecca Ray, for example, has found more than 200 different species of plants and animals in her small urban backyard. To some, her backyard might seem overgrown, but for Rebecca and the species she finds living in her yard, it is a haven of biodiversity.

Rebecca uses the iNaturalist app to document and identify the wild species living around her home. This free online platform is a database of tens of millions of photographs of wild plants and animals around the globe submitted by nature-curious people like Rebecca. When you submit an image, iNaturalist helps identify what you've photographed, so you can learn about what you're seeing. Each observation can become a conversation with others on the platform—like social media for nature lovers—as experts and amateurs alike help identify what you've observed.

Even though she was once afraid of spiders, Rebecca has become an amateur spider expert. Using the iNaturalist app played a key role in building her passion for and knowledge about arachnids, and users around the world now seek her help in identifying the spiders they observe. iNaturalist helped her overcome her fears, learn more, and make exciting connections with other experts.

When you use iNaturalist, you are a citizen scientist. The observations you make become public records of biodiversity that can help scientists with research and inform discussions on big topics such as conservation efforts and climate change. "We are all gathering data for scientists and helping with this massive scientific effort," says Rebecca.

▲ Rebecca Ray examines a spider she found in her backyard.

Getting Squirrely

Dr. Eric Rickart, NHMU curator of vertebrate zoology, is often asked to give advice to youth who are starting out on their scientific journey. For him, a fundamental first step to being engaged in the natural world is to learn how to see things—looking for, not ignoring, the wild things that are around us all the time.

Squirrels are a classic example of an animal often overlooked in our urban environment. Squirrels are everywhere, so people tend not to think much about them. But if you pay attention to squirrels, you can begin to appreciate their fascinating story. The eastern fox squirrel *(Sciurus niger)*, which was once found primarily in the eastern and central United States, arrived in the Salt Lake Valley around 2011. Someone may have deliberately introduced them, and they are now flourishing along the Wasatch Front thanks to the plentiful trees, food, and water available in our urban environment.

When any species is introduced to an area, scientists have questions: How is this species affecting the local ecosystem? What resources are helping this species be successful? Is the species spreading? The curious thing about studying squirrels in urban environments is that, although they can be easy to find, there are some limits to where researchers can go to study them, because much of the land in our cities and towns is private property. Citizen scientists who document the species in their own yards are thus critical to helping scientists get a full picture of the fox squirrels on the Wasatch

▲ Citizen scientist Mary Miller, who looks for squirrels in her neighborhood for NHMU's Fox Squirrel Project, displays a yard sign to help engage others in the project.

◀ The eastern fox squirrel is a relatively new resident of Utah.

Front. Citizen scientists' observations are providing real-time data on where fox squirrels are spreading and how they are behaving in their new home.

Seeing a unique opportunity to study how a newly introduced species can interact with an ecosystem, Eric and NHMU's citizen science team developed a survey to capture community observations of squirrels in Utah. The team initially examined iNaturalist data to track squirrel expansion and eventually designed a web survey to capture more detailed community-based observations and comments on these squirrels. Hundreds of people in Utah have now submitted thousands of observations about the squirrels living near their homes, providing immeasurable value to the study of this introduced species.

Phillip Kinser had been noticing fox squirrels in his backyard, and when he learned that NHMU was asking residents to report sightings and observations of the animals, he was immediately interested. "The NHMU Fox Squirrel Project intrigued me because I could participate in the surveys and provide meaningful information regarding their behaviors, distribution, and ecological effects given their nonnative status." As Utahns like Phillip and his family continue to submit squirrel observations to NHMU, trends about where the species is living and spreading and insights into squirrel behaviors will begin to emerge.

Fireflies in Utah?

Christy Bills, NHMU entomology and malacology collections manager, knows firsthand of the benefits of connecting with, and being inspired by, citizen scientists. An avid science communicator herself, she talks frequently with the public, not only sharing her own passions but also listening to the stories people share.

One species that kept coming up for Christy in conversations with the public were fireflies—in Utah! She had heard rumors for years that fireflies lived in the state. Though many residents were adamant that fireflies did not live in Utah, others told detailed stories of sightings. NHMU's invertebrates collection supported these claims, however, because several specimens of the beetle were collected in the state and stored at NHMU long ago. But, she wondered, were fireflies still here?

Early in her efforts to locate living firefly populations in Utah, Christy spent an entire field season searching from Bear Lake to Moab, but she came up empty handed. She was essentially "staring into the dark," as she describes it, waiting for something to happen, but fireflies were so elusive that knowing about their general habitats wasn't enough to find them easily. The missing link for Christy was people. After asking the community to report sightings of fireflies for her research, Christy received immediate responses from a broad audience, including suburban homeowners, ranchers, and land managers. Armed with community knowledge, her second season of searching for fireflies was much more productive.

Christy recalls a particular night when she was following up on a report made by a homeowner in Springville at the mouth of Provo Canyon. As she pulled up to the address where she was to meet the firefly observer, she found herself in a suburban environment—houses nearby and streetlights glowing brightly in the newly fallen night. This was not a place she would expect to find an elusive insect with particular habitat needs, and she worried that the trip to the site would be a complete bust. But when the homeowner led her to an adjacent empty lot, she saw fireflies! The property was overgrown with plants and had a naturally fed spring. It was perfect firefly habitat hiding within an established suburban neighborhood and a place Christy would have never found on her own. The homeowner was thrilled when Christy verified the observation and was proud to have found and reported something that was of interest to science.

NHMU's Western Firefly Project has confirmed that fireflies—once thought to be rare—are very much part of Utah's unique and varied ecosystems. With help from collaborators at Canyon Country Discovery Center in Monticello, Southern Utah University in Cedar City, Stokes Nature Center in Logan, and Brigham Young University in Provo, the project has confirmed

▲ Many people are surprised to discover that fireflies flash in wet meadows across Utah in late May and early June.

▼ A citizen scientist holds a tiny glowing firefly in her hand.

► With free apps such as iNaturalist to help you document your discoveries, you can be a citizen scientist wherever you go.

firefly populations in twenty-six of Utah's twenty-nine counties. Additionally, the project has yielded the first scientific records of fireflies in Nevada and Wyoming (the first and third driest states in the United States, respectively) and new populations in Montana, Idaho, Colorado, and Arizona.

As Christy notes, this project would not be possible without contributions from citizen scientists. These community members are key to locating this elusive insect and, for Christy, this collaboration with the community could not be more exciting. "If something as charismatic as fireflies is out there and not much is known about them, imagine what else could be out there!"

Who, Me?

Getting started as a citizen scientist can feel like staring into the dark, waiting for something magical to show itself. The key? Find something that excites you and join the conversation! Start to observe what is around you and share the things you see. A simple observation you make today may provide a valuable piece for the broader scientific puzzle, one that may never have been completed without your watchful eye, observant ear, thoughtful mind, or steady hand.

Contrary to what people might think, "the door is open, and we are asking you to come in," Christy says. The citizen science conversation needs your input. And as Eric Rickart notes, as a citizen scientist, you are "becoming part of the scientific community—building on something that has been going on for generations" and exploring and learning more about the world around us. We can't do it without you!

Ellen Eiriksson has worked as an environmental educator and science communicator since the early 2000s. She manages the Natural History Museum of Utah's Citizen Science Program and she enjoys connecting people, communities, and science.

Birds
78

Fungi and a Lichen
107

Invertebrates
(Insects, Spiders,
and Friends)
118

Mammals
146

Reptiles and
Amphibians
163

127 WASATCH FRONT SPECIES TO KNOW

Street Trees
174

Wild Plants and Trees
194

Birds

Yellow bill

White-striped chin

Broken white eye ring

Rusty red breast and dark back

American Robin

Turdus migratorius

Watch an American robin as it runs across a lawn, pauses, cocks its head, and then pounces on a worm. Did it hear the worm or see it? This question has sparked much debate, with studies supporting both sides. Given their excellent eyesight and hearing, robins are probably relying on both senses, although evidence suggests vision may be more important.

Robins are famous for yanking worms out of suburban lawns, but they actually have a varied diet. In spring, they also hunt insects, snails, and spiders. This high-protein diet helps their chicks grow quickly. As summer progresses, robins enjoy a variety of fruits such as crabapples, juniper berries, sumac, mulberries, and Russian olives. Fruit and berries are staples of their diet in the winter as well.

Winter Flocks

We tend to think of robins as harbingers of spring, but along the Wasatch Front, they are our companions throughout the winter too. Some robins do migrate, but many stay put. They seem to disappear every winter because their behavior changes. Instead of foraging in yards, robins form nomadic flocks—sometimes numbering hundreds of birds—that hang out in trees where fruit is plentiful.

When spring rolls around, these flocks split up and males begin aggressively defending a territory in advance of courting females and raising chicks. That's when we hear their melodic "cheerily, cheer up, cheer up, cheerily, cheer up" song that we associate with the first signs of spring.

Easy Pickings

Robins seem to be benefitting from urbanization. Suburbs make great habitat for robins, with their expanses of lush lawns bordered by trees and shrubs. Though robin populations are increasing, individual birds remain vulnerable to a hazard that's a serious threat to less-adaptable species—domestic cats. Because robins forage on the ground, they are easy targets for cats. Predation by cats is actually the number one human-caused threat to birds in the United States and Canada. Robins and many other birds will be grateful if you keep your cat indoors.

Robins are the quintessential early birds. They often start singing well before dawn. While not exactly night owls, robins are one of the last birds you'll hear singing in the evening.

How to Spot Them

Robins are ubiquitous in cities and suburbs along the Wasatch Front as well as in the forests of the surrounding mountains. Look for them on lawns and listen for their iconic song. They nest in trees and sometimes in sheltered areas under house eaves and porches. Keep an eye out for their cup-shaped nests lined with mud.

American White Pelican

Pelicanus erythrorhynchos

You may have heard the limerick about how a pelican's beak can hold more than its belly can. It's true! An American white pelican's pouch can stretch to hold up to three gallons of water. After scooping up fish, they carefully open their beaks to let water drain out while keeping the fish inside. Along the Wasatch Front, you can find these huge birds where there is sufficient open water. If there's a spot to swim, they'll give it a try.

Fishing Buddies

Pelicans often hang out in groups. They work together to herd fish into shallow water and dip their beaks in unison. This strategy increases each bird's likelihood of a successful catch.

Wispy "nuptial crest" on breeding adults

Breeding adults have a plate on the upper bill

Large bill with extendable pouch

Huge white water bird with a long neck

Eating too many fish can make a pelican too heavy to fly. If an overindulgent pelican needs to get airborne to escape a predator, it may have to regurgitate a recently caught meal.

You'll also see groups of pelicans in flight, soaring on their giant wings with hardly a flap. Their wingspan can reach over nine feet! The only bird with a larger wingspan in the United States is the California condor.

Pelicans are very cautious when it comes to raising chicks. Because they nest on the ground, they seek out small islands in lakes that don't have many predators. One of the special places pelicans are willing to nest is Gunnison Island in the super-salty north arm of Great Salt Lake. As a trade-off for the safety the island offers their chicks, pelican parents have to travel more than sixty miles round-trip each day to find fresh water and fish.

Keeping an Eye on Pelicans

Some 10,000 pelicans once nested on Gunnison Island, which made it one of the largest breeding colonies in North America. Unfortunately, today's historically low water levels in the lake have turned Gunnison Island into a peninsula, and coyotes can now reach the nesting pelicans. Scientists at Westminster College installed fifteen PELIcams on the island to monitor the colony. The cameras take photos every three minutes, so researchers need help reviewing thousands of images to identify predators and rarely observed nesting behaviors. Find out how to get involved at Westminster College's PELIcam website.

The Utah Division of Wildlife Resources is also studying our local pelicans. Since 2017, wildlife technicians have fit more than seventy pelicans with solar-powered Global Positioning System (GPS) transmitter backpacks to track their annual migrations to Mexico and learn more about their behaviors. You can follow the paths of individual pelicans with names like Barnabus, Daphne, and Hook on the PeliTrack website.

How to Spot Them

Look for pelicans along the Wasatch Front between February and October. They are most common in the freshwater wetlands around Great Salt Lake. You can also spot them at Utah Lake, along the Jordan River corridor, and at Lee Kay Ponds, Decker Lake, and ponds at city parks and golf courses.

Barn Swallow

Hirundo rustica

The connection between humans and barn swallows goes way back. Barn swallows historically built their mud-cup nests in caves or on cliffs, but about 2000 years ago in Europe, they started constructing nests on structures made by people instead. Barn swallows in North America made the same switch in the 1900s. Today, virtually all barn swallows nest on structures we build, including under the eaves of buildings, under bridges, in parking garages, and, of course, in the rafters of barns.

Mud Masters

Barn swallows build their own interesting structures. A mated pair constructs a nest from hundreds of tiny mud pellets. After locating a good mud puddle, a barn swallow uses its lower jaw like a trowel to gather mud and mix it with

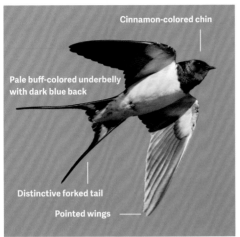

Cinnamon-colored chin

Pale buff-colored underbelly
with dark blue back

Distinctive forked tail

Pointed wings

▲ In this nest full of baby swallows, you can see outlines of the individual mud pellets gathered by their parents.

grass. Then it scoops up a mouthful, flies to the nest site, and attaches the mud pellet to a vertical wall or atop a flat ledge. Building a sturdy mud-cup nest can require 1000 trips to the mud puddle, and a pair of swallows may spend more than two weeks to finish their project!

Barn swallows live much of their life on the wing—feeding, drinking, courting, and even mating in midair. As aerial insectivores, they catch insects in flight, making sharp twists, turns, and swoops in pursuit of their insect prey. They eat primarily flies but also catch beetles, bees, wasps, butterflies, and moths. To drink or bathe in flight, they skim above the water's surface and then effortlessly dip their beaks or whole bodies into the water without missing a wing beat.

Fork-Tailed Flyers

It's easy to recognize a barn swallow in flight: look for its distinctive forked tail created by two long feathers on either side that aid in controlling its acrobatic maneuvers. No other swallow in North America has a forked tail. If you spot a barn swallow at rest, look for its steely blue back, wings, and tail and its buff-colored to reddish brown belly.

As the most abundant and widespread swallows in the world, barn swallows are among a handful of birds that have long lived on every continent (except Antarctica). In the

Americas, they make extended annual migrations from their breeding grounds in Canada, the United States, and northern Mexico to their winter homes in Central America and South America. During migrations, they often travel 600 miles per day, eating on the fly.

How to Spot Them

You can spot barn swallows along the Wasatch Front between April and October. They are common in open areas and near water. Watch for them cruising just a few inches above the ground or water. During the breeding season, you may see a barn swallow gathering mud at a mud puddle.

Wondering who built that mud nest you spotted? Barn swallows make solitary, cup-shaped nests. Cliff swallows prefer communal living and build gourd-shaped mud nests in large colonies.

Black-Capped Chickadee

Poecile atricapillus

Black-capped chickadees are tiny, acrobatic songbirds with lots of energy and big personalities. Their round bodies, oversize heads, and dapper black caps make them easy to recognize and super cute. They are very curious and show little fear of larger animals, including humans. If you put up a new bird feeder, chickadees will likely be the first birds to investigate it.

Oversize head on round body

Black cap and bib

White cheeks

Long, gray tail edged with white

Dinner to Go

Chickadees are rather dainty diners at bird feeders. While house finches sit at the feeder and send shells flying with their strong beaks as they gobble down seeds, chickadees swoop in, grab one sunflower seed, and dart away. In a nearby tree, they drill a hole in the shell with their small, pointed beaks and eat tiny bits of seed while expanding the hole. Chickadees also frequently hide food for later and can remember thousands of hiding spots.

The chickadee's name comes from its famous "chick-a-dee-dee" call. By varying and repeating the four notes in this call, chickadees can convey a variety of messages about food sources, predators, and other flocks of chickadees. The "chick-a-dee-dee" call is just one of sixteen different calls and songs chickadees use to communicate. Scientists are studying this remarkably complex system to learn more about how animal languages—including ours—evolve.

Sounding the Alarm

Chickadees add five or more "dees" to their call to raise the alarm that they've spotted a predator—the more dangerous the predator, the more "dees" they add. Other species of birds recognize and react to the chickadee alarm call, even if they don't have a similar alarm call in their own vocabulary. Nuthatches will even "retweet" chickadee alarms with their own warning call.

Listen for the chickadee mating song in the spring—a high, pure, two-note whistle that sounds like "fee-bee." Though they sound the same to human ears, each male's "fee-bee" song is unique!

If you listen for chickadees, you can often locate other birds too. In the winter, chickadees hang out in noisy mixed-species flocks that move through trees together feeding on insects and seeds. Local birders report that tiny chickadees are often instigators in the "mobbing" of raptors and owls. The chickadees will sound the alarm and then lead a mixed flock to pester the larger bird into going away.

How to Spot Them

Chickadees are widespread, year-round residents of the Wasatch Front that thrive in both urban and less-developed environments.

Look for them in neighborhoods, in parks, and near waterways. In the foothills, watch for them darting through Gambel oaks. Welcome chickadees to your bird feeder with black oil sunflower seeds or suet in the fall and winter. In the spring, look for them nesting in cavities in trees.

Black-Billed Magpie

Pica hudsonia

Iridescent feathers on wings and tail

Namesake black bill

Notably long tail used as a rudder in flight

Black-billed magpies are divas of the suburbs with their stylish black-and-white plumage, wonderfully long tails, and dark feathers that gleam an iridescent blue-green in the sunlight. They often sit conspicuously at the tops of trees or fence posts. They are also very chatty, talking to one another with bill clicks, soft mews, and harsh, high-pitched chatter. When they travel in a flock, magpies constantly call to one another—"I'm here! Where are you?"

Inviting Themselves to Dinner

As members of the corvid (crow) family, magpies are very social, extremely intelligent, and curious about their environment. They figured out long ago that humans are connected to food. They often followed hunting parties of Indigenous peoples on the Great Plains to feast on leftovers at bison kills. In 1804, explorers Meriwether Lewis and William Clark reported magpies boldly entering their tents to steal food. Today, magpies dumpster dive for half-eaten cookies and abandoned French fries.

Magpies' broad appetite and boldness have contributed to their success in suburbs. They eat fruit, grains, insects, and small mammals, and they occasionally raid other birds' nests. Carrion is also an important part of their diet. They often gather around roadkill for a protein fix along with turkey vultures and crows.

Magpie Marriages and Mourning

Magpie pairs mate for life and stay together year-round. Keep an eye out for their large nests that look like jumbled balls of twigs high in the trees. They are one of the few North American birds that build domed nests. Females and males work together for more than forty days on the project, creating different entrances and a nest cup inside. They seem to choose a nest site together, but like all couples, they sometimes disagree. If they don't reach an accord about a good location, each bird will begin building its own nest.

In the fall and winter, magpies gather in garrulous flocks. Their strong social bonds may be behind one of their most remarkable behaviors—the magpie funeral. When a magpie discovers a dead flock mate, its calls loudly and a group gathers. The birds remain together with their fallen friend for ten to fifteen minutes, calling constantly.

How to Spot Them

Magpies live year-round in suburbs along the Wasatch Front, especially where neighborhoods meet less-developed land. Look for them along the Jordan River, on the University of Utah campus, in the foothills, and near pastures. You'll see them perched atop trees and foraging on the ground.

Black-Chinned Hummingbird

Archilochus alexandri

Black-chinned hummingbirds are the only hummingbirds that nest in the valleys of the Wasatch Front. Other local hummingbird species tend to breed in the mountains and visit the valleys only when they arrive and depart during their seasonal migrations. If you see a tiny hummingbird nest in a Wasatch Front neighborhood, you know it was made by a black-chinned hummingbird.

Purple Flash

Adult males are easiest to identify. In the right light, a brilliant purple stripe glows like a jewel at the base of a male's black chin. Their heads, backs, and flanks vary from metallic brown to green. Females and immature males have dull, metallic brown or green backs and grayish white bellies. They look a lot like the females and immature members of other hummingbird species.

Long, curved black bill

Purple throat feathers

Metallic brown-green flanks

▲ As black-chinned hummingbird chicks grow, the spider silk woven into their snug little nest stretches around them.

Adaptable little black-chinned hummingbirds are widespread throughout the West. They live in deserts, forests, cities, and suburbs—just about anywhere they can find flowering plants, tall trees, and water. In the winter, these tiny flyers migrate to central Mexico. They return in the spring as soon as blooming flowers and insect populations provide adequate food.

Flamboyant Flirts, Mercurial Mates

Courting males put on quite a show during the breeding season from May through July. They perform a "pendulum" display, climbing sixty to a hundred feet in the air and descending repeatedly in a U-shaped arc in front of a perched female. Their wings make a whirring sound on each dramatic dive. How could any female resist such romance?

After the courtship show and mating, all the work of nesting and raising chicks falls to the females. Hummingbird nests look like fairy creations. Females build a little cup with spider silk and plant down and camouflage the nest

> Hummingbirds are super-aggressive when it comes to food, because they can't afford to share flowers during times of scarcity. They apply the same rules of combat at feeders.

with lichens, leaves, or flower petals. They usually lay two tiny eggs the size of coffee beans.

These hummingbirds thrive on nectar, but they also eat a wide range of small insects and spiders that provide essential protein, especially for growing chicks. Like human parents, hummingbird mothers know their babies can't build strong bones (and beaks) on sugar alone.

How to Spot Them

Look for black-chinned hummingbirds along the Wasatch Front between April and early October. Listen for them too—their wings make a distinctive, low-pitched hum like the drone of a bee. They readily visit hummingbird feeders and gardens with flowers that offer nectar. During breeding season, watch for males perched high on exposed branches, surveying their territories.

California Gull

Larus californicus

Dark eye

Distinctive red-orange spot on lower bill

Gray-and-black wings with white tips

Greenish yellow webbed feet

The California gull is Utah's state bird thanks to its hallowed place in Utah lore. The gulls are credited with saving the crops of early Utah settlers from hungry Mormon crickets (*Anabrus simplex*) by gorging on the insects until they were full, regurgitating the dead ones, and then coming back for more. The story of the 1848 "Miracle of the Gulls" reflects an ancient relationship between California gulls and Mormon crickets. These insects regularly swarm throughout the Mountain West, and gulls take advantage of the massive food resource. Because the crickets' crunchy exoskeletons are difficult to digest, the gulls regurgitate them.

Dual Citizenship

Although our state bird was named after California, where the majority of the wintering population resides, the largest group of breeding California gulls is found around Great Salt Lake in the summer. This fact, their place in local history, and their hardy versatility all seem like good reasons to claim the California gull as Utah's own.

California gulls are easy to confuse with their cousins, ring-billed gulls (*Larus delawarensis*), which are also common along the Wasatch Front. A California gull has dark eyes, greenish yellow legs, and a red spot on the tip of its lower beak. A ring-billed gull is a bit smaller, with a namesake black ring around its bill.

Land, Air, and Sea

California gulls are "all-terrain" birds. Along the shores of Great Salt Lake, they feed by running through swarms of brine flies with their bills open. They are also acrobatic fliers and can snatch food out of the air. Young gulls practice this skill by dropping sticks midair and swooping down to catch them. In the water, gulls paddle like ducks and can dive below the surface after fish.

The red spot on a California gull's lower beak it key to its chicks' survival. Chicks instinctually know to peck at the spot, which prompts their parent to regurgitate food for them. Several other gull species have similar red spots. The scientist who discovered this behavior and proved it was instinctual won a Nobel Prize for the research!

California gulls eat just about anything, from grasshoppers to garbage. They exploit the many dining opportunities human activities provide, scavenging at landfills, trailing boats to eat discarded fish, and following farmers' plows to grab the insects and small mammals they churn up. Gulls aren't shy about asking for (or demanding) a handout directly from humans either. Keep a firm grip on your sandwich when gulls are around!

How to Spot Them

You can spot California gulls year-round on the Wasatch Front, but fewer are present during the winter when many migrate to California. Look for them around water at reservoirs and ponds or scavenging for food in parking lots, parks, and landfills. You may see resting gulls standing on one leg with their eyes closed.

California Quail

Callipepla californica

California quail aren't originally from Utah. In November 1869, the *Deseret News* reported that General John Gibbon, the commander of Fort Douglas just east of Salt Lake City, "brought to Utah 14 pairs of California quails and set them at liberty, that they might 'increase and multiply.'" They did! Sightings of quail with chicks were reported two years later.

General Gibbon hoped California quail would become a new game animal for local hunters—a common reason humans introduce species to new places. Along the Wasatch Front, however, California quail thrive in suburban and urban neighborhoods where there is plenty of food, cover, and water—and no hunting. Every year, the Utah Division of Wildlife Resources traps urban quail and relocates them to create new populations in places where hunting is allowed.

Comma-shaped topknot feather

Distinctive black-and-white mask on males

White-and-chestnut pattern on the bellies of both sexes

Covey Call

You can see these stout, ground-dwelling birds year-round on the Wasatch Front. In the winter months, they form coveys, large groups that search out seed at bird feeders or forage by scratching through the leaves and snow. If members of the covey get separated, you may hear their famous "Chi-CA-go" reassembly call.

In the spring, the coveys dissolve as males and females pair up to raise young. Their well-camouflaged nests—usually shallow depressions lined with grass—often go undetected under dense vegetation in backyards. The adorable, downy chicks hatch ready for action. They can scurry after their parents right away and fly short distances within ten days.

Cooperative Parenting

Summers are all about family life for quail. Parents lead their large broods of fluffy, brown ping pong balls through yards and across streets—which can be nerve-racking for human neighbors to watch. The males are devoted fathers and often perch high above the foraging female and chicks to act as lookout. When he gives an alarm call, the chicks seem to melt into the landscape.

Despite the efforts of their attentive parents, life is very dangerous for baby quail. Many large broods shrink quickly as chicks fall prey to mishaps and predators, especially house cats. Sometimes two or more sets of parents raise their young together, with all of the adults caring for all of the chicks. Studies show that these mixed families have better survival rates.

How to Spot Them

Look for California quail year-round on the ground or in the lower branches of shrubs and trees. They readily visit bird feeders. They usually forage for dropped seed on the ground but will also use platform feeders. At night, quail often roost in tall trees, especially thick conifers.

Canada Goose

Branta canadensis

Any place with a big lawn near a pond is excellent Canada goose habitat. Because they are one of the few bird species that can digest grass, a lawn is like a big, green goose buffet. Wide-open lawns also let them see threats from a distance. If a predator gets close, the geese can hustle their babies to the safety of the pond.

Canada geese mate for life and are great parents. Their babies (goslings) stay with them for an entire year. The adults molt their flight feathers during nesting season, so they can't fly while they incubate their eggs and when their goslings are relatively helpless. Canada

Black mask and neck with white chinstrap

Black bill, legs, and feet

Brown body with pale chest

Often stand on one leg to conserve heat

Goslings are famous for imprinting on the first creature they see—usually their parents. Because they can walk and swim shortly after hatching, they need to know who to follow to stay safe.

▲ A Canada goose with a yellow neck band or a silver, blue, or red ankle band was relocated at some point.

geese are fierce protectors of their nests and young. They hiss, honk, and flap to warn off potential predators—including humans. This behavior can be quite alarming if it's directed at you. Just remember: it's not personal.

Saved in a City

Not that long ago, Canada geese were a rare sight in many parts of the United States. Populations had declined sharply by the early twentieth century as a result of unregulated hunting and loss of wetlands. One subspecies, the giant Canada goose (Branta canadensis maxima), was thought to be extinct until it was rediscovered on a lake in Rochester, Minnesota, in 1962. The last wild population had survived in a city! A captive breeding program in the 1960s reintroduced the giants throughout their range in the Midwest and beyond.

This conservation effort was wildly successful. Some introduced giant Canada geese took up residence in cities in the eastern half of the United States. Never strong migrators, they found plenty of food and open water that enabled them to skip winter migration and become full-time city dwellers. By the mid-1980s, some cities began to worry about having too many geese.

Some Stay, Some Fly Away

The Wasatch Front has both resident and migratory Canada goose populations. Most of the resident geese belong to a western subspecies called Moffit's Canada goose (Branta canadensis moffitti). These are the geese you see grazing in parks and golf courses from March to November. During the winter, a few other subspecies migrating from the north join our year-round Moffit's flock.

Each June since 2006, the Utah Division of Wildlife Resources has captured hundreds of Canada geese around the Salt Lake Valley. Teams of technicians and volunteers band the goslings and release them in the marshes of Great Salt Lake. The goal of the program is to reduce the urban goose population and increase the flocks that can be hunted. Many of the goslings imprint on geese at the lake and learn to migrate. Wildlife Resources staff members transport the adults farther away, but strong nesting instincts guide about half of them back home.

How to Spot Them

Canada geese are common year-round on the Wasatch Front. You can see them at parks and golf courses as well as around Great Salt Lake, Utah Lake, and the Jordan River.

Cedar Waxwing

Bombycilla cedrorum

Yellow and red "waxy" tips on wing and tail feathers

Crest

Pale yellow belly

Black mask

A cedar waxwing looks like it is dressed for an elegant ball. Its silky plumage shimmers in pale brown and soft gray, with a lemon-yellow accent splashed across its belly. It wears a black mask over its eyes and a stylish crest on its head. The ends of its tail feathers are dabbed in brilliant yellow. Bright drops of red sparkle on the tips of its secondary wing feathers—the common name refers to these red, waxy feather tips.

Fond of Fruit

Cedar waxwings obtain their splashes of red and yellow pigment from the plants they eat. Berries and fruits make up the vast majority of their diet, although they do hunt a few insects in the summer. The cedar waxwing population has actually grown during the last twenty years, in part because people are planting more delicious fruiting trees and shrubs in cities and suburbs.

Cedar waxwings are very sociable. They usually gather in flocks and often build nests in loose colonies. In the winter, they stick together in dense, cohesive flocks that fly and forage as one. A flock will settle on a tree, quickly eat all the fruit, and then move on to the next tree.

The fruit on the Bradford pear trees on Presidents Circle on the University of Utah campus attracts flocks of cedar waxwings every winter. Unfortunately, the large, mirrored windows on a number of nearby buildings create a deadly deception for the waxwings, which, like all birds, cannot perceive the glass and see only more trees and sky in the reflection.

Hot Spot of Death

After a cedar waxwing crashed into a window with a horrific thump during a meeting, a University of Utah professor began recording how many birds hit the mirrored glass on her building. She counted twenty dead birds—mostly cedar waxwings—in the winter of 2017 and dubbed the building a "hot spot of death."

The professor and her students wrote a grant to fund covering some of the windows with a pattern of dots. The birds recognize the dots as an obstacle, but people can still see through the window. The team also launched a citizen science project to identify other hot spots on campus. Their work is a good reminder that both migratory and resident birds, like cedar waxwings, are at risk of window collisions.

How to Spot Them

Cedar waxwings live along the Wasatch Front all year, but they are easiest to spot in winter when they gather in large flocks. You'll often hear their high-pitched whistles before you see them. Look for them in neighborhoods and parks, along the Jordan River, and at the Salt Lake City Cemetery.

Courting cedar waxwings politely pass a berry back and forth between their beaks. The charming ritual starts when the male offers the female a "gift." After a few exchanges, the female usually eats the berry.

Cooper's Hawk

Accipiter cooperii

If you put up a bird feeder in your yard, a Cooper's hawk might stop by for a snack, but it won't go for the sunflower seeds. These hawks love to dine on medium-size birds such as doves and pigeons. They won't pass up smaller songbirds or the occasional squirrel, either. The hawks' adaptations to navigating in thick forests help them hunt in complex urban environments, zipping around buildings and along tree-lined streets.

Thriving in Cities

Populations of Cooper's hawks in cities and suburbs have soared since the 1980s. In some areas, their numbers may now be higher in cities than in forests! The hawks' increasing urbanization paralleled their remarkable recovery from steep population declines in the mid-1900s. People often shot hawks because they saw them as competition for game animals. Plus, the widespread use of the pesticide DDT weakened their eggshells, decreasing the number of hatchlings. In the 1960s, many people worried that Cooper's hawks were headed for extinction.

Along with banning DDT and the shooting of Cooper's hawks, an unplanned change in human behavior helped the hawks rebound. In the 1990s, more people began feeding birds and keeping bird feeders up all year. Research shows this growing backyard bird buffet is a key factor in the hawks' success in cities. When you see a Cooper's hawk snag a bird from a

Large head with black cap

Pale chest with reddish brown barring

ng, rounded tail

> Though very agile, Cooper's hawks can sometimes be injured in high-speed chases. One study of 300 Cooper's hawk skeletons found that more than 20 percent had healed chest fractures.

feeder, you're watching an interaction between two birds, a human, and the $4 billion-a-year birdseed industry.

Shifting Migrations

The abundance of easy prey in neighborhoods may be impacting hawk migration patterns. Many northern cities now report year-round Cooper's hawk populations. Hawks that breed far in the north still migrate, though, and many fly along the Wasatch Front. The ridgelines of the Wasatch Mountains are a great place to see this spectacular phenomenon. Check HawkWatch International's website for more information on how you can join a "hawk-watching" expedition.

One difficulty in spotting Cooper's hawks is telling them apart from sharp-shinned hawks (*Accipiter striatus*)—a challenge that stumps even expert birders. Compare the birds' sizes and shapes: a Cooper's hawk is larger, with a rounded tail, and a large head that sticks out noticeably in front of its wing as it flies. Color pattern can help you too. An adult Cooper's hawk has a lighter gray neck that contrasts with a dark cap atop its head. A sharp-shinned hawk has a continuous dark head and neck.

How to Spot Them

The Wasatch Front has a year-round population of Cooper's hawks. They are common in neighborhoods, parks, and open spaces. At least one nesting pair lives in Liberty Park in Salt Lake City each year. Watch for juveniles in the late summer as they learn how to hunt.

Doves

Eurasian Collared-Dove

Streptopelia decaocto

Mourning Dove

Zenaida macroura

Black collar band at the nape of the neck

Dark gray wingtips

Squared-off tail

Gray-brown head and body

Small brown head and plump body

Gray wings

Pointed tail

Who's that hooting in your neighborhood? Chances are it's a dove rather than an owl. The songs of both Eurasian collared-doves and mourning doves are owl-like, but the mourning dove's call is more haunting. Eurasian collared-doves make a rhythmic, insistent "koo-KOO-kook" call, repeating the same three syllables many times. The mourning dove's call is a soft, drawn-out lament—"hooOOoo-hoo-hoo."

Each bird makes another sound that will help you identify it. Eurasian collared-doves announce their presence with a comically harsh "Hwaaah!" before landing or when they're excited. When mourning doves land and take-off, their wings make a loud, squeaky whistle, perhaps to startle predators or warn flock mates that it's time to flee.

A Tale of Two Doves

Both doves are common along the Wasatch Front, but they have very different backstories. Mourning doves are longtime residents and have generally prospered as humans altered the landscape. Widespread across the country, they are very popular game birds. Hunters harvest more than 20 million every year, but that number is easily supported by their estimated population of 350 million.

Eurasian collared-doves are new to North America. In the mid 1970s, a pet store owner in the Bahamas imported a flock to sell as pets, and some escaped during a burglary. For some reason, the store owner decided to set the rest of the flock free. They made their way to Florida by the early 1980s and began rapidly expanding across the United States. Their first Utah sighting was in Orem in 1997.

Possible Peaceful Coexistence

As often happens when an introduced species spreads, people worried about the Eurasian collared-doves' impacts on other species, especially mourning doves. But studies of collared-doves have yet to show that they have a negative impact on other bird populations. In fact, some studies found that increases in local collared-dove populations were correlated with increases in populations of other dove species. Their population in the United States continues to grow but is estimated at less than five million—a tiny fraction of the mourning dove population.

Mourning doves and collared-doves may easily coexist because people provide a super-abundance of their main food—seeds—at bird feeders and in agricultural fields. Both species are seed-eating machines, consuming 12 to 20 percent of their body weight each day! When a dove can't fit more seeds in its stomach, it stores the rest for later in its crop, an extension of its esophagus.

How to Spot Them

Both dove species are year-round residents of the Wasatch Front. Look for them in yards, parks, and any open area with trees nearby. They forage for seeds on the ground and gobble them up at platform feeders.

Dove parents produce "crop milk," a substance made of sloughed off cells inside the crop that's full of protein and fat. They regurgitate the crop milk to feed their chicks, providing a nutritious start to their young lives.

European Starling

Sturnus vulgaris

Stout body

Iridescent summer plumage

Slender, pointed yellow bill

White spots from winter plumage

European starlings flourish alongside humans—in fact, they tend to avoid undeveloped areas without a human presence. Look for flocks of them patrolling grassy areas with a purposeful air, probing the ground with their beaks every step or two. Starlings love to forage for invertebrates in lawns, but they also eat other foods that humans inadvertently provide, including fruit, grains, livestock feed, and garbage.

Starlings' plumage looks quite different depending on the time of year. In the fall, they grow new feathers with brilliant white tips that give them a speckled appearance. Over the winter, the white tips wear away, leaving dark, glossy feathers that glow iridescent purple and green in the sun. This slick process enables starlings to change to breeding plumage without having to replace a single feather.

The Real Origin Story

You may have heard a captivating story about how starlings arrived in North America. According to this account, all the starlings that live in North America today are descended from about eighty birds released in New York City's Central Park in the early 1890s by Eugene Schieffelin, an amateur ornithologist and Shakespeare fan who wanted all the birds mentioned in the Bard's plays to live in the United States.

Recent research has shown that reality is a bit more complex, however. People repeatedly released starlings in the United States during the late nineteenth century as part of the "acclimatization" movement that tried to transplant species to North America either to see how they would adapt or because they were seen as beneficial in some way. As part of this effort, Schieffelin did release starlings in Central Park, but the Shakespeare connection was invented by an essayist in 1948.

Highly adaptable and intelligent, starlings spread quickly across the country, arriving on the West Coast in the 1950s. Their population grew dramatically, reaching an estimated 200 million birds in North America during the twentieth century.

Rethinking Their Reputation

Being abundant, bold, gregarious, and boisterous has earned starlings a bad reputation in many circles—a reputation that may not always be deserved. Many birders and scientists worry that starlings cause declines in populations of other bird species by outcompeting them for scarce nesting holes in trees. Although starlings do compete fiercely for nest cavities, data hasn't shown that the presence of starlings explains declines in other bird populations, with the possible exceptions of sapsuckers. Habitat loss and fragmentation, however, are proven causes of decreasing populations of cavity-nesting birds.

Starling populations are actually now in dramatic decline. In fact, the North American population dropped 52 percent between 1966 and 2015. This may be part of the pattern experienced by many introduced species—an initial population boom, followed by a decline as the species settles into its new home. It may also be part of the alarming decline of many bird populations worldwide.

How to Spot Them

You can find starlings year-round just about anywhere along the Wasatch Front. Look for them feeding on lawns or perched on powerlines and buildings. They enjoy visiting bird feeders too.

Starlings sometimes fly in huge flocks, or murmurations, that flow and pulsate in mesmerizing patterns across the sky as each bird reacts to those around it. Check out videos of murmurations online!

Great Blue Heron

Ardea herodias

Black head cap with white mask

Long, pointed yellow bill

Characteristic S-shaped neck

Huge, blue-gray bodies and wings

Great blue herons are big! They stand up to four feet tall and can have a wingspan of nearly seven feet. Their size alone makes an impression when you encounter them. They seem improbably large for urban wildlife, but they are a surprisingly common sight at rivers, ponds, and wetlands along the Wasatch Front.

Adaptable Hunters

These stately birds are expert hunters that walk with slow, cautious steps or stand with statue-like patience, stalking prey in shallow water or open fields. With a lightning-fast thrust of its neck and head, a blue heron stabs its meal with its strong bill. They dine mainly on fish but aren't picky eaters. In addition to consuming many aquatic creatures, they eat rodents, lizards, snakes, and birds. An overly ambitious heron can choke to death on large prey that won't fit down its throat.

Great blue herons are highly adaptable, thriving in habitats as diverse as mangrove swamps, desert rivers, and the coast of southern Alaska. They are adjusting well to life in cities across the United States that offer water and safe nesting areas. A close cousin, the grey heron (Ardea cinerea), has even learned to visit the fish market in the heart of the city of Amsterdam in the Netherlands at closing time to dine on discarded fish.

Almost a New Heron

In a random collision of Utah natural and architectural history, a subspecies of great blue heron was named after Utah architect Alberto O. Treganza in 1908—the Treganza blue heron (Ardea herodias treganzai). In addition to designing many prominent Utah buildings in the early twentieth century, Treganza was an avid birder throughout his life. He gathered field notes and heron specimens on Antelope Island from 1905 to 1907, which were used by ornithologists to establish the new subspecies.

The Treganza heron was thought to be a bit paler and smaller than other great blue herons, but scientists later decided these slight differences weren't enough to qualify it for subspecies status. Although Treganza's heron didn't stand the test of time (and the scientific process), many of his buildings are still standing. His Crane Building in downtown Salt Lake City, for example, isn't named after a bird, but sounds like it is!

How to Spot Them

Look for great blue herons year-round on the Wasatch Front, standing motionless along rivers, lakes, ponds, and wetlands. You can also see them stalking rodents in fields. They are a little shy and may fly away when you approach. Visit the Lee Kay Ponds in Salt Lake City and the Eccles Wildlife Education Center at Farmington Bay to see them nesting on trees and artificial nesting structures.

House Finch

Haemorhous mexicanus

If you haven't seen a house finch lately, chances are you can find one at the next bird feeder you come across. These gregarious little birds are common in Wasatch Front neighborhoods year-round and eager customers at bird feeders. Black oil sunflower seeds are their favorite and will attract large flocks.

Questionable Marketing

House finches have made themselves at home in cities and suburbs. They generally seem to benefit from living in developed

Thick, curved seed-eating beak

Bright coral plumage on head and chest for males

Female, with a brown face and streaky belly

areas. Originally residents of deserts and grasslands in the western United States, today they live in cities across the country, thanks in part to a few "enterprising" pet stores in Long Island, New York.

In the early 1940s, these stores tried to sell house finches as songbirds, branding them "Hollywood finches." To escape prosecution for the illegal sales, the store owners set the birds free. During the next fifty years, the eastern population expanded rapidly to the west. When you see a range map for house finches today, it's easy to think they've always inhabited the entire country.

You Are What You Eat

The plants a male house finch eats determine whether his chest, head, and rump are bright red, orange, or mustard-yellow. Birds can't make red and yellow pigments directly, but plants can. A male that eats more plants with red pigments will have more red feathers. Female house finches, which are a streaked gray-brown, definitely prefer the reddest male they can find as a mate. Perhaps his color is a signal that he'll be able to provide lots of food for nestlings.

With their thick, cone-shaped beaks, house finches are experts at shelling seeds. They are fairly dedicated vegetarians, subsisting mostly on seeds, buds, and fruits. They also feed their young a vegetarian diet—an unusual approach in the bird world. Many birds that eat plants as adults feed insects to their fast-growing young to supply them with protein.

How to Spot Them

One of the easiest ways to find house finches is to listen for their melodious song full of warm, bubbling notes. They often end their phrases with a loud, buzzy, rising "vrrreee!" Males sing throughout the year. Look for house finches at bird feeders, foraging on the ground, or dining on sunflowers. When resting, house finches like to perch high in trees or on wires.

Young house finches leave the nest only two weeks after hatching. Prolific house finch parents may raise six broods in a year, though two or three is more common.

House Sparrow

Passer domesticus

The histories of house sparrows and humans are deeply intertwined. When people in the Middle East started farming about 12,000 years ago, house sparrows adapted to eating leftover grain in farm fields. They've lived alongside us ever since. In fact, house sparrows almost never live far from a farm, town, or city, and they disappear in areas abandoned by humans. You can even see the connection between house sparrows and humans in our DNA. Recent research shows that we both developed similar genetic adaptations for processing starchy foods, such as grains, as we settled into an agricultural lifestyle.

Small, round, grayish brown body

Short, straight, pointed bill

Brown-red wings with white and black markings

Black bib

House sparrows have learned how to trigger automatic doors to fly into supermarkets, airports, and home improvement stores in search of a meal. They flutter in front of door sensors or perch on top of them and lean their heads into the infrared beams.

Having lived with us for so long, house sparrows are often quite bold around people. They'll eagerly hop around your feet or alight next to you on a bench, seeking a handout. Frequent customers at bird feeders, they clamor over seeds in noisy flocks. True to their name, they nest in crevices in houses, on outdoor light fixtures, and even on traffic lights. Their simple, cheery "cheep" or "chirrup" song is part of the soundtrack of almost every neighborhood.

Utah's Sparrow Solution

The first house sparrows in North America were released in New York in 1851, but Salt Lake City was one of their earliest homes in the West. In the late 1870s, two prominent local merchants imported house sparrows to eat moth larvae that were destroying Utah fruit crops. The Salt Lake City Council even passed an ordinance protecting the valuable birds in 1877.

Unfortunately for the sparrow boosters, their pest control plan didn't work out as intended because insects are only a small part of house sparrows' diets. People soon came to regard sparrows as agricultural pests. In 1886, the Utah Territorial Legislature began offering a bounty of a few cents per sparrow head, but sparrow populations increased anyway.

House Sparrows vs. Bluebirds?

House sparrows earned a bad reputation among bird lovers for competing for nest cavities in trees and sometimes ejecting or even killing other cavity-nesting birds. When eastern bluebird populations declined in the early twentieth century, many bird conservation societies pinned the blame on house sparrows and advocated gruesome measures for killing them.

House sparrows do aggressively claim nest cavities and can be fierce toward other birds, but no studies have proven that these behaviors cause decreases in other bird populations. House sparrows may have played some role in eastern bluebird population declines, but the main culprit was likely the destruction of the forests that bluebirds depend on for nesting. Fortunately, artificial nest boxes have helped bluebird populations recover dramatically. Now it's actually house sparrow populations that are declining, probably as a result of industrial farming practices that spill less grain and use more pesticides.

How to Spot Them

House sparrows live in Utah year-round and are common in most neighborhoods. Look for them hopping along the ground or at bird feeders. You can easily attract them with food, and they may feed out of your hand.

Lesser Goldfinch

Spinus psaltria

The "lesser" in lesser goldfinch refers to this tiny bird's size, not any quality it lacks. This petite species is not only the smallest North American finch, but it may be the smallest finch in the world. Individuals can weigh as little as a quarter of an ounce—about as much as three pennies. Being so small, they can perch almost weightlessly on slender flower stalks and pluck seeds from flower heads.

Stout, gray bill

Black-and-gray wings with white spots

Yellow bellies year-round on males

Birders affectionately call lesser goldfinches "LEGOs," like the toy blocks—LE for lesser and GO for goldfinch.

Dinner and a Show

Lesser goldfinches specialize in eating seeds, especially those from plants in the sunflower family. They can be acrobatic diners, bending plant stems over and clinging to seed heads upside down. Most songbirds feed on insects in summer, but lesser goldfinches eat seeds year-round. They even feed seeds to their young, although they do mix in some small insects for extra protein.

Unlike their slightly larger cousins, American goldfinches *(Spinus tristis)*, male lesser goldfinches maintain their bright yellow color throughout the winter. In Utah, males have dull, olive-green backs and they wear crisp black caps. Farther east and south in the bird's range, males have glossy black backs, but people occasionally spot "black backs" in Utah too.

Singing Virtuosos

Male lesser goldfinches are talented performers. They incorporate snippets of other birds' songs into their own complex compositions. Researchers have documented songs from thirty different bird species—and a squirrel—in lesser goldfinch songs. About half of each male's song is imitated fragments, another 10 percent is made up of typical lesser goldfinch calls, and musical phrases of the male's own invention make up the rest. Each male may have a repertoire of up to a hundred unique phrases!

Lesser goldfinches are a relatively new arrival on the Wasatch Front. They've been steadily expanding their range northward from the Desert Southwest. In the mid-1990s, they started showing up in winter bird counts in Provo and Salt Lake City. Now they live year-round on the Wasatch Front, probably thanks to the abundance of bird feeders and our milder winters. In the rest of the state, they are mostly migratory, though populations continue to show up in new parts of the state.

How to Spot Them

Lesser goldfinches have become common neighborhood birds along the Wasatch Front and readily visit bird feeders. They especially love thistle socks. You can also spot them feasting in fields of thistle, rubber rabbitbrush, or sunflowers in mixed flocks with American goldfinches and pine siskins.

Mallard

Anas platyrhynchos

Green head feathers and yellow bill on males

Blue band on wings of males and females

Bright orange webbed feet

This duck probably looks familiar. You can find mallards floating on virtually any pond, marsh, or river along the Wasatch Front. Today they waddle through cities across the world thanks to introductions of captive-bred mallards. The fact that there are more records of mallards on the iNaturalist app than any other species in the world reflects their ubiquitous presence—and the ease of photographing them.

Big Dippers

Like many dabbling ducks, mallards often appear to be nibbling at the surface of the water when they feed. They strain water through a series of ridges inside their bills to trap small bits of food. You'll also see mallards dabbling, or dipping their heads below the water and tipping their tails in the air in search of food, but they don't dive beneath the surface. That's the purview of diving ducks.

Mallards eat a wide variety of foods—aquatic plants, seeds, insect larvae, earthworms, and more—which is one key to their

success in cities. Another is their tolerance of humans, which, unfortunately, often leads eager mallards to accept handouts of bread. A bread-heavy diet is the duck equivalent of filling up on nonnutritious junk food and can make them sick. If you enjoy feeding mallards, consider offering them halved grapes, corn, and lettuce, which are more nutritious options.

Mallard Mash-Ups

Almost all domesticated ducks have mallard ancestors. Because they are closely related, escaped domesticated ducks often breed with wild mallards. Mallards sometimes breed with other wild duck species too. A duck that looks like a mallard at first glance but displays an odd color pattern on closer inspection is probably a hybrid of some kind.

Although mallards are very at home in cities, some urban mallards pick up and leave for the country. A study of mallards that had been banded in cities in the Midwest found that 14 percent were harvested by hunters beyond the city limits. Mallards and other animals that move between cities and less-developed areas remind us of the connections between habitats we often see as separate.

How to Spot Them

Visit most any slow-moving body of water in a Wasatch Front city or suburb and you'll find mallards. They love parks and golf courses. Some migrate, but many stay throughout the year. The marshes around Great Salt Lake are important habitat for nesting and migrating mallards.

If it quacks like a duck ... it must be a female mallard. The iconic "quack" call is made only by female mallards. The male mallard's call is quieter and raspier.

Northern Flicker

Colaptes auratus

Signature long bill of the woodpecker family

Bright red "moustache" on males

Black crescent necklace

Black spots across belly and banding on wings

Northern flickers are woodpeckers with unusual habits. Instead of hanging on the sides of trees to hunt for insects under the bark, they forage on the ground. Ants are their favorites, but they won't pass up other insects strolling by. Flickers often search out juicy, nutritious ant larvae underground by drilling into the soil or a sidewalk crack the way other woodpeckers drill into trees.

If Ants Made Horror Movies

Flickers lap up ants with their long tongues coated with sticky saliva—like a bird version of an anteater. Their smooth tongues don't have the barbs that help other woodpeckers spear and extract insects from trees. All woodpeckers have super-long tongues, but

101

flicker tongues are the longest. A woodpecker extends its tongue with the help of a long, flexible bone that starts at the back of its tongue, wraps around the back and over the top of its skull, and then attaches near its nostrils.

When the weather turns cold, flickers add berries and seeds to their diets. Along the Wasatch Front, you'll frequently see them eating the silver fruits of Russian olive trees. Though they don't often visit bird feeders, they may stop by for some suet in the winter.

The Rhythm Section

If you've heard the loud, rapid-fire drumming of a woodpecker in your neighborhood, it was likely a flicker. Flickers drum for the same reasons songbirds sing: to defend their territory and communicate with other birds.

Since drumming is about making a loud noise, not drilling holes, flickers take advantage of metal surfaces, such as aluminum siding, downspouts, and chimneys, to amplify their messages.

Occasionally, flickers drill nests in wood or stucco walls, but they usually excavate holes for their nests in dead or diseased trees with soft wood. Finding a good nest site in cities and suburbs is often a challenge because people tend to remove dead trees. The lack of nest sites caused by development and "snag" removal seems to be a significant factor in flickers' steadily declining populations. Consider putting up a nesting box to attract a breeding pair.

How to Spot Them

You can see flickers along the Wasatch Front year-round, but more often in the fall and winter. These flashy birds wear black "necklaces" and males sport red "moustaches." Look for them on the ground or perched on tree branches in neighborhoods, parks, and open spaces. They are common in the canyons of the Wasatch. You can often hear them from a long way off, either drumming or making their loud "ki-ki-ki-ki" and "kyeer" calls.

Rock Pigeon

Columba livia

Rock pigeons are synonymous with cities. They thrive in the places that seem least hospitable to nature, including freeway underpasses and paved downtowns. They are so common that we often don't see them or we regard them with disdain. Pigeons, however, are anything but commonplace. Their intelligence, navigation skills, and relationship with humans are remarkable. These birds are definitely worth a second look.

Plump body and small head

Red eye

Often iridescent
throat feathers,
color patterns va

Gone Wild in Cities

People started raising pigeons for food more than 5000 years ago. Many cultures came to revere pigeons not only for their delicious meat, but as religious symbols, status symbols, a communication technology, and companions. European colonists brought their precious pigeons with them to North America 400 years ago. Pigeon racing and fancy pigeon breeding continue to have many passionate devotees today.

All the pigeons flapping around cities across the globe are descendants of escaped domesticated pigeons. These escapees tended to hang out around humans, as they'd been bred to do. As we built larger, denser cities, we created great habitat for pigeons. Tall buildings are excellent substitutes for the cliffs that the pigeons' wild ancestors nested on, and because pigeons aren't fussy eaters, all the bits of food we drop on sidewalks ensure that they have plenty to eat.

Pigeons mate for life and are devoted parents. Their unusual way of feeding their young also helps them thrive in cities. Both males and females feed their chicks a nutritious crop milk produced in a pouch in the throat. So instead of having to gather insects or seeds to feed their young, pigeons can provide for their offspring by eating the plentiful food people toss away.

Not "Birdbrains"

Scientists have studied pigeons' intelligence extensively. It turns out that, like many birds, they are very smart. For example, pigeons can learn abstract rules about numbers—an ability thought to be limited to primates. They are also much better at learning the solution to a famous probability problem—known as the Monty Hall problem—than humans.

Pigeons have incredible abilities to recognize visual patterns too. Japanese scientists taught a group of pigeons to differentiate paintings by Monet from the works of Picasso, and a study at a California university showed that they could be taught to diagnose breast cancer on medical slides with the same accuracy as radiologists. They also recognize people's faces and remember how those people treated them.

No Need to Stop for Directions

Pigeons' visual skills may contribute to their amazing ability to navigate back to their home loft from hundreds of miles away. Scientists studying how pigeons' complex navigation system works have tried to befuddle the birds in all kinds of ways. They've even anesthetized birds and put them on a rotating turntable inside an airtight chamber during the drive to the release site. The pigeons still came home.

The latest evidence suggests that pigeons rely on many navigation cues. They use the position of the sun, direction and intensity of the geomagnetic field, and olfactory cues when far away from home. As they near their lofts, they switch to navigating by visual landmarks.

How to Spot Them

Look for pigeons in city parks and neighborhoods, in downtown areas, and beneath freeway underpasses. They are very social birds, so you'll often see them in flocks walking on the ground and pecking at food. When alarmed, the flock may suddenly fly into the air and circle several times before returning to the ground.

Humans have used pigeons as a communication technology for thousands of years. As recently as World War II, messenger pigeons were one of the most secure and reliable forms of communication available.

Western Screech-Owl

Megascops kennicottii

A western screech-owl might be your neighbor. We usually picture owls gliding through dark forests, but a handful of North American owls have learned to thrive in cities and suburbs. With plentiful prey and large trees for roosting and nesting, city life has a lot to offer owls as long as they avoid cars and poisoned rodents.

This diminutive owl is about the size of a quail. The stocky little birds have squarish heads and almost no neck. Their piercing yellow eyes and pointed "ears"—tufts of feathers they can raise or lower depending on their mood—give them a comically stern expression. With streaked gray or brown feathers, they blend into the bark of the trees they perch on.

Feathered "ear" tufts

Square head

Large, bright yellow eyes

Mottled brown and gray body

Don't underestimate the little western screech-owl as a predator. It will occasionally kill prey bigger than its own body, including rabbits.

Element of Surprise

Western screech-owls are adaptable nocturnal hunters. They sit quietly in trees and wait for prey to venture near. Their superb hearing and night vision help them detect even the quietest scurry. The frayed edges on their feathers enable them to fly silently and strike before their prey realizes they are on the menu. They primarily eat rodents, but in the summer they add reptiles, birds, worms, and even large insects to their diet.

These owls are secondary cavity nesters. This means they can't make their own nesting holes in trees. Instead, they depend on woodpeckers, especially northern flickers, to excavate holes they can move into after the woodpeckers leave. They also happily take up residence in nest boxes.

On the Move

A species of the western United States, the western screech-owl's range has expanded slightly eastward across the Pecos River in Texas in recent years. Humans created new habitat for the owls by planting trees in historically open landscapes. This was the case on the Wasatch Front, as well. These owls wouldn't have lived in the grasslands that filled the valleys before humans planted an urban forest.

How to Spot Them

Western screech-owls are fairly common along the Wasatch Front. Look for them in yards, parks, and along urban rivers. They often sit right at the entrance to a tree cavity. It's easiest to spot them in winter when deciduous trees are leafless. Because they are mostly active at night, your best chance at detecting a screech-owl is to listen for its song—a series of short, hollow whistles that speeds up as it goes along. Birders call it the "bouncing ball" song. In the late winter and early spring, you can hear duets of paired owls singing their bouncing ball song back and forth.

Woodhouse's Scrub-Jay

Aphelocoma woodhouseii

White eyebrow and throat markings

Blue head and wings

No crest on head like some of its jay cousins

Lanky body with long legs and tail

Woodhouse's scrub-jays are confident, assertive, and very intelligent. They are famous for being able to remember where they hide, or cache, food for later. They can recall up to 200 different cache locations in their home range. Imagine having 200 pairs of keys and trying to remember different "safe spots" for each one over an area the size of forty-eight football fields!

Caching helps scrub-jays take advantage of temporary food surpluses, such as the piñon nuts in the piñon scrublands where they evolved. Research shows that scrub-jays can also remember how long an item has been cached and whether it is likely to have become rotten.

Social Savants

Scrub-jays sometimes steal other birds' food caches. To protect themselves from thieves, scrub-jays try to be secretive, hiding behind objects to prevent other birds from seeing them make a cache. If a scrub-jay thinks another bird is watching, it will return to its cache later and hide the food in a new location. A scrub-jay won't move a cache if it is certain it was alone.

Scientists studying this behavior think it indicates that these jays not only understand that other birds are able to see what they are doing, but that the other birds could use that information to steal their food. This kind of social awareness is quite rare among animals. Human children don't develop the ability to understand what information others have and how they might use it until they are about five years old.

A Lot to Say

Though they are suspicious of one another, scrub-jays are also very gregarious. They gather in vocal, playful flocks during the winter. They use more than twenty separate types of calls for communicating with one another. You've probably heard a jay make a piercing call that sounds like it's asking, "What?!"

Scrub-jays have adapted well to living with humans. They enjoy a wide range of foods, dining mostly on fruit and insects in the spring and summer and switching to seeds and nuts in the fall and winter. They sometimes build their twig nests in backyards with dense brush or small trees.

You may know the Woodhouse's scrub-jay as the western scrub-jay. In 2016, ornithologists split the western scrub-jay into two species—the California scrub-jay (*Aphelocoma californica*) and Woodhouse's scrub-jay—after research showed these two groups rarely interbreed even where their populations overlap.

How to Spot Them

Woodhouse's scrub-jays are year-round residents of the Wasatch Front. They are common in neighborhoods and in the foothills. Look for them hopping boldly across the ground and silhouetted high in trees, where they act as lookouts.

Woodhouse's scrub-jays will happily eat peanuts, sunflower seeds, and suet at backyard feeders. They will also gladly annoy pets by eating their food too.

Fungi and a Lichen

Aspen Oyster Mushroom
Pleurotus populinus

Overlapping kidney-shaped caps grow atop logs

Grows on aspen or cottonwood trees

Pale, fan-shaped caps project from trunk

Aspen oyster mushrooms grow in clumps on decaying wood. As their common name suggests, they usually grow on aspens and closely related trees such as cottonwoods. Both trees are species of the genus *Populus*, which is the source of this mushroom's species name.

Aspen oysters are pale overall, with broad white or yellow-gray caps. If they grow on a standing tree, their fan-shaped caps often project perpendicularly from the trunk, forming graceful stairsteps up the tree. If they grow on a fallen log, their caps are more kidney-shaped and often overlap. Underneath the cap, off-white gills descend to the upper part of the stalk in parallel ridges. These mushrooms have a distinct smell—a combination of shellfish and a sweet odor reminiscent of anise.

Many people forage, or search for and collect specific mushrooms to eat. The term "foray" is used by mushroom hunters to describe an outing to find, but not necessarily collect, mushrooms. If you are interested in learning more about local mushrooms and attending mushroom foray events, the Mushroom Society of Utah is a great place to start. Never eat a wild mushroom if you aren't absolutely certain what it is.

Enjoyed by Many

The "oyster" part of the mushroom's common name comes from their resemblance to freshly shucked oysters and their slightly slippery texture when cooked. Although they don't taste like their nautical namesake, they are edible and delicious. In fact, the aspen oyster is a close relative of the commercially cultivated oyster mushroom, *Pleurotus ostreatus*, which is sold in some grocery stores.

Many other animals consume mushrooms too. Though our wild neighbors don't exchange recipes for their favorite oyster mushroom sautés, pastas, and soups, they do benefit from the many nutrients the mushrooms contain. A variety of insects, slugs, snails, and even birds and mammals dine on oyster mushrooms.

Mushroom Hunter

It turns out that oyster mushrooms consume some animals—microscopic roundworms called nematodes. The mushrooms produce a toxin in their tiny filaments that reach into the dead wood they live on. When a nematode bumps into a filament, the toxin paralyzes it within minutes. Then the mushroom injects its filaments into the nematode and dissolves it from the inside out with special digestive enzymes. Nematodes are an important source of nitrogen for oyster mushrooms, a crucial nutrient that dead wood lacks.

How to Spot Them

Aspen oyster mushrooms are common along the Wasatch Front in spring and fall. Look for them growing almost exclusively on dead cottonwood and aspen trees.

Elegant Sunburst Lichen

Xanthoria elegans

Lichens grow in colorful patches that resemble crust, leaves, or coral on rocks, trees, and other surfaces. They are actually a combination of two types of organisms, a fungus and algae (green algae or cyanobacteria), arranged in layers like a sandwich—fungus on the bottom, algae in the middle, fungus on top. The fungus provides a moist and protective structure, and the algae harness the energy for photosynthesis.

The elegant sunburst lichen lives up to its striking name. Its flat lobes resemble brilliant

orange-yellow coral and radiate outward like a burst of light. Like many of its cousins, elegant sunburst lichens grow in small, disk-shaped patches that are typically less than two inches in diameter. These tough lichens live in a variety of climates around the globe. They can grow in urban settings, deserts, and even in the extreme cold of Antarctica.

Lichens get their water and some nutrients from the air. Because they don't have roots or protective surfaces to filter out pollutants, they absorb heavy metals from the air as they grow. Analyzing the heavy metals present in lichens can provide a reliable indicator of the air quality in an area and can be used to examine the possible impacts of pollutants on human health.

To Infinity and Beyond!

Research on lichens isn't limited to those growing on our planet. A panel containing elegant sunburst lichens was attached to the exterior of the International Space Station in the year-and-a-half-long Lichen and Fungi Experiment (LIFE). After the lichens were exposed to solar and cosmic radiation in the vacuum of space for eighteen months, 71 percent of them were still alive.

These incredible survival powers are likely related to the lichens' ability to enter a desiccated dormant state and to produce compounds that protect them from radiation.

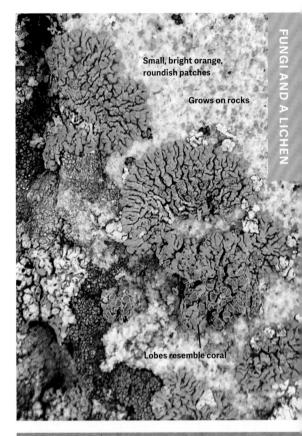

Small, bright orange, roundish patches

Grows on rocks

Lobes resemble coral

Some lichens are more tolerant of pollutants than others, so the presence—or absence—of lichen species can be a good indicator of air quality.

Inky Caps

Common Ink Cap
Coprinopsis atramentaria

Caps split as they age

Furrowed, brownish gray cap

Grows in groups

Mica Cap
Coprinellus micaceus

Shiny particles on young caps

Bell-shaped cap grows more conical with age

Grooves on cap edges deepen with age

Shaggy Mane
Coprinus comatus

White, egg-shaped cap when young

Curling white scales

Ring near bottom of stalk

Inky caps have a dramatic and morbidly fascinating way of releasing their spores. They digest their own caps with enzymes, turning themselves into gooey, inky, black masses. When conditions are right, these mushrooms can appear suddenly—seeming to spring up overnight—and become drippy black parasols within half a day. Because these mushrooms' caps don't broaden as they mature, this self-destruction enables more of their long, tightly packed gills to be exposed to the air so the wind can carry away their spores.

At least six species of inky caps are found in Utah, and many are especially common in urban areas along the Wasatch Front. Their caps are usually taller than they are wide, like the shape of a bell. Their sizes vary, from minute and delicate to as tall as a person's forearm.

Rearranging the Family Tree

All inky caps used to be grouped in the genus *Coprinus* based on the idea that self-digestion and other physical similarities indicated a genetic relationship. It turns out, however, that just because a mushroom's gills liquefy and turn black doesn't necessarily mean it is closely related to other mushrooms that do the same thing.

Recent DNA studies revealed that the genus *Coprinus* included mushrooms that were so far apart genetically, they didn't even belong to the same family, much less to the same genus. So inky caps were divided into four genera—three of which you can see in Utah. But don't worry too much about differences that are undetectable without DNA analysis.

Three to Meet

Three species of inky caps you're likely to meet along the Wasatch Front are the common ink cap, mica cap, and shaggy mane.

Common ink caps have faintly furrowed gray to brown caps and grow in clusters. Their other common names—alcohol inky caps and tippler's bane—allude to a chemical they contain that prevents a person's body from metabolizing alcohol. If you drink a glass of wine with your sautéed common ink caps, violent vomiting is likely to result.

Mica caps also appear in dense clusters, growing on dead wood or emerging from the soil. When young, their brown caps are coated with a distinctive dusting of granules that resemble mica. Delicate white scales curl up from a shaggy mane's cap, seeming to foreshadow the dramatic disintegration that lies ahead.

How to Spot Them

Inky caps can be found in areas with adequate moisture, most often in spring and fall. They grow on lawns, along sidewalks, and at the base of trees (both living and dead), especially along streams. Some species of inky caps are solitary, while others grow in clusters.

You can write with the "ink" produced by inky caps! One Salt Lake City artist drew a picture of an inky cap with inky cap ink.

Morels

Morchella spp.

Yellow-gray to black cap, depending on species

Conical, deeply pitted cap

Light-colored stalk with single hollow chamber inside

▲ Skilled morel hunters display some of their delectable finds.

Prized by mushroom hunters and chefs alike, morels are famously delicious. Both the black and yellow varieties grow in Utah, but don't expect a mushroom hunter to disclose the location of these coveted delicacies. You can recognize morels by their distinctive conical caps that look like sponges or honeycombs and their light-colored stalks. They are actually only distantly related to most things we would consider mushrooms—like button mushrooms, porcini, and chanterelles. Molds and truffles are closer kin.

Finicky to Farm

Though very popular gourmet mushrooms, morels have proven extremely difficult to cultivate on a large scale, probably because of the complexities of their lifecycle. Many mushrooms absorb nutrients from decaying organic matter or from mutually beneficial relationships with tree roots, but morels seem to rely on both.

In the 1980s, a large pizza chain was interested in growing morels commercially and bought the rights to a cultivation method. Their efforts, however, never produced enough morels for the mushrooms to make it onto their pizzas. In the 1990s, the pizza chain sold the patent to a company in Minnesota that runs a modest, thriving commercial growing operation. Today, morels are cultivated at large scale in China and Denmark, but these recent successes haven't yet made it to supermarkets in the United States.

Morel Impersonators

If you forage for morels to eat, be wary of their nonedible look-alikes, which can sometimes be toxic. The easiest way to determine whether your find is a true morel is to slice it in half lengthwise: the whole cap portion and stalk

Although no evidence suggests that picking a mushroom harms the mycelium, the fungus's main body that is hidden below the soil, overharvesting is a potential concern. Please be considerate of these special organisms and don't harvest every mushroom you find.

will be hollow, and the stalk will be attached to the bottom of the cap. The stalk of a nonedible false morel (genus *Verpa*) passes through the inside of the cap, connecting at the top.

Other false morels, such as those in the genera *Gyromitra* and *Helvella*, have convoluted tops that aren't pitted like a true morel, and their stalks are compartmentalized into chambers. Some stinkhorn mushrooms of the genus *Phallus* have pitted caps that look a bit like true morel caps, but the dark, smelly slime covering the caps gives away these mushrooms' true identity.

If you're not 100 percent sure you have a true morel, don't eat it! If you have found a morel, be sure to cook it thoroughly—raw and undercooked morels can make you sick.

How to Spot Them

Look for morels along the Wasatch Front in springtime. They are tricky to spot, because they are well camouflaged and blend in with the ground. Yellow morels grow at lower elevations along streams near cottonwood trees, especially near trees that have recently died. Black morels grow at higher elevations and tend to grow near aspen and conifers, especially Douglas fir, and in recently burned areas.

Mower's Mushroom

Panaeolina foenisecii

Some short gills don't connect to the cap

Cap changes from dark to pale brown as it ages and dries out

Thin stalk with no ring

You've probably seen these delicate brown mushrooms growing in a lawn somewhere. Mower's mushrooms are among the most common and widely distributed mushrooms in North America. Our countless irrigated lawns make excellent mower's mushroom habitat.

Shifting Colors

When young, a mower's mushroom looks a bit like a small golf ball resting on a dainty tee. Their thin stalks typically grow between two and four inches tall, and their broad, conical caps range from about a half inch to a little more than one inch across. If you gently look underneath the cap, you'll see that the mushroom's gills vary from pale brown to darker brown. The gills can be mottled or have pale edges.

The colors of mower's mushroom caps can vary because this species is hygrophanous—a scientific way of saying they change color as they absorb or lose water. Wet caps are dark brown and turn various shades of lighter brown to creamy buff as they dry. Sometimes you'll see bands of different colors on the same mushroom or different colored groups of mushrooms in the same lawn.

Don't Eat Me

It can be difficult to tell little brown mushrooms apart. Mower's mushrooms are not highly toxic, but some look-alikes are and eating them can be dangerous, especially to children and pets. The hallucinogenic mushrooms *Panaeolus cinctulus* and *Panaeolus olivaceus* look similar and share the same habitat. You may hear claims that mower's mushrooms produce hallucinogenic psilocybin compounds, but they don't. It's best to just leave all little brown mushrooms growing in the lawn.

How to Spot Them

Look for mower's mushrooms in grass, especially lawns or other landscaped habitat with abundant irrigation, from late spring through fall. The mushrooms are short-lived and may appear in the morning only to wither under the heat of the sun by afternoon.

What Is a Mushroom?

Fungi are not animals, plants, or bacteria. They are a separate kingdom of organisms made up of as many as twelve million different species—compared to about seven million identified species of plants and animals. Evolutionarily and physiologically, fungi are actually more closely related to animals than plants.

The mushrooms we see above the ground are the reproductive structures of fungi that live in massive underground networks. These networks are made of very abundant tiny filaments that can extend over vast areas. The world's largest living organism, measured by area, is the "Humongous Fungus," a network of honey mushroom filaments that covers about three square miles in Oregon!

Fungi's highly interconnected filaments are extremely efficient at extracting resources and distributing them throughout the network, shifting resources according to demand. Some networks even link plant roots together, including trees in forests, enabling the trees to exchange nutrients and other chemicals with one another underground. This "wood-wide web" may be one of the most important aspects of land plant ecosystems that we still know very little about.

▲ These honey mushrooms growing in Utah are the same species as the Humongous Fungus that covers about three square miles in Oregon.

Pavement Mushroom

Agaricus bitorquis

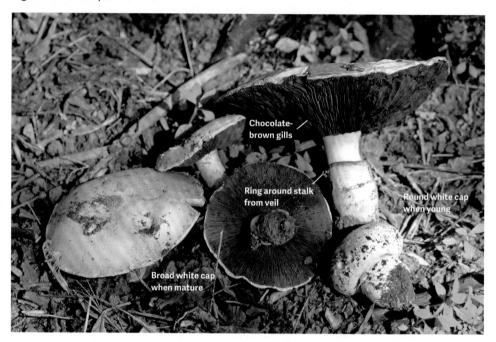

Chocolate-brown gills

Ring around stalk from veil

Round white cap when young

Broad white cap when mature

The pavement mushroom is at home in the city. It seems to prefer growing in hard-packed soil next to sidewalks and roads, but it pops up in gardens and compost piles too. In addition to sprouting next to pavement, this mushroom can grow through it.

Decomposing organic matter in the soil below the pavement attracts and fuels pavement mushrooms' growth. They often mature under the soil and grow straight up. The strength of their internal cell structure enables them to exert enough force to break through asphalt and lift slabs of pavement as they grow. Although they may be damaging the driveway, they are doing important work—breaking down dead things in the soil to provide nutrients to other plants.

A Short, White Veil

Pavement mushrooms start out short and stout. As a mushroom is developing, its gills are covered by a veil, a thin membrane that protects the gills until the spores they contain have matured. Look for a ring on a mature mushroom's stalk where the veil collapsed after the cap expanded.

As it ages, the mushroom's white cap broadens, becoming almost flat. Pieces of soil often cling to the cap. If the mushroom matures underground, only a small part of its cap may be visible above the soil. You may have to dig a bit to find one. You'll know it's a pavement mushroom if its white flesh doesn't change color when you bruise or slice it.

Mushroom Art

Just as you can identify a person by her fingerprints, a spore print can help you identify a mushroom. Try making a spore print with a pavement mushroom. Gently remove the cap, place it gills down on a piece of white paper, and cover it for twenty-four hours. When you lift the cap, you'll see the delicate, dark brown spores "printed" on the paper. Other mushroom species produce black, purple, or white spore prints.

Pavement mushrooms are close relatives of the white button mushrooms (Agaricus bisporus) you can find at the grocery store and are similar in flavor. Pavement mushrooms have the nutritional benefit of being high in amino acids, but they also accumulate toxic heavy metals, so harvesting them in an urban setting is not ideal.

How to Spot Them

You can find pavement mushrooms growing alone or in groups throughout the Wasatch Front in the late spring, summer, and fall. Look for them in gardens, next to paths, or along roads.

> As a pavement mushroom matures, its gills change color—from grayish pink, to reddish brown, to chocolatey brown.

Reishi

Ganoderma sichuanense

Projects from a tree like a shelf

In Utah, grows on Gambel oaks

Red-brown, fan-shaped sporocarp

Reishi mushrooms are from Asia but now grow along the Wasatch Front. So far, Utah is the only place in North America where this species has been observed growing outside of cultivation. Some people speculate that this mushroom was introduced during an outdoor cultivation program somewhere in the Salt Lake Valley.

Deadly for Trees

This mushroom grows from a stalk in the soil near a tree or horizontally from a tree's bark, where it resembles small shelves hanging on the trunk. The mushroom's red-brown, leathery, sometimes shiny sporocarp (the structure where spores are produced) is shaped like a fan. Reishi mushrooms lack gills underneath; instead, each mushroom has a compact layer of whitish, vertically arranged tubes that look like a sponge under a magnifying glass. They are also hard—almost wooden—and can last for more than a year.

Reishi mushrooms are parasites of woody plants. In Utah, they grow on Gambel oaks (*Quercus gambelii*). Because they are not easily eradicated, the appearance of reishi mushrooms means certain death for their host tree—though it may take many years for the tree to die.

Healthy for People

Reishi have been used for thousands of years in Asia to treat a wide variety of ailments, including cancers and high blood pressure, and they are also used for reducing stress and improving sleep. References to their health benefits exist from as early as 100 B.C. Depictions of reishi often appear in ancient Chinese and Japanese art and are associated with royalty, wisdom, and eternal life. (The mushroom's Chinese name is *lingzhi*.)

The reishi industry is quite profitable today, valued at more than $2 billion in the supplements market. The mushrooms are grown commercially and are ground into a powder to make a variety pills, tinctures, and teas prescribed in traditional medicine.

How to Spot Them

Look for reishi growing on benches throughout Salt Lake City or on exposed or buried wood near oak trees. You'll see their actively growing sporocarps from late spring to early fall, but you can find old, woody specimens year-round. Old sporocarps will regrow in subsequent years by adding new layers to their undersides.

Spring Fieldcap

Agrocybe praecox

Spring fieldcaps are common in urban areas but virtually unknown in wild places. They thrive in the ubiquitous woodchips that cover garden beds and park strips in cities and suburbs. This is one of many mushroom species that humans have spread around the world through our landscaping practices.

This mushroom has a pale brown, beige, or yellowish white cap and a white to off-white stalk. You may see the wisps of a thin, white veil hanging from the edge of its cap. Spring fieldcaps often grow in great abundance, sometimes in clusters. They are similar in size to the cultivated button mushrooms sold at grocery stores but have thinner stalks. In dry conditions, the caps develop fissures that give them a distinctive cracked appearance.

These Gills Aren't for Breathing

Some fungi species use structures called gills to disperse spores for reproduction. These rows of papery ridges underneath a mushroom's cap look a bit like fish gills. Because the arrangement and color of gills differ from species to species, they can be helpful in

Pale gills darken to brown with age

Cracked cap

Remnants of the veil that covered the gills

identifying a mushroom. If you're taking photos of a mushroom for iNaturalist or another identification app, try to include a photo of its gills.

The spring fieldcap's tightly packed gills radiate outward from its stalk. They are pale colored when young and become brown at maturity. When reproducing, spring fieldcaps produce copious brown spores that can sometimes create a dusting of brown powder on objects below their caps.

Nature Networking

Spring fieldcaps can grow a network of thick, white strands (mycelial cords) that spread throughout landscaping woodchips, binding the mushrooms together like a net. These cords resemble aboveground roots and function similarly, drawing nutrients from the surrounding area.

Although they aren't poisonous, spring fieldcaps have an unpleasant taste. That's just one reason to avoid eating them. In urban areas, they may accumulate harmful chemicals, including herbicides and heavy metal pollutants from combustion engines. Plus, several toxic mushrooms are similar in appearance.

The spring fieldcap's common name is a pretty direct translation of its scientific name, *Agrocybe praecox*. *Agro* refers to "fields," *cybe* refers to a "head or cap," and *praecox* means "developing or appearing early."

How to Spot Them

The spring fieldcap is named for the season when it emerges. Look for them fairly early in the year. They are common in urban areas across the Wasatch Front, along roads, and in landscaped areas, especially among woodchips.

Invertebrates (Insects, Spiders, and Friends)

Blue Orchard Bee

Osmia lignaria

Covered in little black hairs

Dark metallic-blue body

Carries pollen on its belly, not its legs

If you set out a bee house that includes hollow tubes, this gorgeous, metallic-blue stunner is one of the wild mason bees likely to take up residence there. Blue orchard bees are about the same size as the familiar western honeybees (*Apis mellifera*), but they are plumper, royal blue, and have soft black hairs. They sometimes appear metallic green in the right light. Look for pollen under their bellies instead of on their legs, where many other bees carry it.

Hardworking Moms

Like most wild bees, blue orchard bees are solitary. They don't have a hive to protect so they're unlikely to sting. After they emerge in the early spring, blue orchard bees mate and the females begin the hard work of preparing a home for their young. A mother bee looks for a tube-shaped hole, where she builds a series of little cells separated by mud walls—one cell for each egg. In her brief adult life of a few weeks, she can fill an average of four, six-inch tubes with about eight eggs per tube. She stocks each cell with a supply of pollen mixed with nectar for the larvae to feed on when they hatch. Provisioning her young requires as many as 60,000 blossom visits!

The young bees spend the summer growing and then overwinter in their little cells. The fertilized eggs at the back of the tube develop into females, while the unfertilized eggs near the front develop into males. This enables the males to emerge first in the spring, ready to mate with the females as they emerge. It also provides better protection for the females, which are more precious to the continuation of the mother bee's genes.

A male blue orchard bee has fluffy hairs lining the bottom of his face, creating a dapper bee mustache.

Power Pollinators

Blue orchard bees are super-industrious pollinators and love visiting flowering trees that bloom in early spring. Studies show that they pollinate almonds, sweet cherries, and other fruit trees much more efficiently than honeybees. Scientists at the USDA Agricultural Research Service in Logan are studying how farmers can utilize blue orchard bees to diversify the suite of pollinators available to us and improve our food security.

How to Spot Them

Look for blue orchard bees collecting pollen from blooming trees in the spring. If you're lucky enough to have blue orchard bees nesting nearby, watch for females warming themselves in the morning sun at their nest sites. When they return with a load of pollen, you'll see some charming acrobatics as they unload it.

Bold Jumping Spider

Phidippus audax

When you meet a bold jumping spider, take a moment to gaze into its eyes. Like many spiders, this spider has four pairs of eyes: The two large, forward-facing "principal" eyes looking right back at you see color and detail. The smaller eyes on either side detect motion, the rear set sees behind the spider, and the middle set is a bit of mystery. If your spider has charming bushy eyebrows, it's a male.

These eyes provide bold jumpers with incredible vision that scientists can't resist studying. They've devised all manner of spider eye tests to learn what these arachnids see

Very fuzzy black body with white striped legs

Large "principal" eyes

Emerald-green mouthparts

Keeps legs tucked underneath its body

and how their eyes coordinate. They've learned that bold jumpers see with remarkable resolution for their tiny size—they can see as well as a much larger animal, such as a cat or an elephant. They can also track moving objects with their small front eyes while watching something else with their principal eyes.

Safety Conscious

Bold jumpers' unusually good vision helps them make precisely targeted jumps. Instead of building webs to snare meals passively, these spiders prefer to sneak up on their prey and pounce. Although they can make leaps with great accuracy, they don't take chances. Before jumping, they often secure a strand of silk to the surface they're on so they won't fall if the jump doesn't go as planned.

With their large, expressive eyes and fuzzy little bodies, bold jumpers are about as cuddly as spiders can be. They're mostly black with white stripes on their legs. Their abdomens usually have white or orange markings; if you're lucky, you may see a spider with markings in the shape of hearts or spades! Beneath their eyes, their mouthparts glow a brilliant green, especially in males.

Some people worry that jumping spiders will want to jump on them, but being on or near a person is the last thing a spider wants. That said, this spider can be fun to pick up, very gently, and hold for a few minutes, watching it jump from hand to hand before you release it.

How to Spot Them

Bold jumpers are common along the Wasatch Front throughout the summer. They're active during the day because they depend on vision for hunting. Look for them on flat spaces with an open view for spotting prey. They're not shy about hunting near human structures. They may sometimes venture indoors, but they prefer to be outside, where more food is available. If you meet one inside, it would probably appreciate an escort outside.

Cabbage White

Pieris rapae

The unassuming cabbage white is probably the most common butterfly in the world. Originally from Europe, they now live on every continent except South America and Antarctica. The key to global domination—or at least distribution—for these little butterflies was our love of cabbage, broccoli, kale, and all their delicious cousins.

Epic Journeys

Cabbage whites evolved a close relationship with plants in the *Brassicaceae* family, also known as the cabbage or mustard family,

Females lay eggs on these plants and their caterpillars specialize in eating them. After humans began domesticating members of the cabbage family and moving them over long distances, cabbage white caterpillars went along for the ride.

A team of researchers recently compared the genes of butterflies collected by citizen scientists around the world to unravel the timing of cabbage whites' global conquest. They determined that the butterflies' first long-distance journey was along the Silk Road from Europe to Asia at least 1,200 years ago.

Shadowy black tips on forewings

One or two spots on each forewing

Creamy white open wings

Cabbage whites' next big leap was from Europe to Toronto in the 1860s. A few Canadian caterpillars may have ridden the newly completed railroad to San Francisco in the late 1870s to establish the genetically distinct central California population.

One Spot or Two?

Cabbage whites are exceedingly common along the Wasatch Front. They live in almost any sunny, open area and love our wild mustards, such as tall whitetop (*Lepidium draba*). When their wings are open, they are almost entirely a creamy white, though the tips of their forewings are smudged in charcoal black. If you see two black spots in the center of the forewing, you've found a female; males have a single black spot. When their wings are closed, look for a pale-yellow hindwing.

Females lay single eggs that are tiny, ridged, and oblong, attached to the undersides of leaves. The caterpillars that hatch from them are lime green and camouflage very well with their food plants. To avoid predators, they hang out on the undersides of leaves as they dine. At least two or three generations are born each year, with the last one in the fall overwintering as a chrysalis.

How to Spot Them

You can see cabbage whites almost anywhere along the Wasatch Front, including city parks and backyard gardens, canyon streams, dry foothills, and even in downtown garden beds. They are active throughout the day from March to October. They aren't high flyers, so look for them flying close to the ground.

Cabbage whites are sometimes mistaken for moths. Moths are generally fatter, faster, and fluffier than butterflies, and there are approximately fourteen times more moths than butterflies in any given habitat (remember the four F's). Moth antennae come in many shapes and are often branched and feathery, while each of a butterfly's threadlike antennae ends in a tiny knob.

Common Pill Woodlouse

Armadillidium vulgare

Roly-poly, sowbug, pillbug, potato bug—what do you call the common pill woodlouse? In the United Kingdom, woodlice have more than fifty different common names! Their official common name may be a bit confusing, because woodlice are not closely related to the insects we call lice. In fact, woodlice aren't even insects. They're crustaceans—like shrimp, lobsters, and crabs.

Farewell to the Sea

Woodlice are the only crustaceans that evolved to leave the ocean behind for life on land. However, they still breathe through gills that remove oxygen from water in the air, which is why they usually live in damp environments. Originally residents of the Mediterranean region, common pill woodlice are now found all over the world.

As any kid can tell you, woodlice roll up in a ball when disturbed to protect their soft undersides and seven pairs of short legs. Like the armadillo, from which their genus name is derived, they have rounded gray backs that are divided into segments. Though their vision is poor, small elbowed antennae help woodlice sense what's going on around them.

Family and Friends

Woodlice like hanging out together. Some species even live in family groups, with juveniles helping to clean the family home. Female woodlice have a "brood pouch" like a kangaroo. They lay their eggs in the pouch and the babies hatch inside. A mother woodlouse carries her young, which look like tiny versions of adults, until they are mature enough to be released.

Woodlice feed on decaying wood, leaf litter, and dead animals, helping return nutrients from organic materials to the soil. They also have an unusual ability: they tolerate consuming heavy metals in the soil, such as copper, lead, and zinc, by isolating them in special

Rounded back

Segmented, gray-brown body

Elbowed antennae for sensing the world

Woodlice make great pets! All they need is a terrarium with slightly damp soil, a piece of carrot, some decaying leaves, and maybe a pine cone. Be sure to keep them away from bright light.

tissues in their gut. This means woodlice can serve as the crustacean equivalent of the canary in the coal mine. By testing the woodlice at a site for heavy metals, researchers can detect even relatively low levels of contamination.

How to Spot Them

Look for woodlice where it's dark and damp—under logs and rocks and buried in leaf litter. They prefer to move around at night. Chewed up pine cones and brown leaves are evidence of their snacking. You can spot them in the spring through the fall. They spend the winter underground.

Desert Tarantula

Aphonopelma iodius

The Wasatch Front is at the very northern edge of tarantulas' range in the Western Hemisphere. (Poor Idaho doesn't have any tarantulas at all!) Just one species lives in our area—the desert tarantula, also known as the Salt Lake County brown. This slow-moving gentle giant can be up to five inches long.

Despite their large size, tarantulas are pretty delicate—a fall could kill them. They're also vulnerable to predators because they can't run quickly. Desert tarantulas don't bite defensively, either. Their primary defense is flicking barbed hairs from their upper abdomen at attackers. Like tiny fish hooks, the hairs are very irritating and difficult to remove from eyes, noses, and mouths.

Large, hairy brown body

Barbed hairs on upper abdomen for flinging at attackers

Long pedipalps (sensory organs) look like extra legs

Desert tarantulas are remarkably long-lived for invertebrates. Males live about ten years and females can live up to twenty-five years.

Homebodies

A desert tarantula relies on the comfort of its dark burrow to keep safe. It hangs around the mouth of the burrow to wait for dinner to walk by. Sensing the vibrations of a passing beetle or cricket, it will dash out, subdue its prey by injecting it with venom from its fangs, and bring it back to its burrow to eat. (For a human, the venom is no worse than a bee sting.)

A mature female doesn't need to leave her burrow as long as it's undisturbed. Adult males don't go out until they reach sexual maturity at about ten years of age. After one last molt, a male will leave his burrow in the fall on a final quest for love. Because it's common to see tarantulas on foothill roads and trails in the fall, some people wonder if they are migrating, but they aren't relocating to a new area—they're just looking to pass on their genes.

Dangerous Liaisons

When a male finds a female's burrow, he'll drum at the entrance to entice her to come out and assess him as a mate. It's a dangerous dance. If mating occurs, males use the hooks on their forelegs they acquired in their last molt to hold the female's fangs for safety. Afterward, if she hasn't eaten in a while, he might be her next meal. If she's not too hungry and allows the male to retreat, he'll continue searching for other females until he is killed or dies with the onset of cold weather.

How to Spot Them

Watch for desert tarantulas in the foothills from late August through October, when sexually mature males emerge to search for mates. During this time, they are active both day and night. The rest of the year, look for tarantula burrows with a round entrance lined with silk. If you're lucky enough to find a burrow, please don't disturb it.

Dragonflies

Blue-Eyed Darner

Rhionaeschna multicolor

Big blue eyes in males

Two blue triangles on each brown abdomen segment

Up to 2.8 inches long

Variegated Meadowhawk

Sympetrum corruptum

Up to 2 inches long

Gold markings on female abdomen

Tinted vein on leading edge of wings

At the height of summer, the Wasatch Front's suburban skies fill with dragonflies zooming in all directions like tiny bejeweled fighter jets. Dragonflies are among nature's ultimate flying machines. They can fly forward, backward, sideways, and hover in midair. They achieve this incredible maneuverability by controlling each of their four wings independently, making precision adjustments to the angles of their wings and the length of their wing stroke. They can even stop one or two wings in midflight.

Deadly Hunters

Flying prowess is just one feature of a dragonfly's "supreme hunter" package. The two huge compound eyes that cover most of its head give it nearly 360-degree vision. Keen vision helps a dragonfly judge the speed and trajectory of its prey and adjust its flight path to intercept it in midair. After grabbing dinner with its legs, a dragonfly removes the insect's wings with its sharp, strong jaws and can consume its meal without having to land.

Dragonflies spend their youth as ferocious underwater hunters. The larvae, or nymphs,

have a lower lip that shoots out on a hinge to scoop up prey—kind of like the alien in the movie *Alien*, but much faster. They mostly wait patiently for prey to float past, but they are able to move rapidly by sucking water into their abdomens and squirting it out their rear ends.

A Brand New Me

After spending months or years in a pond or stream, a nymph climbs out of the water and goes through one of the most dramatic transformations in insectdom. It clings to a rock or reed and then splits open down a seam in its back, pulls its wings out of its former body, and takes to the air with an entirely new breathing system and hunting strategy.

Dragonflies are as beautiful as they are fierce. One of the most striking dragonflies in our area is the blue-eyed darner. A male darner has vivid sky-blue eyes and two blue triangles on each segment of its brown abdomen. Females are usually green. The smaller variegated meadowhawk is the most commonly observed dragonfly on the Wasatch Front. Males have red and brown abdomens and tinted veins along the leading edge of each wing. Females have gold markings instead.

How to Spot Them

Look for dragonflies from midsummer through early fall. You'll often find them near still water, but they are strong flyers and may be spotted miles away from water. On cool mornings, you may see a dragonfly holding still as it warms up in the sun. This is a great chance to make close observations, as dragonflies are not usually amenable to hanging out with humans.

> When it comes to kill rates, dragonflies are much deadlier hunters than great white sharks or lions. Dragonflies are successful at taking down their prey 95 percent of the time, while great white sharks have a success rate of 50 percent and lions have a meager 25 percent kill rate.

Eastern Box Elder Bug

Boisea trivittata

Eastern box elder bugs are a gregarious bunch. In the fall, they get together in big box elder bug bashes to sun themselves on the walls of buildings. In the spring, you may see bugs gathering on box elder trees (*Acer negundo*) as they emerge from hibernation to lay eggs. It may be alarming to see so many box elder bugs in one place, but they are completely harmless. Abundance means success in nature, so think of box elder bugs as an amazing success story!

Box elder bugs don't do the cool metamorphosis trick that transforms many insects from larval to adult forms—think caterpillar to butterfly. Instead, their young are just smaller, wingless versions of adults. Baby box elder bugs start out almost entirely reddish orange in color. As they molt and become larger, their black wings appear.

An adult box elder bug is about half an inch long, with a tracery of red on its textured

Long antennae

Oval-shaped body

Red markings on black wings and back

Protruding red eyes

black wings and back. Its small black head comes to a soft point, with dull reddish colored eyes protruding on either side. Its thin, jointed antennae are about half as long as its body.

Staying Off the Menu

The red on a box elder bug's back may be a warning to predators, a trick, or perhaps both. Box elder bugs can release a foul odor from glands on their abdomens when threatened, but they don't make any toxins. Their color pattern, however, resembles that of the milkweed bug (*Oncopeltus fasciatus*), which feeds on toxic milkweed sap and tastes terrible. Box elder bugs' warning/trick deters many predators, enabling them to hang out in large groups without becoming a buffet.

Box elder bugs, like all true bugs, have strawlike mouthparts called beaks. Their beaks lie against their undersides, so you don't usually see them unless they are actively eating. They use their beaks to pierce plants, sometimes sucking nourishment out of fallen seeds or leaves and sometimes out of living trees. Their feeding doesn't harm the plants they dine on, which is pretty considerate.

How to Spot Them

Look for box elder bugs on the trees that they prefer to feed on—box elders and other maples. Box elder seeds are their absolute favorite food. During the summer, you may see box elder bug gathering on sidewalks. In the fall, look for big groups on the sides of buildings. You may even see them out on a warm winter day.

European Firebug

Pyrrhocoris apterus

The Wasatch Front holds a special place in European firebug history. Around 2008, firebugs established their first population in the entire Western Hemisphere in Salt Lake City! No one knows how these intrepid little settlers arrived from Europe, but humans were certainly involved. Perhaps the firebugs were hanging out on some plants that were shipped to Utah. Though new populations have become established in other locations in the Western Hemisphere, Utah's firebug population remains the largest outside their original range in Europe and parts of Asia.

Nice Neighbors

Firebugs seem to be settling into their new home without causing any significant ripples.

Protruding red eyes

Two black spots on short red wings

Unable to fly

They have many predators in Europe, including birds, mammals, ants, and mites, and are probably being gobbled up here too. They eat dry seeds, so they won't damage gardens.

Middle-school students from the Salt Lake Center for Science Education played a big role in gathering the data for the scientific paper formally announcing the arrival of European firebugs in North America.

In the decade after their arrival, firebugs spread from Salt Lake City north into Cache Valley and south to Santaquin—a pretty impressive feat for insects that can't fly. The Natural History Museum of Utah launched a citizen science project on iNaturalist to track their range expansion. The data gathered by citizen scientists will ultimately help NHMU researchers better understand firebugs' ecology in Utah.

Look for the Dots

At first glance, firebugs look similar to the eastern box elder bugs (*Boisea trivittata*) familiar to many Wasatch Front residents. The easiest way to identify a firebug is to look for two black dots surrounded in bright red on its short wings. It also has prominent eyes that seem to emerge from its shoulders. If it flies away, you know it's a box elder bug, not a firebug.

Like box elder bugs, firebugs sometimes gather in large groups. They use a chemical beacon, called an aggregation pheromone, to call a big crowd together. Other chemical messengers, called alert pheromones, trigger an alarm response that causes the group to scatter. In addition to helping keep their members warm and active when temperatures drop, big groups of bugs seem to deter predators.

How to Spot Them

Look for firebugs from March to November. When they mate in April and May, you may spot them pairing end-to-end. Mating can last from twelve hours to a week! Because firebugs don't fly, they are likely to be seen close to the ground in neighborhoods, parks, and open spaces—any place they can find seeds to eat.

European Harvestman

Phalangium opilio

European harvestmen (commonly known as daddy longlegs) are not spiders. They are their own order of arachnids (the Opiliones) and have been around for more than 400 million years. Look closely and you can see that a harvestman isn't a spider: it has two eyes instead of a spider's typical eight, and it has a fused, round body instead of a body with two segments connected by a thin waist. Plus harvestmen can't make silk to spin a web.

Completely Harmless

Have you ever heard that European harvestmen are the most poisonous spiders in the world, but they can't bite you because their

Round body with brown or gray pattern

Eight very long legs

Two eyes

fangs are too small to penetrate human skin? It's an exciting story with the thrill of a threat barely escaped, but none of it is true.

As we've established, harvestmen are not spiders. They aren't poisonous either. Technically, they would be venomous if they could inject venom with their fangs—but they don't have fangs. They have mouthparts that enable them to eat chunks of food, unlike spiders, which can only drink liquefied food.

Finally, harvestmen don't even try to bite people. Their preferred food seems to be soft-bodied invertebrates such as aphids, slugs, or squishy larvae. They will, however, take a crunchy snack as well, so beetles beware. And they will happily munch on dead bugs and rotting plants, which helps keep things tidy.

Stilt Walkers

European harvestmen live up to their daddy longlegs nickname, with eight legs that are incredibly long compared to their bodies. They rely on their second pair of legs to sense the world. Their legs detach easily to help them escape from predators, but they don't grow back. Each time they lose a leg, they develop a different stride suited to their new leg count.

There's some debate about whether or not European harvestmen are new to North America because they are so widespread now, but it seems likely that they were introduced here. The first confirmed record of them on our continent is from Arkansas in 1890. A few other species of harvestmen live along the Wasatch Front, but they aren't very common.

How to Spot Them

European harvestmen are easy to spot in cities and suburbs along the Wasatch Front. They like places with a bit of humidity, such as under leaf litter and rocks or in a moist corner of a basement. They are mostly nocturnal, but you can see them moving in the daytime too. They won't be out in the winter when it's cold.

> The name "harvestmen" refers to the time when you're most likely to see these arachnids—in late summer and early fall, around harvest time. They are also known as shepherd spiders because the males guard the females as they are laying eggs.

European Paper Wasp

Polistes dominula

Slender body and tiny waist

Yellow-and-black pattern on body

Yellow-orange antennae

Long legs

European paper wasps are among the many skilled architects of the insect world. Not only do they build sophisticated structures, they also make their own building material—a sturdy, waterproof paper—by chewing up old wood and mixing it with their saliva. Each spring, new queens emerge from hibernation to build new nests.

A nest starts as just a few hexagonal cells, but it can grow to several dozen cells after the queen's daughters hatch and get into the construction business. The cells are open, so you can see into them from below. They often

▲ European paper wasps build nests with cells that are open from below, unlike the enclosed nests of western yellow jackets.

choose a protected location for the structure, such as under eaves or other overhangs. If you see a round, football-size nest that's completely enclosed in paper, it belongs to a different wasp—the western yellow jacket (*Vespula pensylvanica*).

Not a Yellow Jacket

It can be easy to mistake a European paper wasp for a yellow jacket. They both sport the yellow and black "I have a stinger!" warning colors that many flying insects evolved to deter potential predators. Compared to chunkier yellow jackets, European paper wasps have slender bodies and tiny waists like corseted Victorian ladies. Watch for their long legs trailing elegantly behind them as they fly.

If a wasp is trying to horn in on your picnic fare, it's a yellow jacket. European paper wasps, on the other hand, aren't interested in human food. The adults sip nectar and other sweet liquids, but you may also see them hunting caterpillars and other insects. They chew up their prey and regurgitate the nutritious "bug juice" to feed their young. Because European paper wasps are such effective hunters and often target caterpillars that gardeners

Paper wasps can recognize the faces of their nest mates, a skill that helps them know who's who in the colony hierarchy.

consider harmful, some people install nest boxes for them.

City Wasps

Relatively new to the Wasatch Front, these wasps were first noted in Utah in 1995. They were first documented in North America in the late 1970s in the Boston area. As they do throughout their range in the United States, European paper wasps in Utah tend to stick to cities and suburbs. Their preference for nesting on and in the structures we build may have helped them adapt to life in the city.

How to Spot Them

European paper wasps are busy during the warmth of the day throughout the summer and into the fall. Look for their nests tucked away under overhangs, in pipes, in the gas grill you never use, and in other sheltered spots. As long as a nest isn't in a high traffic area, you can let it be. European paper wasps are not likely to sting unless you disturb their nest.

Garden Snail

Cornu aspersum

Spiral pattern on shell varies from light beige to dark brown

Eye stalks

Tentacles for smelling and tasting

Foot

Humans have a love-hate-love relationship with the unassuming garden snail. On one hand, we love to eat them so much that we carried them from their original home in Western Europe to five other continents. On the other hand, they're great at adapting to their new homes and eating many foods we wish they wouldn't eat, including our gardens and crops. But then again, they're pretty adorable.

Garden snails seem to like us too. In Utah, they live almost exclusively in cities and suburbs, where we create moist environments with lots of fresh green foliage for them to feast on. Their very name suggests our close relationship. If you see a snail cruising the sidewalk or a flower bed along the Wasatch Front, it's almost certainly a garden snail. Their shells have a charming right-hand coil, with colors ranging from darkest chocolatey brown to a delicate tan-beige, often with bands or flecks of yellow.

Mucus Magic

A snail moves about on a "foot" that protrudes from its shell, with help from "snail slime," a mucus with amazing properties. When a snail is at rest, the slime is sticky and helps the snail adhere to whatever surface it's on. But under pressure from the snail's foot muscles, the slime becomes a slippery lubricant that helps it glide along, leaving a sparkling trail behind.

Garden snails produce another kind of mucus to seal off their shells from the outside world when they need to wait out dry periods in the summer or the cold of winter. Slowing their metabolism to a snail's pace, they can hide out this way for months.

All in One

Like most snails, garden snails are hermaphroditic, which means that each individual has both male and female reproductive parts.

During their complex mating rituals that involve shooting "love darts" at each other, both snails exchange sperm and both become pregnant. It's a very efficient system. The fact that every snail can have baby snails helps explain why they're so successful at populating new places.

How to Spot Them

Garden snails like moist, leafy, shady environments. They are most active at night or very early in the morning, but if it rains during the day, you may spot some sliding along the wet pavement or grass. They tend to stay fairly close to the ground, as a fall could crack their shells. The easiest way to find them is to look for their glittering trails.

Snail mucin—or mucus—is a key ingredient in popular skincare products. Some manufacturers try to jazz up their labels by saying their slime is from "black snails" or "Chilean earth snails," but it's really from the humble garden snail.

Hunt's Bumblebee

Bombus huntii

Like all bumblebees, Hunt's bumblebees have adorable fuzzy bodies and heart-shaped faces. They resemble many other bumblebees in the West, but you can identify them by their color pattern. Workers and queens—the Hunt's bumblebees you're most likely to meet—have a yellow head, followed by a yellow thorax with a black band between the wings, and then a distinct abdominal segment pattern: yellow-orange-orange-yellow-black-black.

Royal Duties

Bumblebees' fuzz keeps them warm, enabling them to be active when it's too cold out for other bees. The queens emerge from hibernation as early as March after spending the winter hidden under leaf litter. Watch for burly queen bumblebees flying low over the ground in the spring, stopping often to investigate holes in the ground or in building foundations. They are house-hunting for a nest site.

Once the queen finds a good underground home, she'll gather pollen and nectar to provision her offspring. After a few days, she will have enough food to begin laying eggs. When the queen's adult daughters emerge, they take over foraging and nest construction duties, leaving the queen to lay eggs and incubate her brood.

Workers are often much smaller than their mother, so don't expect to see many big Hunt's

Yellow fuzz on face and back

Distinct order of yellow, orange, and black abdominal segments

Black band between wings

the flower with its jaw and legs and vibrates its flight muscles, essentially turning itself into a living tuning fork. A bumblebee can generate g-forces up to 30 g's this way, resulting in a bee-covering shower of nutritious pollen. Tomatoes, potatoes, and blueberries are just a few of the plants that rely on bumblebees for "buzz pollination."

How to Spot Them

Hunt's bumblebees stick to lower elevations, where the growing season begins earlier. This enables their colonies to become relatively large, so their busy workers are common sights in Wasatch Front neighborhoods. In the summer, they often stay in their nests during the heat of the day, so watch for them in the early evening. Plant a garden with flowers that bloom from early spring through fall to support your local bumblebees.

bumblebees over the summer. In the fall, the new queens and males emerge to mate before the queens search for a spot to spend the winter.

Shake It!

Bumblebees (and some solitary bees) can perform a nifty pollination trick that honeybees can't. Some plants hold their pollen in a tube with a small hole at the top, kind of like a salt shaker. To get to the pollen, a bumblebee grabs

Immigrant Pavement Ant

Tetramorium immigrans

Every spring, battle lines are drawn on sidewalks and driveways across the Wasatch Front as colonies of immigrant pavement ants go to war to establish or defend their feeding territories. Some battles arise as boundary disputes when workers from neighboring colonies repeatedly bump into one another. Others occur as colonies try to expand their territories. The most brutal battles happen when one colony raids another.

It's difficult to tell exactly what's happening when you encounter a roiling mass of pavement ants, because the two sides don't wear uniforms. Except in the case of a colony raid, the fighting seems somewhat ritualized, with lots of ants pulling and tugging at one another. Some ants do get killed, but not as many as you would expect given the numbers on the battlefield.

Founding Mothers

In midsummer, watch for swarms of winged ants emerging from their nests. This time, love, not war, is in the air. The winged ants are the reproductive members of a colony. During their nuptial flight, they hang in a small cloud to mate. After mating, a new queen sheds her wings and finds a suitable crevice in which to found a new colony. She lays eggs that hatch and develop into a first generation of workers about two months later.

As their name suggests, immigrant pavement ants thrive in paved cities and suburbs. Because they like disturbed habitats with a low diversity of plant life and full sun, a sidewalk bordering a lawn is a perfect place for a nest. They also thrive on human food that gets dropped on sidewalks. These ants are generalist scavengers and will eat almost anything they can find in their territory.

Brown-and-black bodies

Workers are about 0.1 inch long

Two round nodes between the thorax and abdomen

All in the Family

Although immigrant pavement ants are now among the most common ants in North America, they are originally from Europe. They were probably shipped unintentionally to the eastern United States in the early 1800s. To find out more about how pavement ants got established here, entomologists collaborated with students in the School of Ants citizen science project to collect ants from across the country and study their genes. The low genetic diversity they found suggests that North America's pavement ants are descended from a single colony or a few closely related colonies.

How to Spot Them

Because they are resilient and will eat a wide variety of foods, pavement ants can live just about anywhere. Look for them on sidewalks and driveways as well as in parks, gardens, and vacant lots. Lift up some rocks and you're sure to see them. They are active during the day, from spring to fall.

▲ Immigrant pavement ants are very protective of their feeding territory and intolerant of nearby colonies. Battles between colonies break out every spring.

Keep an eye out for small cones of loose dirt in cracks or joints in the pavement. Each of these marks an entrance to a pavement ant colony's underground nest.

Ladybugs

Convergent Ladybug

Hippodamia convergens

Often twelve black spots on red wing covers

Two white lines on thorax converging toward a "V"

Seven-Spotted Ladybug

Coccinella septempunctata

Seven black spots on red forewings

Round shape, like most ladybugs

A least one hundred species of ladybugs live along the Wasatch Front. Ladybugs are actually beetles, so they are sometimes called lady beetles or lady-bird beetles. In general, they are small and round, which gives them a friendly appearance. Their heads and antennae are mostly tucked beneath the second section of their bodies, the thorax, enhancing their round shape when viewed from above.

The convergent ladybug and the seven-spotted ladybug are two of the most common species you're likely to meet in Utah. It's easy to identify the convergent ladybug and remember its name if you look for the two white lines on its thorax that converge toward a "V" shape. The rim of its thorax is also bordered in white. Typically, twelve black spots decorate the convergent ladybug's red-orange forewings.

Eat and Run

Convergent ladybugs are often sold to gardeners who want to get rid of aphids. Like most ladybugs, they are voracious predators and delight in devouring these juicy garden pests. If you release enough ladybugs at once, they can reduce the number of aphids in your garden. Within a few days, however, most of the ladybugs will fly away in search of more aphids.

Some convergent ladybugs in Utah migrate to the mountains in the summer. They gather in dazzling groups of thousands on mountain peaks, tuck themselves into cracks and crevices, and enter a nine-month-long dormant phase. In the spring, they return to lower elevations to feast on aphids and lay eggs.

Invited for Dinner

Seven-spotted ladybugs, as you probably guessed, have seven black spots on their bright red–orange forewings—three on each wing and one more that spans both wings just behind the thorax. This species hails from Europe. In the 1950s, efforts began to introduce seven-spotted ladybugs to the United States for aphid control. They finally took hold in New Jersey in 1973 and then spread rapidly across the country.

The first record of seven-spotted ladybugs in Utah is from 1993, so they probably arrived a few years before that. Scientists think local ladybug populations are likely to continue to change. Observations made by citizen scientists on iNaturalist and specimens in museum collections will help us track those changes.

There are many other charming ladybugs to meet along the Wasatch Front. Their descriptive names hint at their great variety: two-spotted, ashy gray, twice-stabbed, spotless, and three-banded, to name just a few.

You can't tell how old a ladybug is by counting the spots on its back, but the number and shape of the spots can sometimes help you figure out which species you've encountered.

How to Spot Them

You'll find ladybugs where they find prey to eat, including gardens and urban parks, deserts, forests, and mountaintops. They tend to prefer open areas. Look for them perched on plants at approximately knee height. They're most common in the summer months.

Mourning Cloak

Nymphalis antiopa

Rich brown wings

Pale yellow wing borders

Line of bright blue spots on each wing

Another common name for the mourning cloak is grand surprise, a fitting moniker for a butterfly that is surprising in so many ways. Mourning cloaks break with typical butterfly protocol by overwintering as adults instead of as pupae, larvae, or eggs. Though they find a sheltered spot in which to spend the winter, it's usually not sufficient to prevent their bodies from freezing. Glycerol in their blood acts like antifreeze to prevent their cells from being damaged by freezing and thawing.

Mourning cloaks start flying again on the first warm days in March, making them among the first butterflies you'll see in the spring.

Mourning cloaks seem to have only four legs, instead of six. They're members of the brush-footed butterflies (Nymphalidae), which have a tiny first pair of legs. The tiny legs are hairy and brushlike.

Their early flight is likely the grand surprise. Because only a few flowers may be blooming when mourning cloaks thaw out, they have adapted to sipping tree sap and dining on rotting fruit. Even in the summer and fall, you're unlikely to spot them nectaring at flowers like most butterflies.

Understated Flair

The rich chocolate-brown color of mourning cloaks' wings helps them warm up in the spring sun. This distinctive color sets them apart from other butterflies on the Wasatch Front, making them easy to identify. Their color also earned them their common name, but these butterflies aren't totally somber in their dress. Their wings are bordered in pale yellow, and bright blue spots adorn the black margin between yellow and velvety brown.

After they warm up, mourning cloaks fly about looking for mates for a few weeks or months before dying. By this point, they may have lived as adults for nearly a year, which is absolutely ancient for a butterfly. Many butterflies live as adults for only a few short weeks.

A Few Tricks up Their Sleeves

When it comes to clever defense mechanisms, this butterfly also steals the show. The undersides of their wings look like tree bark, so when their wings are closed, they virtually disappear on a tree trunk. They also "play dead" when threatened, lying still with their legs tucked in and wings closed until they feel safe to fly away. Most curiously, mourning cloaks can produce loud clicks as they fly away from predators. Perhaps this confuses attackers. A clicking butterfly does seem perplexing!

How to Spot Them

Look for mourning cloaks in suburbs, along waterways, in the foothills, and in canyons. They are common wherever the host plants for their caterpillars grow—willows, cottonwoods, poplars, elms, and birches. You can find their spiky black-and-red caterpillars on these trees, often in groups. Adults can be seen flying through late summer, but they are more common in the spring.

Praying Mantis

Oh, those eyes! It's easy to connect with an insect that appears to look at you and cock its head when you meet. Along with its big eyes, a praying mantis's triangular face, swiveling neck, and first pair of legs held aloft like arms make it seem at once familiar and intriguingly strange. As captivating as its gaze may be, a praying mantis is probably more interested in keeping an eye out for prey than watching you.

Precision Vision

Praying mantises' remarkable eyes are vital to their success as ambush predators. Rather than chasing down their prey, they lurk among small branches and leaves, camouflaged from passing invertebrates. They strike—in less than one-twentieth of a second—with their strong forelegs and bring their unsuspecting meal to their chewing mouthparts.

European Mantis

Mantis religiosa

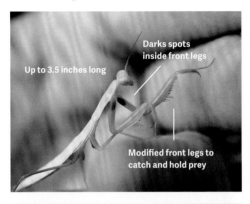

Up to 3.5 inches long

Darks spots inside front legs

Modified front legs to catch and hold prey

Chinese Mantis

Tenodera sinensis

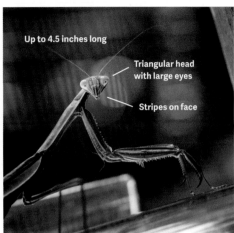

Up to 4.5 inches long

Triangular head with large eyes

Stripes on face

In the fall, praying mantises create a walnut-size egg case called an ootheca (oh-oh-THAY-kuh) that can hold from 100 to 300 eggs. A European mantis's ootheca is long and smooth, while a Chinese mantis's looks like a puffy sphere or cube.

Praying mantises' accuracy in grabbing moving targets is aided by their three-dimensional vision. Unlike all other insects, as far as we know, praying mantises can see in three dimensions, like we do. Scientists discovered this remarkable ability by fitting mantises with tiny 3D goggles! Their 3D vision works completely differently from ours, however, and is highly tuned to motion.

Fair Game

Since they are amazing hunters, are praying mantises good for your garden? Well, they're not bad for it. They aren't picky eaters. They won't pass on a meal, even if it's a pollinator you want in your garden. They also won't pass on a meal because it's another praying mantis. A female mantis, for example, will often bite

the male's head off just after, or even during, mating and then consume his nutritious corpse to support her health and that of her offspring.

By far, the most common mantises along the Wasatch Front are the European mantis and Chinese mantis. People brought them to North America sometime in the late 1800s to control other insect populations. In Utah, both species tend to live alongside us in cities and suburbs.

The Chinese mantis is larger than the European mantis, growing up to 4.5 inches long. It also has handsome stripes on its face. A European mantis has a dark spot on the inside of each front leg. Both species can be tan, brown, or various fashionable shades of green and can change color between molts.

How to Spot Them

If you're keen-eyed enough to see through praying mantises' camouflage tactics, you can find them almost any place where there are insects for them to hunt. In early spring, mantises are very small, making them difficult to spot. As the summer progresses, they grow larger. Late summer and early fall are the best times to meet them.

Ten-Lined June Beetle

Polyphylla decemlineata

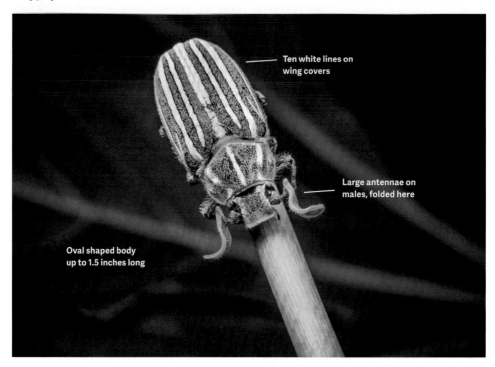

Ten white lines on wing covers

Large antennae on males, folded here

Oval shaped body up to 1.5 inches long

This little tank is one of the largest beetles you'll see along the Wasatch Front. Ten-lined June beetles are members of the famous scarab beetle family (*Scarabaeidae*). They have a smooth, oval-shaped body, with ten white lines on olive-green wing covers. Be sure to count the middle line twice, because it forms two separate lines when the beetle opens its wings. The short lines on the side of each wing cover are also part of the ten.

While the beetle's species name, *decemlineata*, means "ten lines," the genus name, *Polyphylla*, means "many leaves." This is a reference to the males' extravagant antennae that unfold into a fan of multiple "leaves" and look a bit like miniature moose antlers. In addition to giving the males a regal appearance, they are excellent detectors of the pheromones emitted by females that are ready to mate.

A Short Life Above Ground

Each summer starting about June (as their name suggests), adult female beetles begin emerging from the soil and sending out their pheromone signals. They tend not to roam very far and return to the soil to lay eggs once they've mated. The males lead a more adventurous life, flying from dusk until about midnight searching for females. Their strong attraction to lights, however, can deter them from their search and lead them to bumble around your screen door on a summer night.

Adult ten-lined June beetles live for only a few weeks. We don't often see the youngsters of this species because they stay underground, feeding on plant roots. Known as grubs, these pale munchers live underground for a few years, sometimes causing damage to plants.

They survive the frost by moving deeper into the soil. After two to four years, they emerge as adults, ready to look for mates.

How to Spot Them

The best time to spot adult ten-lined June beetles is June through August. You can find them in the foothills, neighborhood parks, and backyard gardens. While the females usually stay on the ground, look for the males flying near lights in the evening.

Ten-lined June beetles hiss loudly when disturbed by forcing air between their back and wing covers. Don't let this display fool you: they are completely harmless.

Western Black Widow

Latrodectus hesperus

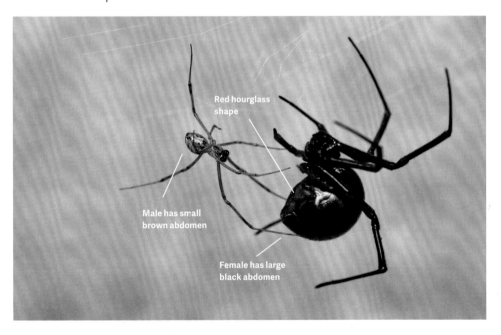

Red hourglass shape

Male has small brown abdomen

Female has large black abdomen

Female black widows' reputation for being dangerous is a bit overblown. They are indeed the most venomous spiders in Utah, and they are fairly common around homes. However, they aren't aggressive and bite people only when poked or pressed upon. If you approach a black widow on her web, she'll try to hide if she can. She'd rather not waste her precious venom on you when she could use it to kill her next meal.

To avoid a black widow bite, don't reach into dark crevices with unprotected hands. If you do get bitten, seek medical help, but don't panic. The small amount of venom a black widow injects is lethal to insects but not to healthy humans.

139

Black widows change the design of their webs depending on how hungry they are. Hungry spiders build sheet webs with more sticky strands for catching prey. Well-fed spiders build more chaotic webs with a few sticky strands that offer better protection.

Good Vibrations

Adult female black widows are famous for their smooth, glossy black abdomens, which are often emblazoned on the underside with a red hourglass shape. Since their weighty abdomens are supported by thin, pointed legs, they move more easily in their webs and prefer not to be out in the open. Black widows can't see very well, but they are very sensitive to vibrations in their sticky webs. An insect flying into a web creates lots of good vibrations.

Black widows build "messy" webs that tend to be coarse and uneven, not flat and symmetrical like those made by more artistic arachnids. Once an insect becomes trapped in a web, a black widow injects its prey with venom to paralyze it and then wraps it in silk. Like most spiders, black widows can't consume bites of their prey. Instead, they inject it with digestive enzymes to liquefy its body and then slurp up the resulting soup.

Femme Fatale?

Black widow males are much smaller than females, with pale brown abdomens adorned with bright white patterns. Despite the implications of this spider's common name, females don't often kill males after mating. In fact, a male spider typically mates with more than one female in its short lifetime.

How to Spot Them

Many spiders are primarily indoor or outdoor spiders, but black widows live in either environment. You can find their webs at the base of sagebrush plants, in garage corners, in window wells, and in many other dark places close to the ground. Black widows are most active at night and easiest to spot in the summer. Because female black widows live longer than a year, they may be active through the winter if they are indoors and prey is available.

Western Conifer Seed Bug

Leptoglossus occidentalis

The western conifer seed bug is a slow-moving, long-legged beauty. With its measured, purposeful gait and flared hind legs that resemble bell-bottoms, it would be at home on any fashion runway. Its wings sport a lush brown sheen and are outlined with a band of alternating light-and-dark bars. Long, dramatic antennae adorn its elegantly narrow head.

Sipping Straw

The western conifer seed bug (WCSB to its friends) feeds on the budding tips of conifer trees and their developing cones. As true

Flared hind legs

Long antennae

Light-and-dark bands

bugs, they use their beaks like straws to pierce plants and sip their juices. (True bugs can also be predators or parasites.) Their feeding doesn't harm trees much, but they can become pests on conifer farms. If conifers aren't available, WCSBs can drink from other trees.

When cool weather arrives in the fall, these insects often gather on building exteriors and even wander indoors looking for a warm spot to spend the winter. Come spring, they'll head outside again to lay eggs on the trees their young need for nourishment. Baby WCSBs, or nymphs, are orange and gradually become brown as they pass through five stages before becoming adults in the late summer.

Stinky, but Not Stink Bugs

WCSBs don't sting or bite, but like many fashion icons, they have a unique "perfume." These bugs give off a strong odor when they feel threatened. Some people call them "stink bugs" because of this smelly defense, but true stink bugs belong to a completely different family. Occasionally, people mistake WCSBs for their blood-feeding cousins, the kissing bugs (*Triatoma* spp.). Kissing bugs aren't common in Utah, though. If the bug's leg has a jaunty flare, you'll know it's a harmless WCSB.

WCSBs are spreading around the world, far from their homes west of the Rocky Mountains, possibly as inadvertent passengers in shipments of timber. They were reported in Iowa in 1956 and reached the East Coast by the early 1990s. Since the early 2000s, they've become common in many places in Europe and have been reported in Japan, South Korea, and China.

How to Spot Them

At about three-quarters of an inch long, WCBSs are fairly conspicuous. Look for them walking near, on, or inside buildings. You can spot them year-round, though more commonly in the warmer parts of summer. If the day is warm enough, they'll go for a stroll even in the middle of winter. Unlike some other gregarious true bugs in our area, they prefer to go it alone, so you won't find them gathered in large clusters.

In flight, a western conifer seed bug makes a loud buzz and follows a wandering path, which makes it easy to mistake it for a bumblebee at first glance.

Western Tiger Swallowtail

Papilio rutulus

One of Utah's biggest and showiest butterflies, the western tiger swallowtail has four vertical black "tiger" stripes across its yellow forewings and delicate tails on its hindwings. Look for sparkling droplets of blue and orange near its tails. You're likely to meet two similar members of the swallowtail family along the Wasatch Front: the aptly named two-tailed swallowtail (*Papilio multicaudata*) and the anise swallowtail (*Papilio zelicaon*), which has a broad black band across the leading edge of its forewing.

Disgusting Disguise

Like all butterflies, western tiger swallowtails start their lives as caterpillars with a difficult job—to eat and grow larger without being eaten themselves. Because they don't have

Four vertical black stripes on wings

Splashes of orange and blue near tails

One delicate tail on each hindwing

Western tiger swallowtail males gather on damp ground or wet spots in the road to get a drink and obtain dissolved minerals, a behavior called "puddling." You can add a puddling station to your yard to help attract butterflies.

▲ The chemicals produced by a western swallowtail caterpillar's fake snake tongue repel and even kill ants and mantids, but they smell pleasantly of pineapple to humans.

wings or fast legs for escaping, they've had to evolve clever strategies to avoid becoming a meal for any number of creatures.

In their first few instars (stages between molts), western tiger swallowtail caterpillars look like bird droppings, with an irregular black-and-white pattern that's so glossy it appears wet. Mimicking bird poop is a widely used and delightfully disgusting habit of many caterpillars and a variety of other insects.

Fake Snake

When they get bigger, a bit over two inches long, the caterpillars look completely different—either green or reddish brown and very smooth. A dark stripe running around their body makes them appear to have a large head. This fake head has two fake eyes, or eye spots, so the caterpillar looks a bit like a snake.

To complete its snake disguise, the caterpillar has a special organ hidden near its head that resembles a forked tongue when turned inside out. Not only does this fake tongue, or osmeterium, look scary to birds and small reptiles, but it also smells awful to ants, spiders, and praying mantises.

The following spring, the western swallowtail again changes its looks, becoming a glorious picture of grace floating through our summer skies. Its fascinating journey from bird poop mimic, to fake snake, to brightly colored butterfly takes less than a year.

How to Spot Them

Western tiger swallowtails are more common in areas with cottonwoods, ash trees, willows, and London planetrees, which their caterpillars need for food. As adults, they pollinate many kinds of flowers. Look for them flying from May to August. Swallowtails tend to fly higher than other butterflies in our area, so you may see them flying ten or fifteen feet above the ground.

White-Lined Sphinx

Hyles lineata

Large, fuzzy body

Tan diagonal band across folded wing

Thin white stripes on wings

It's easy to mistake a white-lined sphinx for a hummingbird. These large, stout-bodied moths hover in midair, uncurling their long, tube-shaped tongues, or proboscises, to sip nectar from flowers. They can beat their wings forty times per second as they hover!

When its wings are still, you can see how this moth got its name. Each dark olive–brown forewing is crossed by a series of thin white stripes along the wing veins. Their fuzzy thoraxes are also streaked with white

lines. Their small hindwings reveal a band of surprising pink.

Round-the-Clock Sippers

Some adult moths don't feed at all, but white-lined sphinxes are a thirsty bunch. They sip nectar from a wide variety of flowers and pollinate many garden blooms and vegetables. Although they prefer to feed at night, you may see them out and about during the day, visiting brightly colored flowers. At night they

▲ The sphinx caterpillar's horn may look like a stinger, but it's soft and harmless.

sip from light-colored flowers that offer more contrast against the darkness.

The relationship between white-lined sphinx moths and columbines (*Aquilegia caerulea*) offers a great example of coevolution between flowers and their pollinators. At lower elevations, where white-lined sphinxes are common, columbine flowers are white. They also have longer spurs with a nectar reward at the base that matches the length of the moth's proboscis. At higher elevations, where it's cooler and wetter, columbines tend to be pale or dark blue. Sphinx moths aren't common up there, but bumblebees that love blue and purple flowers are.

Unicorn Horn

Like the adults, white-lined sphinx caterpillars aren't picky eaters. In fact, if they are having a boom year, they can be a crop pest. The smooth-skinned caterpillars may be various colors—green, red, purple, and black—with an assortment of stripes and dots. They have a distinct and harmless horn that makes them seem like unicorn larvae, but the horn is on their rear end.

How to Spot Them

White-lined sphinx moths are common along the Wasatch Front wherever flowers grow. Watch for them sipping nectar from a variety of plants, from low-growing clover to the top flowers of lilac bushes. You're most likely to see them from April to July at dusk and dawn. They are attracted to lights at night. Look for them resting near a light on a screen door or a wall in the morning.

Woodlouse Spider

Dysdera crocata

Woodlouse spiders have long, bright red fangs for piercing the crunchy shells of their favorite prey—woodlice (also called roly-polies or pillbugs). Their fangs are more than an eighth of an inch long, which is impressive for any spider, let alone one with a half-inch-long body (not including legs). But don't worry—woodlouse spiders are secretive and rarely bite humans. And even if they do, their bite isn't dangerous.

Woodlouse spiders live where they find woodlice—under rocks, logs, paving stones, and in other humid hideouts. Their long fangs can open very wide, enabling them to eat just about anything they encounter, from earwigs

Six eyes

Glossy yellow to beige abdomen

Deep red legs and front part of the body (cephalothorax)

Large fangs

A woodlouse spider has six eyes arranged in an oval shape on its head. The number and pattern of a spider's eyes are an excellent clue to its identity.

and beetles to other hunters including centipedes and spiders. They actively stalk their prey at night and spend the day in a silk-lined retreat, tucked away in a crevice. Adapted to life in the dark, they are quite photophobic and run away from light.

Exceptional Moms

Courtship among woodlouse spiders is a dangerous affair, with couples risking injury from each other's large fangs. The females are very protective moms and guard their egg sacs suspended on silken threads in their retreats. Newly hatched spiderlings stay with their mother in her retreat for the first few weeks of their lives. This level of parenting skills is unusual in the arachnid world.

Like common pill woodlice (*Armadillidium vulgare*), these spiders are originally from the Mediterranean region. They've lived in the United States now for decades but aren't as widespread as woodlice. They seem to prefer living in cities and suburbs, including those along the Wasatch Front.

Falsely Accused

Having a fierce appearance can get you in trouble, even if you are a shy, harmless spider. In 2018, a South Carolina man posted a "public service announcement" about a "deadly new spider," with a photo of a woodlouse spider. Unfortunately, the post went viral. Alerts about supposed threats posed by a newly arrived or previously unheard-of species are a common form of misinformation and "scarelore." Let's hope this one has died down permanently. Woodlouse spiders don't deserve the bad rap.

How to Spot Them

Lift a garden stone, decaying log, or potted plant and you may find a woodlouse spider. They're not as common in hot, dry localities like the foothills. Generations of woodlouse spiders overlap, which means you can spot adults and immature spiders year-round.

Mammals

American Beaver

Castor canadensis

Beavers probably don't spring to mind when you think of urban wildlife, but they are actually quite common in cities with rivers across the United States. They tend to go unseen because they are active mainly at night. If you do spot one, look for its iconic tail.

A beaver's tail is long, flat, black, and scaly. It functions as a multipurpose tool—a rudder for swimming, a balance prop when the beaver stands on its hind legs, a way to signal danger with a loud slap on the water, and a place to store fat for the winter.

Large head to accommodate powerful chewing muscles

Waterproof fur

Wide, flat, scaly tail

Trees for Dinner and Dams

The largest rodent in America is famous (and infamous) for cutting down trees. Each tree a beaver fells gives it access to a large quantity of food—leaves, twigs, and cambium (the soft tissue under the bark). After chewing the cambium off the branches, beavers drag these building materials to their dams and lodges. In snowy climates, they also cache a supply of unstripped branches underwater near their lodge to dine on throughout the winter.

Logging and building dams in urban rivers and ponds often get beavers in trouble with their human neighbors. Beavers are highly effective at modifying their environments in ways that benefit water quality and wildlife habitat. However, they don't consult city planners about how their projects impact parks, streets, trails, culverts, and revegetation efforts.

Helping Beavers and Cottonwoods Coexist

True to form, the beavers along the Jordan River in Salt Lake County have been a source of human controversy. These beavers don't build lodges or dams in the river, because the water is too deep and fast. They excavate burrows in the banks instead. They also have a penchant for cutting down cottonwood trees—both large, old ones and newly planted ones—that are beloved by the community and important for bird habitat.

The Tracy Aviary launched a citizen science project in 2021 aimed at preserving cottonwood trees for birds without removing beavers from the river. Citizen scientists are documenting and monitoring trees affected by beavers along the Jordan River Parkway. The aviary will use the data to identify especially vulnerable trees that need beaver-proof wraps to protect them.

How to Spot Them

Look for beavers along the Jordan River, the Ogden River, and at the mouth of the Provo River. Dawn and dusk are the best times to spot them. It's more common to see signs of beaver activity—including gnawed and felled trees—than beavers themselves, given their nocturnal natures.

Beavers form strong family bonds. A breeding pair lives in a lodge with the current year's kits as well as yearlings, kits from the previous year.

Bats

Big Brown Bat

Eptesicus fuscus

Brown- to copper-colored fur

Rounded, dark muzzle

Black wing membrane

Mexican Free-Tailed Bat

Tadarida brasiliensis

Reddish brown to gray fur

Broad, forward-pointing ears

Long tail extends beyond wing membranes

As they dart after insects under the cover of dark, bats are often overlooked as urban wildlife—even by scientists. Seven of Utah's eighteen bat species have been observed in neighborhoods along the Wasatch Front, but there is a lot we don't know about their lives in cities and suburbs.

The big brown bat is one species you may encounter around town. These bats are happy to roost in the structures humans build, such as under eaves or beneath bridges. They are often solitary but sometimes gather in small groups in the spring and fall. Most of them stick around all year, hibernating through the winter.

The Nightly Routine

Like many bats, big brown bats hunt for insects at night, but not all night long. When they leave their roosts at dusk, the first item on their agenda is getting a drink of water. Then they forage in places where insects gather—over water, near trees, or around artificial lights. After a few hours of grabbing insects out of the air, they take a rest. As dawn approaches, they get another drink and a snack before snuggling into their roost for the day.

Mexican free-tailed bats, also known as Brazilian free-tailed bats, are another species you can spot along the Wasatch Front. Look for them on summer nights, swooping gracefully over the marshes along Great Salt Lake in Davis County. Unlike big browns, these bats migrate south as far as Mexico in the fall.

Hanging Out at School

Mexican free-tailed bats have gained local fame for their habit of taking shelter in school buildings along their migration route. Bats aren't seeking educational opportunities, but rather a large space with high ceilings where they can rest safely. School gymnasiums, which are secluded at night when the bats move in, are ideal spots for groups of migrating bats to gather. They usually stay only a short time before continuing on their journey. Their arrival often makes the local news and sometimes results in kids getting a day off from school.

Like many Utah bat populations, our Mexican free-tailed population is declining.

Colonies in Davis County have shrunk dramatically as the open spaces they depend on are developed. Droughts that dry up urban streams and ponds are also hard on bats, because many bats forage near water. Plus, female bats have to drink extra water in the summer when they are nursing their young. During a twenty-four-hour period, a mother bat may produce as much as a quarter of her body weight in milk! In hot, dry years, fewer mother bats are successful at raising pups.

How to Spot Them

Look for bats at dusk on summer nights near water and places where insects congregate. People often spot them at Fairmont Park, Liberty Park Pond, and Miller Bird Refuge and Nature Park in Salt Lake City. Watch for their fluttering, acrobatic flight patterns.

Bobcat

Lynx rufus

Bobcats have become social media stars along the Wasatch Front. People love posting videos and security camera footage of these elusive creatures—a bobcat elegantly padding along a fence, a bobcat watching her kittens frolic in a backyard, a bobcat nonchalantly greeting the Hello Kitty decoration on a porch. Some of these videos even make the local news.

A few decades ago, bobcat sightings anywhere in the United States were rare. Today, bobcats are popping up in cities across the country. Although bobcats along the Wasatch Front haven't been studied, increased bobcat sightings suggest they are following the national trend.

The New Cat in Town

Why did bobcats move to the city? One reason is that we stopped killing so many of them. As recently as 1970, bobcats could be shot and trapped at any time of year without limit in many states. With bobcat populations declining throughout the country, states began to prohibit or regulate hunting them. This simple solution proved very effective. A 2010 U.S. Fish and Wildlife survey determined that the bobcat population had tripled since the 1980s.

As their populations increased, bobcats began to venture into suburbs and even into urban green spaces. Bobcats are naturally quite adaptable. They live in habitats as varied

Pattern of brown spots and stripes

Small tufts on ears

Short ruff of fur around face

Distinctive bobbed tail

Bobcats are patient and stealthy hunters. They will place their back feet in the same spots where they stepped with their front feet to reduce noise while stalking prey.

as high mountains, deserts, wetlands, and scrublands. Adapting to environments shaped by humans isn't a huge stretch for them.

Keeping to Themselves

Bobcats may be visiting our neighborhoods, but they prefer not to interact with us. A study in Dallas–Fort Worth showed that these shy animals avoided developed areas in the city and tended to move through open spaces and along stream corridors. Bobcats don't typically want to interact with—or eat—our pets either. The chances of Fido or Felix being on the menu are extremely low. Their favorite meal, by far, is rabbit. In the suburbs, they add rats, mice, birds (including ducks), and squirrels to their diets.

Because glimpses of bobcats are often fleeting, they are sometimes confused with mountain lions. But bobcats are much smaller than their apex-predator cousins, weighing an average of twenty to thirty pounds. Their most distinctive feature is the short tail that gives them their name. The small tufts of fur on their pointed ears and ruff of fur on either side of the face lend them a distinguished, nineteenth-century appearance.

How to Spot Them

Along the Wasatch Front, bobcats are most commonly spotted in neighborhoods bordering the foothills or near large open spaces. They are most active at dusk and dawn. Given their elusive nature, seeing a bobcat is mostly a matter of luck. Should you be fortunate enough to encounter one, give it plenty of space.

Botta's Pocket Gopher

Thomomys bottae

Telltale excavated dirt pile

Small eyes and ears

Long, sensitive whiskers for sensing underground

Large incisor teeth

Other rodents use their cheeks for carrying food, but pocket gophers have actual fur-lined pockets with openings on the sides of their mouths. The pockets extend back beyond their shoulders, and the gophers can turn them inside out to empty them.

Spotting a shy Botta's pocket gopher is tricky, but finding evidence of its work in a lawn or open space is easy. Gophers leave fan-shaped piles of dirt at the entrances to their elaborate underground tunnel systems. These master excavators use their claws and teeth to dig, pushing the loose dirt behind them with their back claws. Then they turn around with a somersault and push the dirt out of the burrow with their front feet and chest, creating their hallmark dirt pile.

Subterranean Superstars

Built like blunt torpedoes, gophers are exquisitely adapted for digging and tunneling. Their front claws are long and stout, powered by impressive shoulder muscles. Their lips close behind their large, ever-growing incisors to prevent them from getting mouthfuls of dirt while they dig.

Gophers can't see very well, but sensitive whiskers help them find their way in their dark tunnels. They can run backward almost as fast as they run forward! Their short, hairless tails are very sensitive and probably help guide them.

Except for the dirt piles, pocket gophers' impressive underground infrastructures are invisible to us. They dig long foraging tunnels about four to twelve inches below the surface in their search for roots to munch. Sometimes they pull whole plants underground, which is amusing to watch from aboveground. They also dig tunnels up to six feet deep leading to different chambers: a nest, food storage, and a latrine. Their burrow systems can contain more than 200 yards of tunnels.

Popular Prey

Pocket gophers spend almost all their time underground. They may cautiously pop out of their burrows for a few minutes to forage, but it's always a big risk. Hawks, owls, coyotes, foxes, bobcats, and domestic dogs and cats are eager to make meals of them above ground. Skunks and snakes pursue them in their burrows. In cities and suburbs, they can face traps too. Most pocket gophers survive for only about two years.

Pocket gophers' constant burrowing in search of food can lead to conflicts with humans, but their activity has the important benefit of keeping soil loosened and aerated. Depending on local conditions, a single gopher may rearrange more than two tons of soil in a year, mostly belowground. They also enrich soil with their droppings and leftover stashes of vegetation.

How to Spot Them

You can find pocket gopher dirt piles in lawns, parks, golf courses, and even planted street medians. With luck and patience, you may see one pop its head out of its burrow.

Coyote

Canis latrans

Some urban coyotes have become quite street-savvy, carefully looking both ways before they cross a road. In Chicago, city coyotes have even been observed waiting at traffic lights until the cars stop and then trotting across the street on the crosswalk! Urban coyotes apply the same safety-conscious approach to their interactions with people. They generally avoid us as they move almost invisibly through cities and suburbs.

A Life in the Shadows

To maintain a low profile, urban coyotes have changed their daily activity patterns. In less developed areas, coyotes don't follow a strict schedule and may be active any time of day.

Brown, gray, or tan fur with a pale belly

Large, pointed ears and long, pointed snout

Bushy tail with a black tip

In cities and suburbs, they are active almost entirely at night, when their human neighbors are least active.

Coyotes along the Wasatch Front definitely prefer the night life. They also tend to stick to the edges of our communities near the foothills. Coyotes do venture to the Jordan River in the center of the Salt Lake Valley, usually along natural corridors such as Dimple Dell. Wasatch Front coyotes don't seem to have taken up residence in our parks and neighborhoods as they have in some large cities—at least, not yet.

Not-so-Picky Eaters

There's no particular "urban coyote diet." Coyotes adapt their dining habits to fit the local offerings. In Chicago, for example, coyotes hunt mostly traditional prey, such as rabbits and rodents, and generally avoid trash. But in Los Angeles, garbage makes up nearly 40 percent of coyotes' diets, and cats are often on the menu too. In this respect, the L.A. coyotes are unusual: nationally, data shows that pets make up only a tiny fraction of urban coyotes' diets.

Wasatch Front coyotes may be adding a new item to their diets—eastern fox squirrels. Fox squirrel populations have soared since they were introduced to the Salt Lake Valley around 2011. In fact, one citizen scientist photographed a coyote snagging a fox squirrel near the Salt Lake City Cemetery. Will the growing presence of fox squirrels impact coyotes' hunting habits? It's a question that highlights the dynamic nature of urban ecosystems.

There is one universal truth about coyote eating habits—feeding coyotes is a really bad idea. Intentionally or unintentionally leaving food out for coyotes can make them much bolder around humans, increasing the chances of a dangerous encounter. We should take our cue from coyotes and limit our interactions with them so we can all safely share the same spaces.

How to Spot Them

You're most likely to spot coyotes near the foothills. Look for them on trails behind the Natural History Museum of Utah, at the Salt Lake City Cemetery, or in Dimple Dell. If you're lucky enough to see one, enjoy it from a distance.

Urban coyotes are monogamous and incredibly loyal to their partners. Having two parents devoted to caring for pups helps them successfully raise large litters.

Mountain Lion

Puma concolor

Tan to tawny fur with pale belly

Backs of ears and sides of snout are black

Long, thick tail tipped with black

Mountain lions sit at the top of the food chain along the Wasatch Front, which turns out to be a pretty precarious perch. As large obligate carnivores, they need to hunt, and they require lots of space to find enough prey to survive. Utah mountain lions' main prey is mule deer. Along the Wasatch Front, humans have built neighborhoods in the mule deer's winter range in the foothills, so mountain lions, deer, and people are learning to share the same space.

Habitat Size Matters

Mountain lions face trade-offs when they follow mule deer into neighborhoods. The concentration and predictable location of deer—along with the bonus of occasional roadkill—are a definite plus for mountain lions. A busy road, however, is a big threat. So is the tendency of humans to have a low tolerance for mountain lions, especially those that get lost and wander deep into cities.

The Wasatch and Oquirrh mountains bordering the Salt Lake Valley have a fairly high concentration of these big cats because these areas offer great habitat for deer. But a high concentration doesn't mean their total numbers are high. Each animal needs an average of twenty square miles of habitat to survive—and much more if the habitat is lower quality.

Habitat loss and fragmentation, along with hunting, are major causes of declining mountain lion populations across the Western Hemisphere. Continuing development in and around the Wasatch and Oquirrh mountains could become an increasing problem for our local lions. Identifying critical habitats and ways to connect them is key to the survival of these beautiful mammals.

Coexisting with Carnivores

Security cameras and social media are giving us glimpses of mountain lions' usually invisible movements through foothill neighborhoods. You may find a report of a mountain lion nearby exhilarating, unnerving, or both, but attacks on humans are incredibly rare.

If you live or recreate in the spaces we share with mountain lions, you can take steps to keep yourself, your pets, and mountain lions safe. Avoid jogging or hiking alone at dawn and dusk, when mountain lions hunt, and keep your pets inside at night.

How to Spot Them

Seeing a mountain lion is a very rare privilege. If one is nearby, it will probably see you before you are aware of its presence and get out of your way. It's more likely that you'll come across tracks or scat. Mountain lion scat is about the size of large dog droppings but is segmented and has blunt ends. Occasionally, you might find a scrape, a mark made by a mountain lion with its hind legs, next to its droppings.

Mule Deer

Odocoileus hemionus

Large ears like a mule

White rump with a black tail

Black mask contrasts with lighter face

Tannish brown fur in the summer and brownish gray in the winter

When the snow starts to fly, mule deer venture down from the mountains into neighborhoods along the Wasatch Front. Mule deer depend on annual migrations from their summer mountain habitats to lower elevation winter habitats, where they can avoid deep snow and find food. Because we have encroached upon much of their winter habitat, mule deer have been forced to adapt to life among humans.

Living the Suburban Dream

Neighborhoods offer some great perks for mule deer. Our yards are full of delicious plants that can help sustain deer through the scarce winter and early spring. Tulips, roses, euonymus, and Austrian pine are among their favorite foods. There are also lots of good places to hide and take cover during a season when deer need to conserve energy. Neighborhoods also tend to have fewer predators to worry about. Recent evidence suggests that some Utah mule deer are starting to remain in urban areas through the summer to avoid predators while raising their young.

Life isn't all rosy for suburban mule deer, however. At the top of the list of hazards are busy roads. Collisions between cars and mule deer often don't end well for the deer or the humans. That's why wildlife managers argue that mule deer are actually "the most dangerous animal in Utah."

Human Hazards

Another hazard deer face is well-meaning people who feed them alfalfa, corn, or apples. Unfortunately, this generosity can make deer very sick and can even kill them. Deer are ruminants that ferment their food before they digest it with the help of microorganisms in their gut. In the winter, their digestive systems have a specific mix of bacteria that enables them to process the low-quality foods available to them in nature, such as bark and twigs. Because it takes time for the bacteria mix to adapt to a change in diet, deer that eat tasty handouts can die with a stomach full of food they can't digest.

Kind people also risk becoming baby stealers when they mistake a hidden fawn for an abandoned fawn. Hiding is how fawns stay safe before they are able to run from predators, and they're really good at it. Fawns are scentless, well-camouflaged, and hold still when approached or even stepped on. Mother

> Mule deer can easily leap over most residential fences. Very hungry or frightened deer may even jump eight-foot fences.

deer intentionally graze a safe distance away so they don't attract predators to their babies. If you see a fawn alone, swoon over how cute it is and then quietly leave the area.

How to Spot Them

Mule deer are most active at dawn and dusk in the summer, but they become more active during the day as the weather starts to cool. Look for them near the foothills, in large open spaces, and along urban waterways. A herd of mule deer hangs out most of the year in the Mount Olivet Cemetery near the University of Utah.

Muskrat

Ondatra zibethicus

You've just spotted a mammal gliding gracefully through a river or wetland along the Wasatch Front. Is it a muskrat or a beaver? At first glance, it can be difficult to tell the two apart in the water. If you see the animal's head and back above the surface and a long, slender tail cutting through the water, that's a muskrat. If you see only the animal's head, you're probably looking at a beaver.

On land, it's easy to distinguish between the two animals by their size. An average muskrat weighs about three pounds, while an average beaver weighs around forty pounds. The largest beaver ever trapped weighed 110 pounds!

Similar Tool Kits

Muskrats and beavers are similar in many ways. They are both exquisitely adapted to life in the water, with specialized tails that help

Long, glossy guard hairs that vary from dark brown to yellowish brown

Long, smooth tail

Partially webbed hind feet

them swim, waterproof fur that provides insulation and buoyancy, and the ability to hold their breaths under water for more than fifteen minutes. Both animals have fur mouth flaps that close behind their front teeth so they can chew underwater. They have clear membranes that close over their eyes—like natural swim goggles—and can seal off their ears and noses

Sometimes other animals use the top of a muskrat's mounded cattail lodge as a solid spot to rest upon in a marsh. Muskrats also build burrows with underwater entrances in riverbanks.

A Few Tricks of Their Own

Muskrats have their own unique traits. They build lodges out of cattails and other aquatic plants, rather than out of branches and logs like beavers do. They don't cache food for the winter, so they must forage all year long. Though they are mostly vegetarian, they occasionally eat fish, insects, shellfish, and amphibians.

Muskrats also have adaptations that help them survive in urban waterways. They can tolerate some water pollution and they reproduce prodigiously. Muskrats can raise three litters per year, with up to ten pups per litter.

How to Spot Them

Look for muskrats year-round in marshes, ponds, and rivers along the Wasatch Front. They are most active at dawn and dusk, but it's common to see them during the day as well. If you notice tracks near water with a distinct tail-drag line between the left and right paw prints, they were probably left by a muskrat.

when they dive. They both build lodges and dine on aquatic plants.

For all the traits they share, muskrats and beavers are not closely related. Sure, they are both rodents, but more than 40 percent of all mammals are rodents. Muskrats and beavers are actually a great example of convergent evolution. As the two species evolved, each independently developed a set of similar characteristics that works really well in their watery habitat.

Pronghorn

Antilocapra americana

When explorers Meriwether Lewis and William Clark first encountered American pronghorns, they weren't quite sure what to make of the unfamiliar animals. In their journals, they called them "antelopes" and "goats." That's how pronghorns got saddled with a scientific name that means "American antelope-goat." In fact, the pronghorn is a one-of-a-kind species with no close relatives on this or any other continent.

Home, Home in the City

Pronghorns are iconic symbols of the wide-open spaces of the American West, immortalized in song as "antelopes" frolicking with deer and buffalo (which are really bison) in their "home on the range." Along the Wasatch Front, you can catch a glimpse of these remarkable animals within or near cities.

The best-known place for spotting pronghorns is on Antelope Island in Great Salt Lake, just a short drive across the causeway from Syracuse. However, pronghorns are common along Interstate 80 between the Salt Lake City Airport and about 8000 West, along the Bacchus Highway in the southern part of the Salt Lake Valley, and near Eagle Mountain in Utah County. With the exception of Antelope Island, all these areas are being rapidly developed. Pronghorns may lose the wide-open spaces they need to survive along the Wasatch Front.

Both males and females have horns

Large eyes set high on skull

White markings on face and neck

White rump

Although the pronghorn population as a whole is doing well today, they nearly went extinct in the late 1800s as a result of market hunting (similar to the slaughter of bison) and habitat loss. Their seemingly boundless population of 30 to 40 million had declined to about 13,000 by 1920. Locally, Utah passed legislation to protect pronghorns in 1898, and by the 1940s their populations began to recover.

A Need for Speed

For pronghorns, surviving in wide-open spaces with little cover depends on being able to spot and outrun predators. A pronghorn's giant eyes see the world as we would with the help of eight times magnification binoculars. They can detect movement from four miles away.

Should a sneaky predator get too close, pronghorns can sprint away at up to sixty miles per hour. They are second in speed only to cheetahs among land animals, though they can maintain high speeds far longer than cheetahs can. Curiously, pronghorns are much faster than any of their predators. Why are they so overpowered? Pronghorns evolved alongside the now-extinct American cheetah in the Pleistocene. Today they race the ghosts of those ancient predators.

How to Spot Them

Look for pronghorns along Interstate 80 west of Salt Lake City, in the Oquirrh foothills, and along the west side of Utah Lake. During the winter, they gather in large herds, and in the summer, you'll see smaller groups or individuals. It can take a sharp eye to spot them because they blend into the landscape.

American explorer John Charles Frémont named Antelope Island after the pronghorn he hunted there in 1845. Pronghorn later became extinct on the island and were reintroduced in 1993.

157

Raccoon

Procyon lotor

Gray-brown coat

Rump higher than head

Black face mask

Banded, bushy tail

Raccoons are true city dwellers. Their populations are usually denser in cities and suburbs than in less developed areas. They can even survive in the concrete jungle of city centers—a rare feat for a medium-size wild animal. Just like their human neighbors, raccoons are clever, curious, and eager for a free meal.

Many wild animals that thrive in cities dine on the food we throw away, but raccoons have elevated accessing garbage to an art form. Stories abound of raccoons foiling every attempt to deter them. What might seem like raccoon superpowers, however, are really a combination of their boldness, persistence, and dexterous little hands.

Test Me

Raccoons are neophilic, which means they tend to see new objects and situations as opportunities rather than threats. And once they start trying to figure out how a new object works, they don't give up. A scientist documented one raccoon working for six hours to find a way to open a tricky garbage can. With strong, nimble fingers, a raccoon can pry and twist its way past can lids and many other obstacles. Just ask the experts who designed the City of Toronto's "raccoon-proof" compost bin!

Living in cities may actually be making raccoons smarter. Cities and suburbs are filled with challenges that reward a raccoon's boldness and persistence with a tasty meal. A study designed to test raccoons' problem-solving skills found that urban raccoons were much more likely to approach a puzzle and solve it than raccoons living in less-developed areas. Is this a learned behavior or an example of how cities are driving evolution? Scientists plan to follow up with studies of baby raccoons to find out.

Thanks for the Habitat!

There's a long-running debate in Utah about whether raccoons lived here when European-American settlers arrived or were introduced later. Good historical evidence shows that raccoons resided in Utah in 1847 but were quite rare. They tended to be confined to wooded areas near water. As people created reservoirs, ponds, and canals, they also created more habitat for raccoons.

Utah's raccoon population has grown dramatically since the 1950s, but the national trend is even more impressive. According to one estimate, the North American raccoon population swelled fifteen to twenty times between the 1930s and 1980s!

Raccoons' success in cities and suburbs can lead to tensions with their human neighbors. (For example, raccoon feces can transmit harmful parasites, so don't touch it!) Raccoons, however, aren't the evil geniuses portrayed in headlines warning that "raccoons are taking

Raccoons have a hunched shape when they walk or run that's easy to recognize even from a distance. Their back legs are longer than their front legs, which raises their rumps up higher than their heads.

over cities." They're simply furry, masked mammals taking advantage of all the resources in the environments we've built.

How to Spot Them

Raccoons are active mainly at night—another trait that sets them up for success in cities—so it can be tricky to find them. Look for them and their little hand-shaped tracks near urban waterways, but don't be surprised if one shows up in your neighborhood.

Red Fox

Vulpes vulpes

Red foxes are the most widely distributed carnivores in the world. They live throughout the Northern Hemisphere in almost every habitat imaginable. The latest habitats they've learned

to exploit are those we've built. Our suburbs provide a mosaic of resources that meet all of a fox's survival needs—grassy fields for hunting mice, trees and shrubs for cover, streams

Large ears with black tips

Red, black, or gray fur

Bushy tail with white tip

Black legs and feet

for water and safe travel routes, and lots of denning options in parks or under buildings.

Evolving in Cities

Red foxes are on par with raccoons in their ability to thrive in human environments. As adaptable omnivores, foxes aren't picky eaters. In suburbs, they add birds, insects, and fallen fruit to their typically rodent-heavy diets. They also happily dine on garbage when it's available. Unlike many more skittish animals, foxes tend to approach new objects in their environment to investigate them—a handy trait for discovering new food sources.

Red foxes offer one of the numerous examples of how urban wildlife is not only adapting to, but actually evolving in, cities and suburbs. Researchers studied foxes in southern England, where the mammals have been living in cities since the 1930s. They found that city foxes have distinctly shorter, wider snouts than rural foxes. This new trait likely results in stronger jaws that are helpful in scavenging and accessing a broader range of foods in cities.

Family Values

Red foxes hunt alone, which helps them keep a low profile, but they usually live in tight-knit family groups. Both parents work together to care for their kits. Sometimes older siblings, usually females from the previous year, help with "kit-care" too. Summer is a great time to look for foxes during the day, because the kits are out playing, exploring, and learning how to hunt under the watchful eyes of a parent or big sister.

As it turns out, red foxes don't always have red fur. They can also be black, gray, or even a mix of colors. You'll know you've spotted a red fox if the animal's long, bushy tail sports a white tip. Coyotes' tails have black tips.

Red foxes have incredible hearing. A fox can detect a rodent beneath several feet of snow and then dive headfirst into the snow to grab it. Check out videos of this amazing, and sometimes hilarious, hunting technique online!

How to Spot Them

Red foxes are active mainly at night, but they occasionally enjoy a bit of sunbathing. Dawn and dusk are the best times to spot them. Look for them near large open spaces. People often report fox sightings at Crestwood Park, Big Cottonwood Regional Park, the Salt Lake City Cemetery, and the Ogden Nature Center.

Striped Skunk

Mephitis mephitis

A striped skunk is a stout little animal about the size of a house cat, with a wide rump and a bit of a waddle when it walks. People who keep them as pets describe them as curious, adorable, stubborn, and absolutely fearless. Skunks' charming confidence comes from being armed with a chemical defense that can disable almost any threat they face—except cars.

Large, bushy tail

Two large white stripes on black body

Narrow white stripe on forehead

Warning Stripes

Skunks, however, are reluctant chemical warriors. Their distinctive fur is a good example of aposematic, or warning, coloration: "Remember me? Stay away!" When harassed, skunks issue repeated warnings—raising their tails, stamping their front feet, and hissing and lunging at their adversary—before deploying their weapon of last resort.

Most predators learn to stay away from skunks, especially if they've been sprayed in the past. Great horned owls, which don't have a sense of smell, are really the only creatures that successfully prey on them. Skunks' smelly reputation enables them to punch above their weight and steal food from even the largest carnivores. There are well-documented instances of skunks successfully fending off mountain lions for access to a deer carcass.

Suburban Smorgasbord

Striped skunks thrive in suburban areas across the United States, thanks to their bold natures, nocturnal habits, and flexibility. As opportunistic omnivores, striped skunks will eat almost anything. In suburbs, they find plenty of mice to hunt and lawns full of grubs to dig up with their long, curved claws. A buffet of pet food,

Domestic dogs are one of the few predators that have a hard time learning to avoid messing with skunks—another good reason to keep dogs inside at night!

garden produce, and garbage pairs well with the tasty mice and grubs.

Along with abundant food, skunks can easily find water in the suburbs. And spaces under decks and sheds make great dens, where skunks can retreat during the day or in bad weather. Aside from fewer cars, what else could a skunk ask for?

How to Spot Them

It can be challenging to spot skunks because they are nocturnal. Watch for them at dusk on the edges of open spaces or near urban waterways, including the Jordan River or the mouth of the Provo River. You can also keep an eye out for skunk scat. It looks a bit like cat droppings, averaging one to two inches in length and often containing a wide variety of undigested foods.

Tree Squirrels

Two different tree squirrels make their homes in the Wasatch Front. American red squirrels made their way to our urban forests from the conifer forests in the Wasatch Mountains. Though native to Utah, they didn't live in the dry valleys of the Wasatch Front until humans planted conifer trees there. Eastern fox squirrels traveled a bit farther to get here.

New Neighbors

Originally from the eastern United States, fox squirrels were likely brought to Southern California as pets (or maybe dinner) around 1904. Since then, people have transported

them to cities across the West. Fox squirrels didn't arrive in Utah until quite recently; they were first sited in 2011 along the Jordan River in Salt Lake City.

As fox squirrel populations increased, Natural History Museum of Utah scientists saw an opportunity to study how populations of a recently arrived species grow and spread. They asked citizen scientists to observe squirrels in their neighborhoods, noting behaviors and interactions with their environment. Collecting this data is the vital first step in understanding how fox squirrels fit into the ecology of our neighborhoods.

American Red Squirrel

Tamiasciurus hudsonicus

Less bushy tail

Dark reddish-brown back

White eye ring

Pale cream-colored underside

Eastern Fox Squirrel

Sciurus niger

Back fur is grizzled gray and orange

Large, very bushy tail

Underside is pale yellow to bright orange

Much larger than a red squirrel

Small but Mighty

It's easy to tell fox squirrels and red squirrels apart. A red squirrel has distinctive white eye rings that heighten its cartoonlike cuteness. Its cream-colored underbelly contrasts with the reddish, grayish, or rust-colored fur on the rest of its body. It's the smallest squirrel in our area, measuring twelve to sixteen inches long, tail included.

Don't let red squirrels' diminutive size and adorableness fool you into thinking they are pushovers. These tough little rodents aggressively defend their territories. Listen for their rapid, chattering calls that sound like they are scolding the entire neighborhood. They may even throw pine cones down at you!

Fox squirrels are big and bold—about twice the size of red squirrels. The fur on their backs is grizzled gray and orange, and their belly fur color ranges from pale yellow to bright orange. A fox squirrel's tail is nearly the same length as its body and is very bushy and orange—like a fox! Fox squirrels use their luxuriant tails to communicate their excitement, alarm, or frustration with expressive swishes and twitches.

How to Spot Them

Both squirrel species spend lots of time in trees and on fences and powerlines. They are built to climb and are most comfortable up high. You're more likely to see red squirrels in areas with established conifer trees—their preferred habitat and food source. Larger parks and open spaces along the Wasatch Front are common places to spot them, although they live in neighborhoods too. If you have fox squirrels in your neighborhood, it's hard to miss them. They are quite comfortable around humans. Fox squirrels prefer deciduous trees, where they build nests, called dreys, from clumps of dry leaves high in their branches.

Tree squirrels have double-jointed rear wrists that enable them to climb both up and down vertical surfaces with ease.

Reptiles and Amphibians

American Bullfrog

Lithobates catesbeianus

Large, bulging eyes

Large tympanum (eardrum)

Long legs for jumping

Large body with olive-green and brown back

The American bullfrog is truly an impressive creature. The largest frog in North America, it measures up to eight inches long and weighs in at more than a pound. These superb hunters stalk a wide variety of prey. Unlike most amphibians, they are hardy enough to thrive in environments modified by humans. And they can leap distances of ten times their body length!

Bullfrogs have remarkable powers of reproduction. Females can lay up to 20,000 eggs at a time, which is four to ten times more than most frogs. Moreover, predatory fish apparently don't find bullfrog tadpoles very tasty. Big, bold, hardy, and fertile—all this adds up to a frog people love to hate.

Making a Big Splash

Bullfrogs are blamed for wreaking ecological havoc wherever humans introduce them. As excellent generalist predators, they can both consume and outcompete local amphibians. They can also carry chytrid, a fungal disease that can devastate other amphibian populations.

Humans have introduced bullfrogs from the eastern United States into many western states as well as many other countries. Sometimes people intentionally brought bullfrogs with them as a source of delicious frog leg dinners. In some western states, they may have been accidentally spread by fish-stocking programs. No one knows exactly who introduced bullfrogs in Utah or when, but there have been breeding populations here since the early 1970s.

Extenuating Circumstances

It's important to understand how bullfrogs impact other species and to decide how to manage their populations humanely, but it's also important not to make them into scapegoats. After all, individual bullfrogs don't have bad intentions—they are just trying to survive in the place they find themselves. And although introduced bullfrogs may be one factor behind Utah's declining amphibian populations, there are many other factors at play, including habitat destruction, pollution, and climate change.

How to Spot Them

Bullfrogs are among the few amphibians that thrive in urban areas. They prefer slow-moving, shallow water with lots of vegetation, so look for them in human-made ponds or on the edges of small lakes. They like warmer weather and are observable from April through September. Bullfrogs hunt during the day and at night. During the breeding season, follow their distinctive bellowing calls in the evenings to find them. Some people say their call sounds like the hum of a Jedi lightsaber.

> Frogs can't turn their heads from side to side to look at something. Instead, their large, bulging eyes perched atop their skulls give them a wide frame of vision. When a frog swallows food, it pulls its eyes down into the roof of its mouth to help push the food down its throat!

Barred Tiger Salamander

Ambystoma mavortium

Barred tiger salamanders (also called western tiger salamanders) are the only salamanders in Utah. If it looks like a lizard but has moist skin, you've found a tiger salamander. Their color is variable, but they tend to have dark bodies with yellow, tan, or green stripes on their backs, resembling a tiger pattern. Some individuals, however, prefer the simple elegance of a single dark body color to the flashiness of tiger stripes.

Moist skin

Dark body with yellow, tan, or green stripes

Broad, flat head and wide mouth

In addition to being fashionable, barred tiger salamanders are adorable. They have broad heads with wide mouths that appear to be smiling. Their faces may remind of you of the "smiling" Mexican axolotl (*Ambystoma mexicanum*) of Internet fame, and, in fact, these two salamanders are closely related.

Salamanders don't have ears and their eyesight is rather poor, so they rely on smell and tactile senses to navigate the world.

Forever Young

Another trait barred tiger salamanders and their Mexican cousins share is paedomorphosis—they can mature into adults while retaining characteristics of their juvenile phase. Salamanders start their lives as completely aquatic creatures with external gills and large fin tails. These larval salamanders are often marketed as "mud puppies" and are used for fishing bait.

Most barred tiger salamander larvae undergo metamorphosis and become adults. They lose their gills, develop lungs, and move onto land. But they can also develop into sexually mature adults while staying in an aquatic environment with gills. Some populations in Utah have both metamorphosed adults that live on land and paedomorphic adults that never leave the water. The Mexican axolotl, on the other hand, is entirely paedomorphic.

Shape-Shifters

Barred tiger salamander larvae have another shape-shifting trick they can deploy to survive tough times. Most salamander larvae eat plants, but if their pond begins to dry up, food is limited, or the density of larvae is high, they can change into a "cannibalistic" form with a bigger mouth and small teeth that help them eat larger prey—including their siblings. This high-protein diet keeps them from starving to death and helps them mature faster so they can escape the pond before it dries up.

How to Spot Them

Barred tiger salamanders like moist areas. Look for them near springs, ponds, and lakes. They spend much of their time underground in burrows or under logs and rocks. They are also at home in sprinkler boxes and window wells. The terrestrial adults are primarily nocturnal. You'll typically see them in the spring and summer months. You can find the juvenile and paedomorphic adult forms in all but the coldest months at the edge of the water or just under the mud.

Boreal Chorus Frog

Pseudacris maculata

Boreal chorus frogs are often heard, but seldom seen. In early spring, male frogs begin calling even before all the snow has melted. Their loud calls resemble the sounds made by running your fingernail along the teeth of a comb, from the thicker teeth toward the thinnest teeth: "Rrrreeeet! Rrrreeeet!"

During the peak of the breeding season in the spring, the frogs call during the day. Later in the summer, you'll hear them mainly at

Brown, green, or gray body with dark streaks or spots

Dark line extends from nose, through each eye and down each side

Minimal webbing between toes

Many frogs have webbing between their toes to help them swim, but chorus frogs have little pads on their toes that enable them to climb small blades of grass in search of tasty insects.

night. Although it may sound like hundreds of male frogs are calling, it's probably only a group of ten or fifteen.

Boreal chorus frogs are difficult to spot because they are only about an inch long, plus they are well camouflaged. Their body colors can vary and may be gray, brown, or green, and the spots that cover their backs may merge into stripes. Usually, a very distinct stripe runs from the tip of the frog's nose, through each eye, and down each side—like someone got a little too excited with an eyeliner pencil.

Frog-cicles

One of the coolest things about these little frogs is that they can partially freeze in the winter and revive in the spring. In the northern parts of their range, where temperatures drop below zero in the winter, the frogs can't dig far enough down into the mud to avoid the freezing conditions. So, as winter begins, the frogs slow down their metabolisms until their heartbeats and breathing stop.

Molecules that act like antifreeze prevent the liquid inside the frogs' cells from freezing. If this liquid froze, the cells would burst. The liquid outside their cells actually does freeze, but special proteins control the growth and size of the ice crystals to prevent cell damage. No one knows what signals the frogs' hearts to start beating again when they thaw in the spring. As soon as they're defrosted, the mating season begins.

How to Spot Them

Boreal chorus frogs are one of the few frogs that live in urban areas. During the breeding season, look for them in the water in marshes, temporary pools, and ponds. In the summer, they may take shelter under rocks and logs or in clumps of grass, but they never stray too far from water. If you're determined to see a boreal chorus frog and don't mind getting muddy or wet, follow their calls on a summer night. If you shine a flashlight around, you may see the bright reflections of their eyes.

Gopher Snake

Pituophis catenifer

At first glance, gopher snakes are easy to mistake for rattlesnakes. Each of these snakes has a dark, blotchy pattern running down its back that contrasts its lighter body color. If a gopher snake feels threatened, it will try to convince you that it actually is a venomous rattlesnake. The harmless snake will coil up, shake the tip of its rattle-less tail, inflate its neck and flatten out its head to look more like a rattlesnake, and make a loud, buzzing hiss that sounds like a rattle.

Gopher snakes hope predators will be fooled by their rattlesnake performance and

No rattle on tail
Tan body with dark brown blotches on back and sides
Long, thin body
Narrow head

leave them alone. This is a great example of mimicry, when one species looks or behaves like another, often as a defense against predators. Unfortunately, people are also inclined to fall for the act and sometimes try to kill harmless gopher snakes.

Long, Thin, and Rattle-less

To determine whether you're looking at a gopher snake or a rattlesnake, check out the shape of its head. A rattlesnake has a very triangular head, while a gopher snake's head is narrow and fairly uniform in width. A rattlesnake, of course, has rattles, and its tail is quite wide compared to the narrow, tapered tail of a gopher snake.

Gopher snakes are also much longer and thinner than rattlesnakes. In fact, they're Utah's longest snake, at up to seven feet in length. If you're unsure of which snake you've encountered, the best idea is to back away to a safe distance. You'll both be happier.

Putting the Squeeze on Prey

Although they would like you to think they are venomous, gopher snakes are actually constrictors. They kill their prey by wrapping it in tight coils that cut off blood flow to its brain. They dine mainly on small mammals, as their

> Gopher snakes are sometimes called blow snakes in Utah because they "blow up" their neck with air and "blow out" a hiss to deter predators.

name suggests, but they will eat a variety of prey, including birds, eggs, and lizards.

Gopher snakes are active hunters, not ambush predators. They search out small mammals in their burrows and hiding places and often follow prey down into their dens. They are great burrowers, excellent tree climbers, and good swimmers.

How to Spot Them

Gopher snakes are very widespread and live in many different habitats. They are among the most commonly observed snakes in Utah. You can spot them in the foothills along the Wasatch Front, as well as at the edge of developed areas and in vacant lots. These snakes are active during the day, but they tend to seek shelter underground on hot summer afternoons. Look for them from March through October, depending on the temperatures.

Great Basin Rattlesnake

Crotalus oreganus lutosus

Venture into any of the foothills or canyons along the Wasatch Front and you may see—or hear—a Great Basin rattlesnake. You can identify a rattlesnake by looking for its wide, triangular head and, of course, the rattle at the end of its tail. These rattlesnakes also tend to have thick bodies and are usually two to three feet long. Their main body color can vary quite a bit, from light cream to tan or gray. A series of dark blotches runs down their back.

Dark blotches down back
Wide, triangular head
Rattle on end of tail
Thick body

Night Vision Without Googles

Rattlesnakes often hunt small mammals at night with the aid of an amazing superpower. Pit organs below their nostrils enable them to sense infrared radiation, or heat. They can detect tiny temperature differences down to 0.001 degree Celsius! Rattlesnakes can "see" images of their warm prey—like an infrared camera—in the dark because nerves transmit the information gathered by the pit organs to the same area of the brain that receives nerve impulses from the eyes.

After mating, a female rattlesnake carries fertilized egg sacs inside her body and later gives birth to live young. Rattlesnakes are outstanding mothers, by snake standards. Most snakes provide little or no care for their young, but rattlesnake mothers stay with their babies and actively defend them until they shed their skin for the first time, about a week or two after birth.

Long Rattle, Long Life?

You may have heard that you can determine a rattlesnake's age by counting the segments in its rattle, but this is a myth. Each time a rattlesnake sheds its skin, it adds a new interlocking segment to its rattle. Snakes shed often when they are young and quickly growing. Mature snakes may shed several times per year, depending on the food supply.

Snakes can also lose rattle segments, which are delicate and break off fairly easily. A long, tapered rattle, however, is a sign that a rattlesnake has been around for a while. Captive snakes have been known to live up to twenty years.

How to Spot Them

Look for Great Basin rattlesnakes in a variety of habitats, including exposed hillsides, forests, fields, and rocky outcrops. Near areas inhabited by humans, you may see them in rock piles, woodpiles, and burrows, but they usually avoid disturbed areas. They are most active in the morning and evening. Sometimes rattlesnakes stretch out on roads to warm themselves on the asphalt—sadly, this leads to many squashed snakes.

Keeping People and Snakes Safe

Rattlesnakes rely on camouflage to hide from both prey and predators. They are likely to stay still when they sense an approaching human in an effort to remain unseen. They have no interest in engaging with humans and rarely strike or bite. The majority of snakebites occur when people try to kill or handle snakes. If you are lucky enough to see a rattlesnake, taking a few precautions will prevent unpleasant encounters.

- Slowly back away from the snake and allow it to move off. Choose a different path if it doesn't leave.
- If you hear a rattle, stop and visually locate the snake before you move.
- Take a photo from a safe distance and submit it to iNaturalist.
- If a rattlesnake bites you or a companion, stay calm and seek medical attention as quickly as possible. Don't use a tourniquet or ice, and don't try to suck out the venom.

Northern Rubber Boa

Charina bottae

You'll probably have to venture into the canyons or mountains of the Wasatch Front to see a northern rubber boa. These snakes are fairly rare in our dry foothills and valley floors, preferring to live in moist forests. They made the cut for this urban guide because they are great snake ambassadors. Docile, slow, and nonvenomous, they can help people who are uncomfortable around snakes feel more at ease.

With a tube-shaped body that tapers slightly at each end, a rubber boa looks like a snake made by a child rolling out a ball of clay. At first glance, it may be difficult to tell its tail from its head. Small, shiny scales give these snakes their namesake rubbery appearance. Their skin is often loose, like it's a couple sizes too big. This unique appearance makes rubber boas easy to identify.

Small, shiny scales

Tan or olive-brown color

Blunt tail that resembles a head

Stinky Defense

These snakes have a reputation for never biting in self-defense. When under attack, a rubber boa may release a terrible-smelling musk from its vent (the common opening to its digestive and reproductive systems) to disgust a predator into leaving it alone.

Its other defense is rather charming in its naiveté. A rubber boa will curl up in a ball around its head and wave its blunt tail in the air as a decoy head. It will even pretend to strike with its fake head. Unfortunately for rubber boas, predators rarely fall for this trick.

Snake Legs?

The rubber boa is the northernmost member of the famous boa family. More tolerant of cold temperatures than most snakes, its range extends all the way into Canada. Adult males have tiny remnant limbs on either side of the vent—boas are one the few groups of snakes that maintain vestiges of their hind limbs, evidence of their evolution from lizards.

Baby rubber boas are usually pink and become darker as they age. They may not feed for more than a year, subsisting on stored energy provided by their mothers until after their first hibernation.

Rubber boas prey mainly on small mammals, including mice and shrews. They capture and constrict adult prey with their coils, but prefer to eat baby rodents in their nests, using their tail to fend off the mother as they attempt to consume the entire litter.

How to Spot Them

Rubber boas are common in the Wasatch Mountains, but they can be difficult to spot. They are shy, largely nocturnal animals, and they spend a lot of time underground in burrows. The best way to find one is to flip over rocks or watch for them on roads in the evenings. They are active earlier in the spring than other snakes. Look for them from March through October.

Turtles

The story of turtles along the Wasatch Front is slippery, full of gaps, and constantly changing. There are questions about which turtles were introduced, when and how they got here, and whether populations of new species are becoming established. If you see a turtle, be sure to take a photo and post it to iNaturalist. Your observations will help create a more complete picture of our turtle populations.

Liberated Turtles

By far, the most common turtles in our area are pond sliders and a closely related subspecies, red-eared sliders. Sliders get their name from their habit of sliding off rocks and logs into the water when they sense danger. They are fairly large turtles, with females growing upwards of twelve inches long.

Sliders have oval shells that are patterned and colorful when they are young and become darker and muted as they age. Look for a tracery of irregular yellow stripes covering their green skin. You'll know you've spotted a red-eared slider if you see a jaunty red dash behind each eye.

No one knows for sure when sliders were introduced into Utah's waterways, but they were almost certainly former pets. Red-eared sliders are the most popular turtle in the pet trade globally. When little pet turtles grow into big turtles that need big aquariums, some pet owners illegally release them.

Murky Origins

Farther north along the Wasatch Front, you may see painted turtles. They are smaller than sliders, at five to ten inches long. Unlike sliders, they often have red markings along the rim of the upper shell and quite a bit of red on the lower shell.

Scientists disagree about whether painted turtles have lived in Utah for a long time or were introduced more recently. Both sides in this debate may be correct. It's likely that painted turtles are native to northern Utah and

Pond Slider
Trachemys scripta

Shell color ranges from greenish yellow to gray, brown, and black

Oval-shaped shell

Yellow stripes on dark skin

Red-Eared Slider
Trachemys scripta elegans

Red dash behind each eye

Bright colors on shell and skin on young turtles

Painted Turtle
Chrysemys picta

Edges of shell are smooth, not serrated

Red markings on the rims upper and lower shells

Yellow stripes on face, neck, and legs

that unwanted pet turtles have been added to their populations. Like sliders, painted turtles are very popular in the pet trade.

Keep your eyes out for another turtle that may become an established population in Utah. Common snapping turtles (*Chelydra serpentina*) have already been observed in Salt Lake, Davis, and Utah counties. These turtles don't have any of the colorful markings of sliders or painted turtles, and they grow much larger and have huge, heavy heads. Over time, populations of other turtle species may become established here too.

How to Spot Them

Pond sliders and painted turtles prefer slow-moving fresh water. Look for them in natural or human-made ponds and along the

As a result of their slow metabolisms, many turtles can spend all winter at the bottom of ponds capped by ice. They extract oxygen from the water by moving it across body surfaces flush with blood vessels—especially areas near their rear ends.

Jordan River. These turtles love to bask in the sun and often gather in groups on logs or rocks during the day. At night, they rest underwater. They are active between March and November, depending on the temperature.

Western Terrestrial Garter Snake

Thamnophis elegans

Despite their earthy name, western terrestrial garter snakes can be very aquatic. If you see a swimming snake in Utah, it's probably a garter snake. These snakes often live near streams, ponds, and wetlands, but don't be surprised if you spot one in a forest, desert, meadow, or urban backyard. They thrive in many different habitats. Some people call them garden snakes because they often turn up in in yards and gardens.

Body color varies—light brown, gray-green, or black

Bodies may have black or red dots

Stripe down each side

Yellow, light orange, or white stripe on back

171

Western terrestrial garter snakes vary quite a bit in appearance, but they almost always have "pinstripes"—a white, yellow, or light orange stripe running down their backs and a matching stripe along each side. Their main body color varies and may be light brown, gray-green, or black. Some have a sprinkling of black or red spots between their stripes.

Chow Down

In mid- to late summer, female garter snakes give birth to live young. Baby snakes are immediately on their own with a big challenge ahead of them. They need to eat enough food before cool weather sets in so that they can survive winter brumation—the reptile equivalent of hibernation—without starving to death.

Garter snakes will eat almost any live prey that fits in their mouths, including insects, worms, slugs, fish, lizards, frogs, small mammals, and birds. They can even safely consume toads that secrete toxins that would kill many predators.

A Little Venomous

Garter snakes are slightly venomous, but they don't pose a threat to humans. They inject their venom with small fangs located at the back of their mouths. They have to "chew" on their prey to inject enough venom to immobilize it while they swallow it whole.

Garter snakes try to avoid becoming dinner themselves by blending into their surroundings. But if a predator (or a human) grabs a garter snake, it may deploy a stinky defense to make itself seem less appetizing. "Musking" involves releasing a foul-smelling combination of feces and musk from the vent, the common opening to the snake's digestive and reproductive systems.

How to Spot Them

Garter snakes are very common in neighborhoods and open spaces along the Wasatch Front. They are active during the day from April through October. They emerge in the morning sun to bask and warm up and then hunt throughout the morning and afternoon. On hot summer afternoons, they may take shelter under shady shrubs or rocks.

Whiptails

New Mexico Whiptail

Aspidoscelis neomexicanus

Western Whiptail

Aspidoscelis tigris

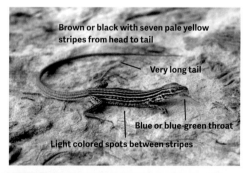

Brown or black with seven pale yellow stripes from head to tail

Very long tail

Blue or blue-green throat

Light colored spots between stripes

Light brown, yellowish, or gray back with marbled dark markings

Very long tail

Yellow or cream-colored belly

Evolutionarily speaking, the New Mexico whiptail is a young species. It first appeared in New Mexico's Rio Grande Valley between 200 and 1000 years ago, when western whiptails hybridized with little striped whiptails (*Aspidoscelis inornatus*). Both parent species contain males and females, but New Mexico whiptails are all female!

All baby New Mexico whiptails are clones of their mother. They are born from unfertilized eggs she buries in sandy soil. Though there are no males to mate with, females continue to engage in mating behaviors with one another, which appears to stimulate the production of eggs. Females that don't "mate" lay fewer eggs.

Hitchhikers or Escapees?

New Mexico whiptails were first documented in Utah in the early 2000s in Lehi, Sandy, and North Salt Lake. The isolated Utah population is much farther north and west than any known New Mexico whiptail population. Because there is no *way* these lizards could have walked from New Mexico to northern Utah on their own, humans had to be involved.

A researcher at the University of Utah kept New Mexico whiptails in a lab in the 1970s. Some speculate that a few of these lizards made a daring escape or were illegally released. Or maybe a New Mexico whiptail was accidentally transported on some plants—a very common way for species to move around. Because they reproduce asexually, it takes only one New Mexico whiptail to start a population in a new location.

Mostly Tail

Western whiptails also live along the Wasatch Front. Both lizards have extremely long tails, which can be twice as long as their body. The end of a young lizard's tail is bright blue and fades to brown with age.

The patterns on their backs can help you tell these lizards apart. The New Mexico whiptail has light-colored lines on its back, giving it a striped appearance. The western whiptail also has light-colored lines, but they are less distinct and tend to overlap with spots, creating a marbled or reticulated pattern.

Although whiptails can shed their tails to distract predators, they deploy this trick much less often than other Utah lizards. The length of their tails makes this a very costly defense.

How to Spot Them

New Mexico whiptails do well in urban habitats. Look for them in parks and along the base of foothills. Western whiptails live in a variety of habitats, but they avoid areas with dense vegetation. Both lizards like very warm weather, so look for them from late May to early September. They are active during all but the hottest parts of the day.

Street Trees

Ashes

Green Ash

Fraxinus pennsylvanica

▲ Ashes have rounded crowns and can grow very large in urban forests.

Ash trees make up 15 to 20 percent of urban trees in Utah, so you're likely to meet some along the Wasatch Front. They were heavily planted during the last half of the twentieth century and are some of our largest neighborhood trees today. In Salt Lake City, ash trees provide the most shade canopy per tree in the urban forest.

White Ash

Fraxinus americana

Each leaf is a group of leaflets

Leaflets are pointed with toothed edges

Seeds shaped like canoe paddles

Don't worry too much about figuring out exactly which ash species you've encountered—the tree won't mind. The differences between green and white ashes are often subtle and variable. Start by learning the ash basics and enjoy observing these stately trees throughout the seasons.

Lots of Leaflets

In the summer, ash trees are covered in plumes of compound leaves. Each ten-to-twelve-inch-long leaf is made up of five to nine smaller leaflets that grow in pairs directly opposite each other on a stalk. One single leaflet stands alone at the top of the compound leaf. Each leaflet has a pointed tip and a gently toothed edge. If you're looking at a white ash, the underside of the leaf may be paler than the upper side.

174

Ashes put on quite a show in the fall. The leaves of green ashes blaze in bright yellow, while white ashes can sport yellow, orange, or even purple leaves. Female trees wear luxurious pendants of dangling seeds shaped like little canoe paddles. As the trees age, their gray bark becomes deeply furrowed with ridges that interlace to form narrow diamond shapes. This distinctive bark pattern can help you identify them in winter.

Threat on the Horizon

Utah's ash trees may be living on borrowed time. Emerald ash borer beetles (*Agrilus planipennis*) have killed tens of millions of ash trees in North America since they were first detected in Michigan in 2002. The adult beetles munch harmlessly on ash leaves, but the larvae feed on the tree's inner bark, disrupting its ability to move water and nutrients. Virtually all trees die within a few years of larval infestation.

Emerald ash borers have been living just next door in Colorado since 2013, but they hadn't been detected in Utah as of 2022. Many forestry professionals think it's only a matter of time until they arrive here. Researchers are working to find ways to control beetle populations and the damage they cause. Individual trees can be treated with insecticides, and stingless Asian wasps are already being used as a broader biological control in thirty states. After the parasitoid wasp lays eggs inside emerald ash borer larvae, her babies eat their host from the inside out. The wasps seem to be killing 20 to 80 percent of the larvae in ash trees without causing problems for other species.

MATURE SIZE: 50–60 feet tall and 25–40 feet wide
BARK: Gray and furrowed
LEAF: Compound, five to nine leaflets
FLOWER: Purple, in small clusters
FRUIT, SEED, CONE: Clusters of winged seeds

Austrian Pine

Pinus nigra

Austrian pines are famously tough. They tolerate heat, cold, pollution, salt, poor soils, and even some drought. It's telling that an Austrian pine was the very first tree planted in the Great Plains Shelterbelt. This wall of twenty million trees that extended from Canada to Texas was planted during the 1930s Dust Bowl in hopes of slowing the winds that carried away precious topsoil. It's hard to think of worse growing conditions than those of the Dust Bowl.

Originally from the rugged mountains of Southern Europe, Austrian pines were being planted in North America as early as 1759. Since then, they've become popular trees in cities across the United States for their beauty and ability to tolerate the stresses and toxins of urban life. Look for Austrian pines growing either singly or in groups in yards, parks, school grounds, and commercial developments across the Wasatch Front.

From Pyramids to Umbrellas

Young Austrian pines have a pyramid shape—wide at the bottom and tapering to a point at the top. As they get older, their top starts to round out and they become more oval shaped. They may even develop an umbrella-like flat top. Older trees often lose their lower

Long needles in bundles of two

Yellow male pollen cones

▲ This Austrian pine has the pyramid shape of a young tree. Older trees often lose their lower branches, but people sometimes prune them away.

branches, exposing the deeply furrowed, puzzle-piece bark on their trunks. Usually gray or brown, the bark of the oldest trees may include swirls of pale pink.

Pine needles grow in bundles, rather than individually like fir or spruce needles. When you meet a pine, counting the number of needles in a bundle will give you an idea of its identity. Austrian pine needles typically grow in bundles of two and are four to six inches long. If you take a close look at a pair of needles in a bundle, you'll see that each is a half-circle in cross section and that the two needles fit together to form a cylinder.

Keep an eye out for cones on or around the tree. Small, yellow male cones produce pollen each spring. They grow in dense clusters at the base of the tree's candles, the poetic name for the pale upright buds on branch tips—the tree's spring growth. Female cones mature about eighteen months after they are fertilized, changing from green to brown and then opening to release their seeds. When you find them on the ground, they will be two or three inches long and will have a small prickle at the base of each scale.

Facing a New Stress

Recently, black pineleaf scale (*Dynaspidiotus californica*) insects have been attacking Austrian pines across the Wasatch Front. The insects usually target trees that are already under stress, especially from lack of water—a problem that could become more widespread as Utah's climate becomes hotter and drier. Fortunately, several effective treatments are available.

MATURE SIZE: 50–60 feet tall and 20–40 feet wide
BARK: Gray or brown, furrowed, and platelike
LEAF: Bundles of two needles
FLOWER: Small yellow male cones and larger female cones on same tree
FRUIT, SEED, CONE: Dark brown cones, 2–3 inches long, with open scales

Blue Spruce

Picea pungens

▲ A blue spruce is cone shaped, with densely packed branches covering the entire trunk.

Single, sharp needles

Cones hang downward

Honey-colored cones with stiff, papery scales

What makes a blue spruce blue? You may have noticed that blue spruces growing in the Wasatch Mountains are often more green than blue, while the spruces in yards across the Wasatch Front vary in color. They can be blue-green, silvery gray, or powdery blue.

A blue spruce's needles are actually green. The intensity of a tree's blueness depends on the concentration of its bloom, the powdery white wax that coats its needles. The nursery industry has bred blue spruce cultivars that produce more bloom to satisfy our desire for shimmering silver-blue trees.

Fading Bloom

The bloom on spruce needles is similar to the bloom on blueberries, grapes, and plums—you can rub it off and see the base color underneath. The bloom on spruce needles often weathers away over time. Pesticides and air pollution accelerate the process. The new growth that emerges each spring has a fresh coat of bloom, so a blue spruce may look bluer in the spring than later in the year.

Blue spruces usually grow in a solid, sturdy cone shape. Their dense, horizontal branches often descend all the way to the ground. Squirrels and birds like to nest in these trees because of the protection offered by their thick foliage. Owls roost in their dim interiors during the day. Many cultivars can grow up to sixty feet tall, but some top out at fifteen to twenty feet, with dwarf trees reaching a diminutive six feet tall.

When you meet a blue spruce, shake hands gently. Its needles are very sharp and can break the skin. The tree's species name, *pungens*, comes from the Latin for "piercing" and warns of its prickly nature. Try picking a needle and rolling it between your thumb and index finger. Unlike fir needles, which are flat, spruce needles spin because they have four sides. Look for small male pollen cones all over the tree and papery, golden-brown female cones at the top.

Home to a Champion

The blue spruce became Utah's state tree in 1933 after a decade-long battle in the state legislature between spruce advocates and box elder advocates from Box Elder County. Though the aspen replaced the blue spruce as our state tree in 2014, Utah still has a special blue spruce connection as the home of the "national champion tree"—the biggest blue spruce in the world! Growing in a remote location in the Ashley National Forest in Wasatch County, it is 129 feet tall, with a trunk circumference of nearly 17 feet.

MATURE SIZE: Varies widely depending on cultivar
BARK: Gray and flaky or scaly
LEAF: Single, stiff, sharp needles about an inch long
FLOWER: Small yellow male cones and larger female cones on same tree
FRUIT, SEED, CONE: Golden brown cones, 2–4 inches long, with papery, ragged scales

Box Elder

Acer negundo

Three lobes will separate to become individual leaflets

Drooping male flowers with dark anthers

The fact that an entire county in northern Utah is named after box elder trees is a good indication of how common they are in our state. Since box elders are both a popular cultivated species and an abundant wild tree, you can find them almost anywhere along the Wasatch Front. People plant them in yards and somewhat less frequently along streets. They thrive on the banks of streams flowing through our cities and in mountain canyons. They shade parks and other open spaces and even happily sprout in vacant lots.

Maples with a Twist

Box elders are unusual members of the maple family. Most maples have simple lobed leaves, shaped like the famous maple leaf on the Canadian flag. Box elder trees have compound leaves composed of three, five, or sometimes seven leaflets on a stalk. The leaflets vary from having jagged toothed edges to being more deeply lobed. Sometime people confuse box elder leaves growing on small branches at the base of the tree's trunk with poison ivy's "leaves of three."

Box elders also differ from their other maple relatives by having separate male and female trees. Male trees bloom in early spring just before their leaves emerge. Their flowers droop in clusters of long, wispy, yellow-green tassels. Female flowers look similar but are more reddish green and emerge along with the tree's leaves.

The female flowers develop into samaras, double-winged helicopter seeds, that hang in dense curtains in the late summer and fall. The two wings of the seeds form a sharp "V" shape, unlike the broader "U" shape or straight line created by other maple samaras.

▲ Mature box elders often have multiple trunks and broad crowns that can look a bit disheveled.

Free Room and Board

Box elder seeds are not only fun to watch twirl-ing through the air, they provide sustenance for squirrels and a variety of birds. The seeds are also the favorite food of eastern box elder bugs *(Boisea trivittata)*, harmless black-and-red bugs that gather in large groups on female box elder trees in the spring to lay their eggs.

Because these hardy trees grow very quickly, box elders were a popular choice in rapidly growing cities and suburbs across the United States that wanted green canopies in a hurry. More recently, however, they've fallen out of favor because, like many fast-growing trees, their wood is weak and their limbs break easily in storms. Falling limbs can be a serious hazard in neighborhoods and leave behind an uneven crown that some people find unat-tractive. On the other hand, box elders' weak wood offers cavity-nesting birds valuable opportunities to create cozy homes.

MATURE SIZE: 30–50 feet tall and wide
BARK: Brown with shallow ridges; young stems are green
LEAF: Compound, with three to five (sometimes seven) irregu-larly toothed leaflets
FLOWER: Drooping green tassels on separate male and female trees
FRUIT, SEED, CONE: Winged seeds in pairs at a sharp angle

Bradford Pear

Pyrus calleryana 'Bradford'

It's easy to spot Bradford pears in the spring. They are among the first trees in our urban forests to burst into bloom, with clusters of flowers covering every branch in small white pom-poms. If you pick one, you'll have a lovely little bouquet of five-petaled flowers with Sputnik-shaped bursts of stamens. To some people, the blossoms smell awful—like fish or rotting meat. To others, they smell like spring.

Bradford pears are unassuming trees in the summer. Their glossy, green leaves have a simple oval shape that tapers to a point, with small, blunt teeth along their edges. The trees stand out again in the fall when their leaves light up in spectacular shades of red, orange, purple, and yellow. Their small, hard fruits soften up after the first frost to provide food for hungry birds.

Small fruit on slender stem

Glossy, leathery leaf surface

Oval leaf with toothed edge tapers to a point

Pears Everywhere

Bradford pears' beautiful spring and fall displays, combined with their incredible hardiness and low cost, made them extremely popular along the Wasatch Front. They were the most common species noted in a 2014 survey of trees in six neighborhoods in the Salt Lake Valley. In some newer developments, all the street trees are Bradford pears. You'll also see them in parking lot islands and industrial parks because they can tolerate intense heat and pollution.

Our national love affair with Bradford pears began in the 1960s. The U.S. Department of Agriculture Plant Introduction Station bred the Bradford pear cultivar from shoots of the wild Callery pear *(Pyrus calleryana)* carefully collected in China in the early 1900s. Their original plan was to crossbreed the hardy Callery pear with orchard pears to produce fruiting pear trees that could resist fire-blight disease. Although this endeavor didn't pan out, their work with the Callery pear did produce what seemed like the perfect street tree.

▲ Limbs of a Bradford pear often grow vertically and give the tree an egg shape.

It's Complicated

Cities across the United States fell head-over-heels in love with the Bradford pear, but, like all romantic relationships, this one turned out to be complicated. By the 1980s, it became clear that Bradford pears have problems with weak limbs. Their branches grow vertically at such narrow angles that wind and snow can easily snap them off. The tree also began to draw flak for being overplanted. These two factors often lead urban forest professionals to use the word "despise" when discussing the Bradford pear.

The tree's PR really took a nosedive when concerns arose in the eastern United States about wild hybridized forms growing outside of cities. Birds spread the seeds, which grew into dense, shrubby, thorny thickets resembling the ancestral Callery pear. Luckily, we don't seem to have wild populations in Utah, perhaps on account of our dry climate. Don't be surprised if you see headlines villainizing the Bradford pear, but remember that they reflect just one part of our relationship with this tree.

MATURE SIZE: 30–50 feet tall and 20–35 feet wide
BARK: Brown and shiny when young, gray-brown and slightly ridged with age
LEAF: Glossy and dark green, 1.5–3.0 inches long, oval with a toothed edge
FLOWER: Showy white clusters
FRUIT, SEED, CONE: Small, round, russet-colored fruit

Golden Rain Tree

Koelreuteria paniculata

The golden rain tree is a showstopper. In late June or early July, it erupts into a fireworks display of bright yellow blossoms—a rare color for a flowering tree. Small blossoms growing in clusters on long, upright stalks cover the entire tree. This profusion of midsummer blooms seems extravagant, especially in our dry valleys.

The blossoms create a lovely yellow carpet when they fall to the ground, but the show isn't over yet. Next come the dangling bunches of three-sided seedpods that look like delicate paper lanterns. They start off green, turn pinkish red, and eventually fade to a soft brown, adorning the tree throughout the winter.

The golden rain tree's leaves get in on the act too. They emerge in rich bronze-pink to purple colors in the spring. In the summer, they become bright green, feathery affairs up to eighteen inches long and composed of seven to fifteen leaflets attached to a single stem. Individual leaflets have toothed edges and a variety of deeply cut lobes. In the fall, the leaves turn a warm yellow to yellow-orange.

▲ A medium-size tree with a round shape, the golden rain tree glows brilliant yellow in the summer.

More than a Pretty Face

The golden rain tree isn't only about good looks. It's a survivor that tolerates drought, heat, air pollution, road salt, and a wide variety of soils—all qualities that make it a popular street tree. Long before it grew in urban forests, this tree shared other gifts with humans.

Long leaves comprising many leaflets

Seedpods look like paper lanterns

People made yellow dye from its flowers, a black dye from its leaves, and strings of beads from its small, round seeds. Tea made from the flowers was traditionally used as an eye wash to combat conjunctivitis.

These trees hail from forests in the temperate regions of eastern China. People there began planting them around temples and palaces as well as to mark the tombs of important officials. The showy tree caught the eye of Pierre d'Incarville, a Jesuit priest who introduced the species to France in 1747.

Thomas Jefferson was the first to plant a golden rain tree in North America. In 1809, he received a shipment of seeds from Madame de Tessé, a French aristocrat and fellow plant lover with whom he often traded plants. He wrote to her in 1811 to report that a seed had germinated and later planted the seedling in his garden at Monticello.

MATURE SIZE: 20–40 feet tall and 25–40 feet wide
BARK: Light gray-brown and ridged on older trees
LEAF: Compound, with 7–15 lobed leaflets
FLOWER: Showy yellow clusters
FRUIT, SEED, CONE: Papery, three-sided seedpods

Honey Locust

Gleditsia triacanthos

Rows of 20–30 small leaflets per leaf

Leathery seedpod

Oval-shaped leaflet

▲ Honey locusts have open, airy canopies, with crowns that are wide and often flattish.

Honey locusts' thin, airy canopies and lacy leaves create flickering, dappled shade on city streets. Their distinctive compound leaves make them easy to spot. Each leaf comprises a stalk of twenty to thirty small leaflets, each about an inch long, oval, and with gently toothed edges. Sometimes each leaflet is itself a little stalk of tiny leaflets, amplifying the tree's lacy appearance.

Leathery seedpods are another honey locust hallmark. Inside the twisting brown pods are beanlike seeds and a sweet pulp that gives the tree the "honey" part of its name. Honey locusts are actually part of the legume family (*Fabaceae*)—think beans and peas—whose members are famous for their pods and compound leaves. If the tree you spotted doesn't have seedpods, it could still be a honey locust. Many modern cultivars have been bred not to produce pods.

MATURE SIZE: 30–70 feet tall and wide
BARK: Dark gray, with long flat plates that curl along the edges
LEAF: Compound, with 20–30 small, oval leaflets
FLOWER: Green to brown, hang in 2-inch-long clusters resembling furry caterpillars
FRUIT, SEED, CONE: Brown, leathery seedpods, 12–18 inches long and 1 inch wide

Mastodon Defense System

Though delicate in appearance, honey locusts are fierce at heart. When they grow wild, sharp thorns up to four inches long cover their trunks. Scientists think these huge thorns evolved to protect the tree from browsing Ice Age megafauna, such as mastodons. Acacia trees in Africa have similar thorns to protect themselves from modern elephants.

The trees that grow on city streets are descended from a natural thornless hybrid. Though they've lost their weaponry, thornless honey locusts haven't lost the toughness that enables them to thrive in harsh urban conditions—one of the reasons they are the most common street trees in Manhattan and downtown Chicago.

Heritage Trees

Honey locusts have a long history on the streets of the Wasatch Front. Their seeds arrived in the Salt Lake Valley along with the first groups of European-American settlers. According to one account, the first tree settlers planted in their new home was a black locust (*Robinia pseudoacacia*), a cousin of the honey locust. Purportedly, they planted the tree the very day they arrived in 1847 on the lot where Brigham Young later built his Beehive House.

Though that black locust is gone, you can still visit a honey locust planted in 1849 on the northeast corner of 800 South and 1000 East in Salt Lake City. It's one of Utah's Heritage Trees. People can nominate trees to this distinguished list for their historic significance, age, or size. An interactive map maintained by the Utah Division of Forestry, Fire, and State Lands shows the location of these trees and tells their stories.

Lindens

American Linden

Tilia americana

▲ The linden's creamy flowers and yellow-green bracts illuminate the tree in late spring. Their crowns tend to be shaped like a bell or a pyramid.

Let your nose guide you to the delight of a linden tree in bloom. Lindens take center stage in June, well after most trees in our urban forests have wrapped up their spring floral shows. You may not see the delicate bunches of creamy yellow blossoms immediately, but their sweet, citrusy fragrance will grab your attention from more than a hundred feet away.

When you get closer, you'll hear that you aren't the only one drawn to the linden's perfume. The entire tree may be abuzz with bees feasting on the flowers' nectar. Look for butterflies and hummingbirds joining the party as well. If you turn over a leaf, you may see aphids

Littleleaf Linden

Tilia cordata

Papery bract that grows with the flowers

Beginnings of pea-size fruits

Lopsided heart–shaped leaves

MATURE SIZE: 40–60 feet tall and 20–30 feet wide
BARK: Gray-brown with furrows
LEAF: Heart-shaped with toothed edges
FLOWER: Small, pale-yellow clusters, intense fragrance
FRUIT, SEED, CONE: Small, round fruit attached to a papery bract

enjoying a sugary sap snack. Because they have to drink a lot of sap to obtain the amino acids they need, aphids squirt excess sugary liquid onto whatever is below the tree. (Pro tip: Don't park under a linden.)

Many Gifts

Humans have long enjoyed the bounty of lindens' sweet nature. Linden flowers make a refreshing tea with floral and lemon flavors. Its leaves—especially young, tender ones—make a tasty addition to a salad. The honey that bees produce from its blossoms is prized for its distinctive sweetness, accompanied by minty and woodsy notes. Lindens have also shared medicines made from their flowers, leaves, wood, and charcoal to treat a wide variety of ailments.

Two members of the linden family are common along the Wasatch Front: the American linden and its European cousin, the littleleaf linden. As you might guess, the littleleaf linden has smaller leaves (1.5 to 3 inches wide) than the American linden (4 to 6 inches wide) and doesn't grow quite as tall. Otherwise, the two trees are very similar in appearance.

One telltale sign you've met a linden is the papery wing, or bract, on the stem supporting a cluster of flowers that turn into pea-size seeds. This little wing helps the seeds fall farther from their parent. Linden leaves are shaped like lopsided hearts with toothed edges. In the summer, the top of the leaf is a dark glossy green, while the underside is pale and a little fuzzy. Lindens aren't the showiest trees in the fall—their leaves usually turn a muted green or pale yellow.

London Planetree

Platanus × acerifolia

▲ Stately London planetrees have distinctive pale limbs. Mature trees are very tall and often have an oval silhouette.

Toothed edges

Large leaves with deep lobes

Pairs of bumpy seed balls

MATURE SIZE: 70–100 feet tall and 65–80 feet wide
BARK: Gray-brown flaky scales shed to expose mottled, peeling patches of white, gray, and green
LEAF: Maple-shaped with three to five lobes
FLOWER: Small, inconspicuous red pom-poms
FRUIT, SEED, CONE: Bumpy seed balls about an inch in diameter hang from long stalks in pairs

London planetrees are tall, elegant, and understated. They don't participate in the exuberance of showy spring flowers or the gaudiness of bright fall leaves. They prefer gracefully shading grand boulevards with their canopies. Their long, smooth branches are dappled in mosaics of light green, gray, tan, and cream. You can really appreciate the distinctive look of their pale limbs when the trees lose their leaves in winter.

These trees initially hide their smooth inner bark under rough, flaky outer bark that easily peels away from the tree. Sometimes you'll see what seems like an alarming amount of peeled-off bark on the ground, but don't worry—the trees aren't sick. The outer bark is brittle and can't expand when a tree experiences a growth spurt, so it naturally cracks and falls off. Losing bark may also help a tree get rid of pests and pollutants.

Pairs of Pendants

Despite their stately reserve, London planetrees do have a whimsical side. Their inconspicuous flowers turn into one-inch balls of densely packed seeds. Like fuzzy dice on a rearview mirror, the balls dangle in pairs from long stems. The bumpy seed balls start off green, turning brown in the fall. Some of them cling to the tree throughout the winter like muted Christmas ornaments. In the spring, the seed balls break up and the individual seeds fly away on bits of feathery fluff.

The origins of the first London planetree are a bit of mystery. The tree is a cross between related trees from two different continents: the American sycamore (*Platanus occidentalis*) and the oriental sycamore (*P. orientalis*) from Southern Europe. The first hybridization may have occurred in sixteenth-century Spain, but there is also evidence that the first London planetrees sprouted in the garden of a London aristocrat in the mid-1600s. Several London planetrees planted in the late 1600s still grow in England today!

London's Love Affair

Londoners fell in love with London planetrees in the eighteenth and nineteenth centuries. In the 1920s, they comprised nearly 60 percent of the city's trees. These hardy urbanites withstood the choking pollution of the industrializing city, and their peeling bark sloughed off grime and soot.

London planetrees are common in the urban forests of the Wasatch Front. Take a stroll under the elegant rows lining Main Street in both Farmington and Brigham City. Though London planetrees love water like many large-leaved trees, they have proven surprisingly tolerant of Utah's hot, dry summers and have become some of the largest, most recognizable, and most beloved trees in cities across the Wasatch Front.

Northern Catalpa

Catalpa speciosa

▲ The northern catalpa has thick, angular limbs with a narrow, irregular crown.

The northern catalpa brings a taste of tropical lushness to the dry Wasatch Front. Hailing from the Midwest, this tree is the northern-most member of the tropical *Bignoniaceae* family. Its huge, heart-shaped leaves can be up to a foot long on young trees.

In late May and June, big, orchidlike flowers cover the tree in tiered bouquets of up to thirty flowers each. The individual white blossoms have frilly, ruffled mouths, with speckles of yellow and purple-pink running down their throats.

Large, heart-shaped leaves

Spike of trumpet-shaped flowers

Speckles and stripes in flower throats

Bean Trees

In late summer, the flowers transform into green seedpods up to two feet long—the famous "beans" that inspired the catalpa's "bean trees" nickname. The pods ripen to brown in the fall, and many adorn the tree throughout the winter. If you break open one of the pods that has fallen to the ground, you'll find flat, winged seeds with a "beard" on each tip.

In addition to their hundreds of dangling seedpods, northern catalpas' distinctive shape makes them easy to recognize, even in the winter. Their limbs tend to be very thick, giving the tree a husky appearance. Sparse branches often grow in sharp, angular shapes, like a spooky tree in a kid's Halloween drawing. Sometimes limbs grow very long and reach dramatically skyward.

Catalpa Craze

Northern catalpas grow quickly. If you plant one, it might be shading your house in just ten years. The tree's rapid growth helped propel it into the national spotlight during the "Catalpa Craze" of the late 1800s. At that time, alarm was spreading about a "timber famine" resulting from massive deforestation in the eastern United States. The search was on for a "miracle tree" that would grow quickly and produce strong, rot-resistant wood for fence posts and railroad ties.

Enter the northern catalpa! After a pair of railroad-men-turned-catalpa-evangelists began promoting the tree's real virtues with over-the-top hype, railroad companies created huge catalpa plantations. Newspapers and seedling salesmen encouraged farmers to plant them too.

MATURE SIZE: 40–60 feet tall and 20–40 feet wide
BARK: Scaly gray-brown with furrows as trees age
LEAF: Heart-shaped with a smooth edge, 6–12 inches long
FLOWER: Showy, trumpet-shaped, up to 2 inches long in clusters
FRUIT, SEED, CONE: Long seed-pods resemble beans

The Catalpa Craze eventually fizzled out in 1910s. Although the trees grew quickly at first, their growth slowed as they got older, and their trunks were too short and curved for railway ties. They made a lot of great fence posts, though. Today northern catalpas continue to grace the streets of cities across the country. Their sound structure and strong wood make them a safe and sturdy tree for neighborhoods and parks. Even trees with large, hollowed-out cavities are unlikely to fail in storms.

Norway Maple

Acer platanoides

The deep, luxurious shade cast by a Norway maple creates a welcoming refuge on a hot summer day. The tree's large and abundant leaves overlap to form a dense canopy. Their ability to throw shade—in the nicest possible way—is one reason Norway maples are among the most common trees in urban forests along the Wasatch Front and all across North America.

In addition to providing deep pools of shade, Norway maples create lovely splashes of yellow along our streets. In the spring, entire trees appear to glow as bouquets of tiny yellow-green flowers burst into bloom. In late fall, their leaves may turn a pale yellow. Norway maples tend to be among the last trees to keep their green leaves in the fall and among the first to leaf out in the spring.

Helicopter Seeds and Milky Sap

Norway maple seeds and leaves are typical of the maple family, with their own unique twists. The two lobes of their samaras, the helicopter seeds, form a nearly straight line, while other maples tend to have U-shaped samaras. Look for five lobes on their broad leaves. Small

Two lobes of "helicopter" seeds form nearly a straight line

Broad leaves with five lobes

Spiky tips at the ends of major leaf veins

MATURE SIZE: 40–50 feet tall and 35–50 feet wide
BARK: Gray and tightly ridged
LEAF: Broad with five lobes
FLOWER: Small, yellow clusters
FRUIT, SEED, CONE: Winged seeds in pairs at a wide angle

▲ Norway maples have a short trunk with a symmetrical, very dense canopy.

spikes protrude around the edges of the leaf where each major leaf vein ends. To confirm you've met a Norway maple, pick one of its leaves, pinch the stem, and watch for milky sap to seep out.

Botanist John Bartram imported North America's first Norway maple seedlings in 1756 and began selling them. He even supplied two seedlings to George Washington to plant at Mount Vernon. Norway maples turned out to be hardy survivors well-suited for many urban environments. They grow quickly and tolerate air pollution, poor drainage, salt, and a range of soil conditions. Even a small square of soil in a sidewalk can be a sufficient home for this tree.

189

Tree Tragedy

The popularity of Norway maples really took off in the wake of a tree tragedy. In the 1940s, Dutch elm disease began decimating millions of elm trees in urban forests as it marched across the country. Many communities planted resilient Norway maples to replace their beloved elms.

The story is a bit different along the Wasatch Front, where we planted lots of Norway maples without our urban forests having to suffer the ravages of Dutch elm disease. In fact, the Norway maple is the most common street tree in several Wasatch Front communities, including Salt Lake City. Unfortunately, the species is not very drought tolerant. Many Norway maples in Utah begin to decline before their fortieth birthdays, never reaching their full potential.

Purpleleaf Plum

Prunus cerasifera

An explosion of pale pink blossoms covers purpleleaf plum trees in early spring. The name of a popular cultivar, 'Vesuvius', advertises the purpleaf plum's eruption of blooms. Or maybe the blossoming trees are more like puffy pink clouds, as the 'Thundercloud' cultivar declares. Whether you prefer volcanoes or clouds of blossoms, spend a moment soaking in the splendor of a purpleleaf plum in spring.

After you admire the blossoms from afar, take a look at one up close. Each flower has five petals surrounding a burst of numerous stamens. You may spot some early pollinators, such as blue orchard bees, sipping nectar and gathering pollen from these fragrant blooms.

Outstanding Color

Purpleleaf plums are common along the Wasatch Front, planted individually in yards, in groups in commercials developments, or in colonnades along streets. Their leaves, which can be deep purple, violet-red, or purple-green, add distinctive colors to the landscape. The individual leaves are oval shaped with slightly pointed tips and fine, jagged teeth along their edges.

In the summer, some trees bear small, dark purple plums about an inch in diameter. The plums are edible, but most people leave them for birds to enjoy. As ornamental trees, purpleleaf plums were bred for good looks, not good fruit.

Members of a Delicious Family

The ancestor of the purpleleafs, the cherry plum *(Prunus cerasifera)*, grew wild in the Balkans, Caucasus, Iran, and Iraq. The cherry plum is also likely the ancestor of the European plum *(Prunus domestica)* that people have been growing for its tasty fruit for more than 6000 years.

Plums are not the only members of the genus *Prunus* that bear delicious fruit. Cherries, apricots, peaches, nectarines, and almonds all belong to this genus, which includes 430 species. They are united by bearing fleshy fruit surrounding a pit containing a seed. (In the case of almonds, we eat the seed instead of the fruit.) The purpleleaf plum's oval, finely toothed leaves and five-petaled flowers are also traits shared by many other members of the genus.

Prominent, spiky stamens

Five-petaled pink blossoms in spring

MATURE SIZE: 15–30 feet tall and 15–25 feet wide
BARK: Smooth and dark purple to silver-gray when young, rough and very dark gray with age
LEAF: Purple, oval-shaped, about 2 inches long with toothed edge
FLOWER: Showy, light pink, about an inch in diameter
FRUIT, SEED, CONE: Small, dark, round fruit with a pit

▲ Purpleleaf plums are small trees with dense, symmetrical canopies and crowns that are either rounded or vase shaped.

Quaking Aspen

Populus tremuloides

Round leaf with a gentle point

Flat stems that cause leaves to turn, or "quake"

▲ Quaking aspens grow in a slender, oval shape, with branches that often begin higher on the trunk, exposing dramatic white bark.

Quaking aspens grow in glorious stands on mountainsides across Utah, rustling gently in summer breezes and blazing brilliant yellow in the fall. You'll also see lots of aspens planted in yards across the Wasatch Front, bringing a bit of mountain beauty to our valleys. Aspens are easy to spot, with smooth, white bark marked with thin black lines and prominent black knots. The bark of young aspens may have a greenish cast, hinting at the chlorophyll that lies just underneath it. When sunlight penetrates the thin outer bark, the tree can photosynthesize, even without leaves—a handy trick for adding to its winter energy reserves.

Why Quake?

The key to aspens' famous trembling leaves is the shape of their stems. The long stems are flattened rather than rounded, enabling the leaves to twist and turn in the slightest breeze. But why have leaves that quake? No one knows for sure, but turning leaves may help the tree with photosynthesis and pest control. One scientist tried stabilizing aspen leaves so they couldn't move and learned that still leaves were more likely to be damaged by insects than leaves that fluttered.

Utah has a special connection to the aspen. It replaced the blue spruce as our state tree in 2014, when fourth-grade aspen lobbyists from Monroe Elementary in Sevier County successfully argued that the aspen was more representative of the entire state because it grows in all twenty-nine Utah counties and forms 10 percent of the state's forest cover.

Many and One

Utah is also home to the Pando aspen clone that spreads across 106 acres in the Fish Lake National Forest. Pando contains 47,000 genetically identical trees connected by a single root system. Although the individual trees live less than 100 years, the Pando clone has survived for 80,000 years or more. Weighing in at about 5990 metric tons, Pando is in the running for the heaviest known organism on Earth.

For as much as we love having aspens as our neighbors, they don't thrive at the lower elevations in the valleys of the Wasatch Front. They aren't adapted to the hotter, dryer conditions here, and they don't tolerate alkaline, compacted soils. Growing in these tough conditions increases their susceptibility to insect and disease attacks and shortens their lifespan.

....

MATURE SIZE: 40–50 feet tall and 20–30 feet wide
BARK: Smooth and green-white to cream colored when young, gaining black lines and knots with age
LEAF: Oval to nearly round, 1–3 inches wide with fine teeth along the edges
FLOWER: Small, gray catkin
FRUIT, SEED, CONE: Small capsules that release cottony seeds

Wild Plants and Trees

Annual Honesty
Lunaria annua

Purple-pink cross-shaped flowers

Heart-shaped, toothed leaves

Lower leaves attach with a stem

▲ Annual honesty's semitransparent seedpods "honestly" reveal the seeds inside.

Annual honesty has lovely flowers, but its seedpods really steal the show. They start off as thin, green discs but turn a translucent silvery brown as they dry, shimmering in the sun. Their resemblance to coins inspired two of the plant's common names—money plant and silver dollar plant. You could also imagine the pod as a full moon, the source of the plant's genus name, *Lunaria*. The common name, honesty, may refer to the fact that the see-through seedpods don't hide their contents.

Garden Favorite Gone Wild

Annual honesty has long been a popular ornamental plant. The white-flowered variety even received the coveted Award of Garden Merit from the Royal Horticultural Society. It spreads easily by seed, so it's not surprising that annual honesty has taken to growing wild in cities. It's quite common east of the Mississippi River and along the West Coast. The Wasatch Front is one of the few places in the dry Intermountain West where you can regularly find it growing beyond garden beds.

Before its seedpods appear in midsummer, annual honesty puts on a spring display of intensely pink-purple flowers. (The white variety is rare here.) Each flower's four petals, arranged in a cross shape, tell you that annual honesty is a member of the mustard family. Most mustards have very small flowers, so annual honesty's three-quarter-inch blossoms are quite showy by comparison. Growing in clusters atop two- to three-foot stems, the bright blooms often tower over other spring urban wildflowers.

Pollinator Pleaser

Annual honesty is popular with the pollinator crowd. Its fragrant flowers attract long-tongued bees, butterflies, and moths. The caterpillars of cabbage white butterflies (*Pieris rapae*) munch on its heart-shaped, toothed leaves. Humans can also munch on these bitter leaves. The plant's flowers make a colorful addition to a salad and its famous seeds can be ground into a mustard substitute.

How to Spot Them

Annual honesty can be difficult to identify before it blooms because its leaves resemble

Annual honesty's translucent seedpods made it a favorite in medieval European gardens. Victorian women painted miniature scenes on the papery pods. They are still considered chic in floral arrangements today—just check Etsy.

those of many other mustard plants. Watch for flowers starting in mid-April and the green seedpods forming in June. The dried seedpods can remain on the plant into the fall and winter. Annual honesty tolerates moist soils, so look for it along streams and places that get a bit of irrigation. It's common in parks, open spaces, and neighborhood parking strips.

Broadleaf Cattail

Typha latifolia

If you had to select just one plant species to grow on your deserted island, cattails would be an excellent choice. Following the lead of North America's Indigenous peoples, you could put cattails to many valuable uses. Virtually every part of the plant is edible, from its starchy rhizomes (underground stems) to its protein-packed pollen. Its fibrous, water-proof leaves make excellent baskets, sleeping mats, cordage, and woven walls. The fluff from the seeds provides great insulation and padding. Dipped in fat, the dried flower stalk becomes a torch.

Maturing female spike packed with seeds

Old male flower spike

Long, flat, narrow leaves

Wetland Keystone

Humans aren't the only species that find cattails incredibly useful. Cattails play a key role in wetland ecosystems. Muskrats munch on their rhizomes and use their leaves to build lodges. Many birds perch on and build nests among cattails. Deer, raccoons, cottontails, and turkeys use them for cover. Below the water, amphibians and fish find shelter and safe places to lay eggs between their stalks.

Cattails' most recognizable feature—their brown "tails"—are made up of thousands of tiny flowers. The male flowers grow at the top of a slender spike, with the female flowers just below. These flowers don't need to be brightly colored or offer nectar for pollinators, because they rely on wind for pollination.

After the male flowers release their clouds of yellow pollen in early summer, they fall away. The green female flowers turn brown as they mature into the iconic cattail. Every tail contains more than 200,000 tightly packed seeds, each with a tuft of fluff. If you pull a mature cattail apart, it will expand into huge mounds of fluffy seeds.

Breathing Underwater

While many plants are concerned with getting enough water, cattails face the challenge of getting enough oxygen. Most of the time, their rhizomes grow underwater in low-oxygen soils. Cattail leaves and stems have large, hollow cells that create passageways to their rhizomes. They allow the rhizomes to "breathe" by exchanging gases through the parts of the

> You can boil young cattail flower stalks and eat them like corn on the cob. They are reported to taste like artichokes.

plant growing above water. If you break a leaf or stalk, you can see the cells that make up a cattail's "scuba gear." Unfortunately, it won't help you escape from a deserted island.

How to Spot Them

Look for cattails growing around ponds, wetlands, slow-moving rivers, and sloughs. They are abundant in the marshes around Great Salt Lake. The Great Salt Lake Shorelands Preserve and the Eccles Wildlife Education Center at Farmington Bay are excellent places to see cattails and explore wetland ecosystems.

Chicory

Cichorium intybus

Chicory blooms in refreshingly cool colors on warm summer days. Its flowers, usually sky blue and lavender, can surprise you in colors of brilliant blue, white, and, rarely, pale pink. Each individual flower head blooms for less than a day. On particularly hot days, flowers may give up before noon. Since each flower is open so briefly, chicory plants make a lot of them. If you look at its branching stems, you'll see that they are covered in buds waiting for their day in the sun with pollinators.

Ragged Sailors

Each petal on a chicory flower head is actually a separate ray flower. The five teeth on their blunt petal tips give the flowers a ragged edge, like someone carefully trimmed their circumference with tiny pinking shears. One of chicory's common names, ragged sailor, is

a delightful allusion to both the fringe and the color of its flowers.

During its first year, you might mistake chicory's low ring of toothy leaves for a large specimen of its close cousin, the common dandelion *(Taraxacum officinale)*. But the long, thin stems that rise from the ring in the plant's second year (and every year afterward) definitely don't belong to a dandelion. Climbing up to six feet tall, these gangly stems are sparsely covered with small leaves that lack the dandelion teeth of the plant's lower leaves.

Gourmet Greens and Bitter Beverages

You may have eaten the leaves of domesticated chicory in a fancy salad. Radicchio, Belgian endive, and wild chicory are all different

Gangly, branching stems

Many buds ready to bloom

Toothed petal tips
on blue flowers

variations of the same species. You can eat the leaves of wild chicory too. Very young leaves are similar to dandelion greens and make a tasty addition to a salad. Older leaves are better cooked, as they can be intensely bitter.

Perhaps you've consumed chicory as a beverage. Its roasted roots have been ground to make a coffee substitute since the late 1700s whenever coffee was difficult to obtain as a result of military conflicts and economic downturns. The residents of New Orleans took to drinking chicory to satisfy their coffee craving when the Union navy blockaded the city during the Civil War. It's still popular in several iconic New Orleans beverages today. Drinking chicory coffee, however, won't give you a caffeinated energy boost.

How to Spot Them

Chicory seems to love growing on roadsides, but really any disturbed area with enough sun and well-drained soil will do. You can spot them along trails, in meadows, and occasionally in neighborhood parking strips. Along

Chicory root is grown today for its inulin, which is used to increase fiber content and cut back on sugar and fats in processed foods. Chicory inulin also adds creaminess to low-fat ice cream.

the Wasatch Front, chicory usually starts blooming in June, gains momentum through the late summer, and continues flowering into October. Look for the white variety in City Creek Canyon.

Common Dandelion

Taraxacum officinale

Do you make a wish when you blow on a puffy dandelion and watch its seeds float away on the wind? There are hundreds of tiny parachuted seeds on a single dandelion, and each is an engineering marvel. The filaments in the fluffy parachute create a vortex that's more effective in preventing the seed's descent than a solid parachute. Dandelion seeds hold the world record for long-distance plant seed travel, with some traveling more than fifty miles.

Dandelions are ubiquitous—in part because of their abundant seeds—and instantly recognizable. Their English name comes from *dent de leon*, French for "lion's tooth," and refers to the uneven, toothy serrations on their leaves. The shiny leaves attach at the bottom of the plant, forming a ring around a hollow stem. A bright yellow flower head sits atop the stem, like a lollipop of sunshine. Though it looks like one bloom, it's actually a cluster of many tiny ray flowers.

Long, hollow stem releases milky substance when cut

Bright yellow flower head

Toothy serrations on leaves

Valuable, Delicious, and Beautiful

Our relationship with dandelions is ancient. For millennia, people in Europe and Asia valued dandelions for their many medicinal properties and as a delectable, highly nutritious food source. European settlers brought them to North America as early as the 1600s.

Every part of a dandelion is edible. The leaves make a delicious bitter salad green. The root can be roasted or ground up and used as a coffee substitute. The flowers are tasty when fresh and heavenly when battered and fried. Dandelions are still grown as a food crop today. Look for dandelion greens being sold at farmers markets and gourmet grocery stores.

With the rise of manicured lawns, dandelions were demoted to despised "weeds." Their decline in status is purely a cultural preference. People once found them beautiful. In Europe, they were a beloved garden flower and the subject of many poems. An early guidebook to New York City's Central Park gushed about how dandelions made the lawns look like a green lake reflecting a starry sky.

Multiple Backyard Benefits

Dandelions can actually play a beneficial role in backyard ecosystems. Their long, strong taproots break up compacted soil and bring nutrients to the surface for other plants to use. They're also good for pollinators, especially in early spring when there's not much else blooming.

Because adults don't care how many backyard dandelions kids pick, children often have a close relationship with these plants. A rich child-lore of songs, games, and superstitions has sprouted up around dandelions, from stringing dandelions into necklaces and crowns, to popping off dandelion heads, to blowing on the dry seed heads and making lots of wishes.

Dandelion leaves have long been used as a diuretic. They're quite effective. One of their French names, *pissenlit*, means "pee the bed."

How to Spot Them

Dandelions prefer disturbed areas such as lawns and empty lots, and they also grow along trails. In early spring, look for their characteristic toothy leaves popping up from the ground. (This is when the leaves are least bitter for eating.) They flower in March and start to set seed soon after. Their rapid lifecycle means that you can find dandelion flowers and seed heads most of the year.

Common Reed

Phragmites australis

In Utah, the common reed is better known by its genus name, *Phragmites*. This plant isn't a reed anyway, but rather a very tall grass. It's from the same family (Poaceae) as the Kentucky bluegrass (*Poa pratensis*) growing in a lawn near you, but its stiff, hollow stems are often more than twelve feet tall.

Phragmites have long, pointed leaves that grow directly out of the stems, alternating sides as they climb. In late summer, drooping plumes of purple flowers appear at the top of the stems. They turn golden when long, silky hairs appear to help disperse the plant's seed. The fluffy seed heads look a bit like ostrich feathers. They remain as the stems dry to golden yellow in the fall and often persist until the next spring.

Golden, feathery seed head

Tall, hollow stem

Long, flat leaves with pointed tips

One Key Difference

Several subspecies of *Phragmites australis* live in North American wetlands. Most have been here a long time, but one arrived more recently from Eurasia. The different subspecies are very similar in appearance and are difficult to tell apart. One way they clearly differ, however, is that the Eurasian subspecies grows in large, very dense stands—so dense that duck hunters get lost in them and other wetland plants can't grow in them.

When Great Salt Lake flooded in the 1980s, its wetlands filled with super-salty water that most plants can't tolerate. The open, sunny mudflats left behind when the floods receded were perfect for the Eurasian phragmites. Its presence in Utah was first documented in 1993. Soon land managers began to worry that the spread of this subspecies would reduce the diversity of the wetland habitats that millions of migratory birds depend on at Great Salt Lake.

Changing Wetland Habitats

Studies of wetlands in other states suggest that large, dense stands of Eurasian phragmites deprive some marsh birds, including rails and bitterns, of nesting areas. They can also take over mudflats and fill in areas of open water that other wetland birds require. But some birds happily make their homes in phragmites—just ask a red-winged blackbird or a marsh wren.

Utah spends hundreds of thousands of dollars each year removing phragmites around Great Salt Lake to maintain the wetland habitats needed by a variety of marsh birds. Because eradicating the plants is impossible at this point, land managers must strategically choose sites to treat. Without monitoring and maintenance, the phragmites will return.

In different environmental contexts, land managers value phragmites for the ecological services it provides. Its ability to soak up excess nutrients and heavy metals makes it useful for cleaning up agricultural and industrial wastewater in Europe, where declining populations of phragmites are cause for alarm. In Louisiana, land managers are considering planting Eurasian phragmites to stem a crisis in coastal erosion.

How to Spot Them

Phragmites is very common along the Wasatch Front. Look for it in wetlands, around ponds, along rivers (especially the Jordan), and near Utah Lake. Their tall stems stand throughout the winter, so you can see them year-round.

> People around the world have made lots of useful things from phragmites, including arrow shafts, flutes, woven mats, pipe stems, thatched huts, hats, baskets, and dinner.

Common Sunflower

Helianthus annuus

Yellow ray flowers

Brown disk flowers

Multiple flower heads and stalks

Wavy, heart-shaped leaves

Friendly yellow sunflowers line roadsides across the Wasatch Front in late summer. You can even spot them growing along the concrete medians of Interstate 15, which is a pretty tough place to survive. But sunflowers have lived in rougher places. Because they can pull heavy metals out of the soil and store them in their tissues, they are planted on contaminated industrial sites as clean-up crews. Fields of sunflowers even harvested radioactive metals from soil around Chernobyl after the 1986 nuclear disaster.

Invisible Bullseye

A sunflower's daisylike flower head is made up of hundreds of tiny flowers. What look like yellow petals are many individual ray flowers. Their job is to attract pollinators to the tiny, seed-producing disk flowers in the center. When insects look at a sunflower, they see a dark bullseye pattern around the central disk advertising delicious, free nectar. This target pattern, created by pigments at the base of the ray flowers, is invisible to us because we can't see ultraviolet light.

Each disk flower in the center is a little tube that opens into five petals. These tiny flowers are arranged in interconnecting spirals that are not only mesmerizing, but mathematically precise. Each disk flower is oriented exactly 137.5 degrees from the last—the famous golden angle of geometry—which enables the sunflower to pack the most seeds possible into its flower head.

A Blooming Compass

To attract the most pollinators, mature sunflowers face east to capture the warmth of the morning sun. You can use a mature sunflower as a compass if you happen to be lost. Sunflower buds, however, behave differently. They follow the sun across the sky from east to west each day, turning back to the east overnight. So if your sunflower compass is still a bud, you'll have to take the time of day into account to figure out what direction it's pointing.

Sunflower flower heads grow atop tall stalks covered with little white hairs. Unlike modern domesticated sunflowers, the wild versions have multiple stalks and multiple flower heads. They can grow to more than nine feet tall in a single summer. Wavy, heart-shaped leaves droop from the stalks on long stems. Tiny hairs give the leaves a sandpapery feel—a rough texture for a tough plant.

How to Spot Them

Look for sunflowers in sunny locations with disturbed soils. They are common in open spaces, in vacant lots, in the foothills, along roads and trails, and even in parking strips. They bloom from late June through October but are at peak flower power in August and September.

Indigenous peoples in North America domesticated the common sunflower about 4000 years ago. Across the continent, Indigenous peoples either grew sunflowers or harvested nutritious seeds from the wild versions.

Creeping Woodsorrel

Oxalis corniculata

Small and demure, creeping woodsorrel grows low to the ground, spreading horizontally via underground runners. Its leaves are composed of three charming, heart-shaped leaflets, each with a crease down its center. They can be bright green, deep purple, or a blend of both colors. At night, the leaflets fold down along their crease and "reawaken" in the morning. Maybe that's why one of this plant's common names is sleeping beauty.

Because its leaves look like shamrocks, some people mistake creeping woodsorrel for clover (*Trifolium* spp.). None of the common clovers on the Wasatch Front, however, have heart-shaped leaflets. When the plants are in bloom, it's easy to tell them apart. Creeping woodsorrel has bright yellow flowers with five petals, while our local clovers have round heads of many tiny flowers in white, pink, or purple.

A Tangy Treat

You can eat creeping woodsorrel leaves, stems, and flowers either raw or cooked. Both the plant's common name, sorrel, and its genus name, *Oxalis*, mean "sour"—which is just how it tastes. Woodsorrel's pleasant lemony flavor makes it a refreshing snack on its own and adds a nice tang to a salad. Its bright colors make a lovely garnish on a plate.

As with any plant you gather for food, make sure your woodsorrel is free of pesticides and herbicides. And don't go on an all-woodsorrel diet. It contains oxalic acid, which can bind to calcium in your body and cause a variety of problems if you eat too much of it. If you're susceptible to kidney stones, avoid plants containing oxalic acid.

Bright yellow flowers
with five petals

Leaves can be bright green,
deep purple, or a blend

Leaves made of three
heart-shaped leaflets

Thanks for the Ride!

Creeping woodsorrel is common across the globe today. Its exploding seed capsules, sticky seeds, and long flowering period make it a very successful colonizer. In modern times, it has spread through the horticultural trade as a stowaway in potted plants.

Because creeping woodsorrel is so ubiquitous, its origins were lost to history and a subject of debate until 2019. Using museum specimens, historic literature, archaeological records, and the plant's use in traditional medicine, researchers identified Asia as its original home.

How to Spot Them

Look for creeping woodsorrel growing low to the ground in lawns, gardens, rock walls, crevices in cement, and other disturbed areas. It likes moderately moist soil, so it is very common in gardens and wherever irrigation reaches. You can find it sprouting in early March. Watch for flowers from late spring through early fall.

Creeping woodsorrel can make a good garden ground cover. It holds moisture in the soil, and its flowers provide nectar for bees and small butterflies—plus, you can harvest and eat it if it gets too thick.

Crossflower

Chorispora tenella

Crossflower's name perfectly describes its four pink or purple petals that grow in the shape of a cross. The only problem with this common name is that almost every other member of the mustard family also bears four-petaled flowers in the shape of a cross. Most wild mustards, however, have tiny white or yellow flowers, so crossflower's pink, half-inch-diameter flowers stand out among its kin. The slender petals with crinkly edges contribute to the flowers' showier-than-your-typical-mustard feel.

Self-Slicing Seedpods

Crossflower has distinctive seedpods too. Long and slightly curved, they attach directly to the plant's stem. As seedpods replace its flowers, the plant begins to look like a many-pronged hat rack. Most long, narrow seedpods break open lengthwise, like pea-pods; crossflower pods, however, split into horizontal sections—like slices of bread—that contain one seed each. This unusual trait is the source of the plant's genus name, *Chorispora*, which means "separate seed" in Latin.

These plants can also have a distinctive odor, which is why they are sometimes called musk mustard. Some people describe the smell as resembling melted crayons or a wet dishrag. Others don't notice a strong scent at all.

A Variety of Spicy Leaves

Crossflower leaves embrace variety. Even on the same plant, the leaves can be long with rounded tips or more egg-shaped. The edges can have deep lobes, shallow lobes, or no lobes at all. They are usually a bit wavy and sprinkled with small hairs. One thing all crossflower leaves share is their deliciousness.

Urban foragers rave about their flavor—earthy, like mushrooms, with a hint of spicy radish kick—and recommend the plants to beginning foragers. If you decide to try some, snip off the top four to six inches of the plant,

Cross-shaped pink flowers

Slender, curving seedpods

Wavy petals

Blue mustard is a very common, but potentially confusing, name for crossflower. Along the Wasatch Front, its flowers are definitely pink or purple, not blue.

flowers and all. Make sure the plants are free of herbicides and pesticides.

Utah is at the heart of the crossflower's North American range. It was first collected in Colorado in 1916, where it likely arrived as a stowaway in a shipment of grain from Eastern Europe or Western Asia. It thrives in full sun and dry soils, so it easily adapted to its new home in the Intermountain West.

How to Spot Them

Crossflower overwinters as a low ring of leaves so it can get a jump start on spring. Look for its pink flowers from March through May along the Wasatch Front. It likes sunny, disturbed areas and is common in neighborhood lawns, along trails and roads, and in open spaces.

Curly Dock

Rumex crispus

Curly dock takes its name from the "curly" edges of its leaves. Their wavy margins look a bit like a crispy piece of bacon. The plant's species name is also a reference to its leaves—*crispus* means "curled" in Latin. In addition to being wavy, curly dock leaves are large, growing up to a foot long. Each is fairly narrow compared to its length and comes to a pointed tip.

Look for curly dock's leaves growing in a ring low to the ground soon after the snow melts. (These first leaves can be less curly than those that appear later.) In late spring, a stalk bolts from the center of the ring, rising up to four feet tall. It starts off green but soon turns red and usually branches at the top. Wavy leaves climb up the stalk in an alternating pattern, growing smaller as they ascend.

By June, tiny green flowers—often tinged with pink—appear at the top of the stalk. Individually they're rather inconspicuous, but thousands grow together to form large clusters that spiral dramatically around the stalk. In the fall, the flowers transform into three-sided seed capsules. The stalk and its whorls of seeds turn shiny and reddish brown as they dry. They both remain throughout the winter, their deep, rich color adding a striking accent to a snowy landscape.

Spikes of small green flowers, often tinged with pink

Red stalk

Long, pointed, wavy leaves

Curly dock seed capsules have three papery, heart-shaped wings that help them float on the wind or in water. The seed inside can survive in the soil for more than fifty years.

Rhubarb's Cousin

Curly dock is popular with urban foragers because every part of the plant is edible. The first leaves that appear in the spring make a tender, tart salad green. You can peel the stalk and use it like its close relative, rhubarb. The immature seeds can be eaten fresh, while the dry seeds can be ground up, chaff and all, and used like a grain. Curly dock has many medicinal uses too. For example, an iron supplement can be made from its roots, and its leaves can soothe insect bites and nettle stings.

Originally from Europe, curly dock now thrives across the globe in areas with temperate climates. Because its seeds need bare ground to sprout and its seedlings don't compete well with other plants, it tends to grow in places where human activity creates regular disturbances.

How to Spot Them

Look for curly dock in disturbed sites with moderate moisture, such as parks, meadows, and vacant lots and along trails, roads, and creeks. You can see it year-round because of its persistent stalks. Watch for curly dock's first leaves sprouting in early spring and its flowers blooming June through October.

Curlycup Gumweed

Grindelia squarrosa

Five or six rows of tiny hooks at the base of flower heads

Gummy white resin on buds and flower heads

Bright yellow flower heads

Curlycup gumweed is super sticky. Its leaves are dotted with glands that produce a gummy resin that collects in little white pools on its flower buds and young flower heads. It doesn't make sticky resin so it can stick to things, but rather to keep hungry herbivores away. The resin, along with other chemical defenses, tastes terrible to grazing animals. It may also deter crawling insects that want to munch on the plant's leaves and flowers.

Harmless Hooks

The "curly cup" at the base of each flower is easy to recognize. It consists of five or six rows of tiny hooks. Before the flower buds open, they look like pincushions and seem a bit menacing. The spiky hooks are actually bracts, specialized leaves that take different forms on different plant species. Curlycup gumweed's iconic bracts secrete the resin that puddles on buds and young flowers.

Growing up to three feet tall, large plants look shrubby with many stems and flowers. Bright green leaves with short, dull teeth attach directly to the stems. The appearance of curlycup gumweed's bright yellow flowers varies along the Wasatch Front. Sometimes, you'll see just a disc flower about one inch in diameter. Many people think of a disc flower as the "center" of a daisy or sunflower, but it's really many tiny, tubular flowers. The disk flower is usually surrounded by a burst of yellow ray flowers—what we often think of as petals.

Late Bloomers

This plant can tolerate both heat and cold. It starts blooming in midsummer and keeps on flowering through the fall. Along with many other plants in the aster family (Asteraceae), gumweed is able to survive in cold weather because it contains sugars that enable it to withstand much lower temperatures than other plants without freezing.

Historically, Indigenous peoples in North America treated a variety of ailments with curlycup gumweed. In Utah, the Goshute, Shoshone, Paiute, and Ute peoples all used the plant to treat coughs. An 1893 medical journal article recommended a closely related gumweed for treating asthma. Modern herbalists make tea and tinctures from curlycup gumweed flowers to use as an expectorant or to treat dry cough.

How to Spot Them

Look for curlycup gumweed in dry, sunny, disturbed areas. It's common in the foothills

Curlycup gumweed is very drought resistant. Its populations actually tend to increase during droughts as competition from thirstier plants decreases.

and in larger open spaces, but it pops up in neighborhoods too. Watch for flowers from June through October. Dead, dried plants remain upright through the winter until the following spring.

Deadnettles

Henbit Deadnettle

Lamium amplexicaule

Rounded, toothed leaves

Flowers stand vertically at the top of the plant

Leaves grow like collars around the stem

Purple Deadnettle

Lamium purpureum

Green and purple heart-shaped leaves

Leaves overlap

Flowers peek out between leaves

While "deadnettle" sounds like a good name for a dangerous toxin or a heavy metal band, it actually refers to the benign nature of these plants. Their leaves look a bit like the leaves of stinging nettles, but they don't have any stinging hairs, so they are safe, or "dead," nettles. (They're actually members of the mint family.)

The "henbit" part of henbit deadnettle means exactly what it sounds like—chickens

like to eat it. Purple deadnettle takes its name from the purplish leaves that grow at the top of its stalk. You may also hear it called red deadnettle.

Getting an Early Start

Henbit and purple deadnettles share a lot in common. Originally from Europe, they are both early bloomers, emerging in garden beds and at sidewalk edges as soon as the snow melts. They soak up the moisture of spring rain and take advantage of direct sun before other plants can leaf out and shade them. Their early-spring flowers provide food for hungry pollinators. As soon as the weather warms up, they turn yellow, wither, and die.

Both plants are small in stature, from four to twelve inches tall. Their elegant flowers look like tiny orchids. Long, slender tubes in colors from pink to purple have white throats and scalloped lower lips peppered with purple spots. It's worth the effort to kneel down and take a close look.

Circles or Hearts?

The easiest way to tell henbit and purple deadnettles apart is to inspect their leaves. Henbit leaves are rounded with large, rounded teeth. They often grow in pairs of leaves arranged like collars around the stem with large spaces between collars. A cluster of leaves grows at the top of the stem. Flowers emerge nearly vertically from this cluster, like a profusion of antlers.

Purple deadnettle leaves are heart-shaped or triangular. They crowd densely along the

Deadnettles' square stems are a dead giveaway that they're members of the mint family. Though edible, they're a bit boring and grassy compared to other plants in this delicious family.

stem, with each pair of leaves rotating ninety degrees from the pair below or above. The young leaves at the top of the stem have a purple tint but become green as they age. Flowers peek out horizontally between the top few layers of leaves.

How to Spot Them

Look for deadnettles in neighborhoods all along the Wasatch Front in gardens, lawns, cracks at the base of walls, and vacant lots. They prefer disturbed areas with plenty of sun and moisture. They usually flower from March through May, but you may spot a few blooming in the fall when temperatures cool down.

Dwarf Mallow

Malva neglecta

The unassuming dwarf mallow is a cousin of the famous marsh mallow *(Althaea officinalis)*. Ancient Egyptians were the first to boil marsh mallow roots with honey to create a sticky, sweet concoction. The French created puffy marshmallows in the 1800s by whipping dried marsh mallow root with sugar, water, and egg whites. Though the marsh mallow got all the glory, dwarf mallow's roots will work just as well for your confectionary needs.

Dwarf mallow can send its long, sturdy taproot down into compacted urban soils. It thrives in lawns across the Wasatch Front, where it grows in low mats to avoid

lawnmower blades. If a dwarf mallow grows in a spot lawnmowers can't reach, some of its stems may extend upward while others spread along the ground.

Salad Stowaways

Dwarf mallow leaves look crinkly with their wavy shapes and toothed edges. They can have shallow lobes or be nearly round. Like the roots, the leaves are edible, but they're rather bland compared to many other wild urban greens. You may find a few accidental young dwarf mallow leaves in salad mixes from a farmers market or fancy greens from a store.

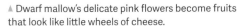

▲ Dwarf mallow's delicate pink flowers become fruits that look like little wheels of cheese.

Go ahead and eat these stowaways—they are super nutritious.

Dwarf mallow's dainty flowers come in white, pink, and pale lavender. Their five petals form a funnel and are often streaked with pink lines. They resemble the flowers of dwarf mallow's cousin—the hibiscus—only much smaller. (You'd need a lot of them to make a lei!)

Cheese Mimicry

The flowers turn into flat, round fruits divided in segments, like tiny wheels of cheese. These fruits are the source of some of dwarf mallow's other common names—cheese mallow and button weed. Some people along the Wasatch Front call them "cheesies." They have a fresh, nutty flavor and are a much healthier snack than marshmallows. If you want to try them,

The leaves and roots of mallow plants contain slimy, gelatinous mucilage similar to that of okra. You can use mallow leaves to thicken a soup or stew. Mallow mucilage has also been used as a medicine for its soothing properties.

pick them when they are green from a location you are sure is free of herbicides and pesticides.

How to Spot Them

Dwarf mallow loves lawns, but you can also find it growing in gardens and other disturbed, sunny areas. They usually start flowering in May and bloom through October. The stems and leaves can remain green through the winter, surviving under a blanket of snow.

Gambel Oak

Quercus gambelii

Leaves have seven to nine curvy lobes

Grows in dense thickets

Often small and shrubby in the foothills

If the Wasatch Front adopted an official tree, it would probably be the Gambel oak. Dense thickets of twisting Gambel oaks flourish in the foothills and lower canyons of the Wasatch and Oquirrh mountains. You can also spot remnant stands of wild trees in yards in many East Bench neighborhoods on the Wasatch Front—a reminder that the lower benches were once covered in these trees.

Rising from the Ashes

Gambel oaks are exquisitely adapted to life in the dry foothills. They like full sun, thrive in rocky soils, and are very drought tolerant. They bounce back quickly after a fire thanks to the ligno-tubers in their root systems, which contain dormant buds and a supply of starch. When the aboveground part of the tree dies, the ligno-tuber leaps into action, sending up many new shoots. Periodic burning actually benefits Gambel oaks, as thickets return larger and denser after a fire.

Wildlife along the Wasatch Front depends on Gambel oaks. Thickets of oak trees provide cover and shelter for a variety of birds and mammals. Mule deer dine on oak leaves in the summer and rely heavily on twigs in the winter when food is scarce. The abundant acorns are a jackpot for birds, including Woodhouse's scrub-jays and black-billed magpies.

Historic Hybrids

The Wasatch Front is home to some unique and famous hybrid oaks, a cross between Gambel oak and Sonoran scrub oak (*Quercus turbinella*). What makes those hybrids so special is that Sonoran scrub oak doesn't grow in northern Utah—at least, not today. Looking at climate records, scientists believe this oak grew along the Wasatch Front in the past. How long ago the hybrids were "born" remains a

The Natural History Museum of Utah helped create a conservation easement to protect an old grove of Gambel oaks with unusually tall trees on the southwest corner of the museum's site.

topic of research, with estimates ranging from 750 to 7500 years ago.

Gambel oaks are easy to recognize. Their leaves have the typical oak shape with seven to nine pairs of curvy lobes. Tree height depends on how much water it gets. In the dry foothills, these oaks may be only six feet tall, but in wet canyon bottoms, they can easily grow to thirty-five feet tall. Though they produce acorns, northern Utah oaks mostly reproduce clonally by sending up shoots from their roots. That's how the stands of hybrid trees have survived for so long.

How to Spot Them

You can't miss Gambel oaks on any walk in the foothills or lower canyons of the Wasatch Front. They also grow in open spaces close to the foothills.

Great Mullein

Verbascum thapsus

When you meet a great mullein, be sure to feel its leaves. The dense covering of tiny hairs on its giant, silver-gray leaves gives them a velvety texture. Several of the plant's common names, such as bunny ears, flannel leaf, and woolly mullein, refer to its luxuriously soft leaves. These leaves have a long history of being used as cozy insulation and padding in clothing and shoes. In a pinch, they make great toilet paper. Keep great mullein in mind the next time there's a toilet paper shortage or you're on a hike without other options.

A Candle of Flowers

In the first year of its life, a great mullein plant grows a ring of large leaves low to the ground. In its second year, it sends up a single leafy stalk that can grow up to three to six feet tall. At the top of the stalk is a dense spike of yellow, five-petaled flowers. They bloom a few at a time throughout the summer, starting at the bottom of the spike and spiraling irregularly to the top. Each individual flower blooms for just one day, opening before dawn and closing by midafternoon.

Great mullein is one the first plants to appear on disturbed sites following a fire or a construction project. It doesn't remain part of the community for long if many other plants move in, because it needs a lot of sun and is easily outcompeted by other species. That's okay with great mullein, though, because it's ready to return after the next disturbance. Each plant produces more than 100,000 tiny seeds that fall near their parent, creating a rich seed bank in the soil. The seeds can remain viable for more than a hundred years.

Embraced in its New Home

Originally from Europe and Asia, great mullein was likely introduced to North America several times as a medicinal herb. In the mid-1700s, Virginians grew great mullein to make a poison from its seeds for killing and harvesting fish. Great mullein spread rapidly and became so

Great mullein has many uses and many colorful common names that describe the plant. The names candlewick, big taper, and our lord's candle all refer to the practice of dipping the mullein's flower stalk in fat and using it as a torch.

Flower spike

Tall, leafy stalk

Large, velvet, silver-gray leaves

▲ Great mullein flowers open first at the base of its flower spike and continue blooming to the top.

well established that a plant book published in 1818 described it as a North American species. Indigenous peoples in North America recognized its many medicinal properties and used the plant to treat a variety of ailments.

How to Spot Them

Look for great mullein in sunny, dry, disturbed areas, such as trails, roadsides, and vacant lots. It's common in the valley, foothills, and canyons of the Wasatch Front. Watch for its ring of leaves growing in early spring. The flowers usually bloom June through September. Even after the plant dies back in winter, you can still see the dried stalks with their brown seed capsules.

Myrtle Spurge

Euphorbia myrsinites

Bright green bracts surround inconspicuous yellow flowers

Bracts fade to pink as weather gets hotter

Long stems grow along the ground

Gray-green triangular leaves

Myrtle spurge is infamous along the Wasatch Front. It was once promoted as an ideal water-wise plant for Utah gardens because it prefers hot, dry sites and is able to grow in poor, rocky soil. These same traits help it thrive in the sunbaked Wasatch foothills.

When myrtle spurge began to grow beyond Salt Lake County gardens and along the benches, alarm spread about the threats it could pose to the environment. Many organizations launched annual "Purge the spurge" weed-pull campaigns, and regular stories appeared in local media warning residents of the "scourge" unleashed in the foothills. The plant's milky sap, which can cause blisters and burns, is often called out as a particular concern—though it would seem to be more of a problem in gardens than in the foothills.

In the Spotlight

The recipient of all this attention is a succulent with blue-green, almost triangular leaves that spiral along its stems. The stems grow to about eighteen inches long, staying low to the ground with just the last few inches turning upward. Clusters of tiny, yellow, star-shaped flowers grow at the ends of the stems. Bright, lime-green bracts—a specialized kind of leaf—surround the inconspicuous flowers. As it gets hotter, some of the bracts take on a pinkish tone.

Myrtle spurge is now very common in disturbed areas along the Wasatch foothills and can grow in great profusion. On steep, rocky, south- and west-facing slopes, it forms dense stands where little else grows. On less exposed sites, it often settles in with a mix of other plants. It doesn't tend to grow in wetter habitats along the Wasatch Front or very far from human activity.

Unclear Impacts

Myrtle spurge has definitely changed the appearance of the Wasatch foothills in places. The significance of its ecological impacts on plant and animal communities is less clear because they haven't been studied yet. They may be difficult to untangle from the broader ecological impacts of human activities and climate change on the Wasatch foothills and canyons. Indeed, they are a reflection of, rather than the driver of, this change.

One question researchers could ask is whether myrtle spurge is providing any services now that it's here. It's possible that its roots are helping prevent erosion on steep slopes. Although mammals can't eat it,

perhaps other species are benefitting from its presence. Many bees and butterflies visit its flowers, and birds are reported to eat its seeds.

A better understanding of myrtle spurge's impacts in different habitats along the Wasatch Front could help guide how we manage it. Efforts to eradicate myrtle spurge are expensive, time-consuming, and, in areas with large populations, probably futile. Given the limited resources we have for managing the dynamic Wasatch foothills, maybe we'll decide that we want to keep myrtle spurge out of some places and let it be in others.

How to Spot Them

Look for myrtle spurge in foothills all along the Wasatch Front and in Lower City Creek, Emigration, and Millcreek canyons. They are most prominent on south- and west-facing slopes that get a lot of sun. They bloom in April and May, but you can see them year-round if they aren't covered in snow.

Prickly Lettuce

Lactuca serriola

Prickly lettuce plants can differ in leaf shape, stem color, and height, but their prickles will always help you identify them. On a mature plant, the prickles are easy to spot. Tiny teeth and short prickles run around the edges of each leaf. If you turn a leaf over, you'll find a neat row of longer prickles marching down its thick, white midrib. A sprinkling of prickles covers the plant's stem, particularly at the base.

Before the prickly lettuce's stem sprouts later in the spring, it's easy to mistake the plant for a common dandelion *(Taraxacum officinale)*. They both grow as a low clump of oblong leaves that ooze milky sap when you break them. Though young prickly lettuce leaves don't have prickles around their edges and lack the deep lobes of older leaves, they still have a distinct prickly midrib on their undersides.

Tiny prickles around leaf edges

Leaves can have deep lobes

Thick, white midrib with prickles

▲ Many of the leaves of mature prickly lettuce plants are oriented perpendicular to the ground—a strategy that helps them avoid losing water in the hot midday sun.

Solar Panels

Prickly lettuce leaves use a nifty trick to help them conserve water in the summer heat. The mature leaves tend to orient themselves north to south and turn on edge, perpendicular to the ground. If you look at the base of the leaves, you can see how they've twisted to achieve this alignment, which gives the plant a somewhat two-dimensional appearance. Growing in this precise way enables the leaves to soak up the eastern morning and western afternoon sun but avoid the baking rays of the midday sun that would dry them out.

In midsummer, clusters of small, yellow flowers appear on branches atop the plant's stem. What look like petals are actually individual ray flowers with five small teeth on their blunt ends. Like the flowers of their dandelion relatives, prickly lettuce flowers turn into seeds with fluffy white plumes that float away on the wind. Mature plants vary widely in size, from one to seven feet tall, depending on growing conditions.

Deprickled Lettuce

Prickly lettuce is the main wild ancestor of domesticated lettuces (*Lactuca sativa*). About 6000 years ago in the Middle East, people began growing prickly lettuce and selecting for plants with bigger leaves, shorter stems, reduced bitterness, and no prickles. Today, scientists are investigating reintroducing some of the prickly lettuce genes lost during domestication to help cultivated lettuces become more resistant to drought and disease. There are no plans to bring back the prickles, however.

How to Spot Them

Prickly lettuce is abundant across the Wasatch Front year-round in yards, parking strips, parks, open spaces, and vacant lots—wherever it can get enough sun and a bit of moisture. Their first small leaves often sprout in the fall and survive through the winter. In spring, they enter their dandelion look-alike phase. Watch for flowers in May through September. The stalks die in the fall, just as the next generation starts growing.

Purslane

Portulaca oleracea

Shiny, green, teardrop-shaped leaves

Red stems

Small yellow flowers with four or five petals

Purslane is a succulent adapted to thrive in areas with high-heat and low-moisture, such as a typical Wasatch Front sidewalk. It forms a low, spreading mat with teardrop-shaped leaves, reddish stems, and yellow flowers. The flowers become small green capsules full of tiny black seeds.

Global Culinary Superstar

People have enjoyed eating purslane for thousands of years. Its delightfully tart flavor adds zing and crunch to dishes of almost any cuisine. It's often used as a pot herb in stews and soups, but it's also enjoyable as a fresh, crisp salad green. Not only is purslane delicious, it's a nutritional powerhouse rich in vitamins and minerals and is perhaps the best plant source of omega-3 fatty acids. Count yourself lucky if purslane grows in your yard for free. If not, you can buy it at specialty stores or farmers markets.

Purslane has a look-alike, spotted spurge (*Euphorbia maculata*), which is bitter and caustic. Pay close attention to the plant you're gathering if you plan to eat it. Purslane leaves are shiny and very plump. Spotted spurge leaves are dull, soft and flimsy to the touch, and they sometimes have a purple spot. They are also much smaller, about a quarter inch long, compared to purslane's half-inch to one-and-a-half inch leaves. Make sure that any plants you collect are free of pesticides and herbicides and give them a hearty rinse before you eat them.

Sharper in the Morning

Purslane tastes slightly different depending on the time of day you collect it. That's because purslane has an adaptation common in desert plants called crassulacean acid metabolism,

Purslane grows all over the world today, but it likely originated in the Middle East. Archaeological evidence suggests it was growing in North America by 1400, but no one knows how it first arrived here.

also known as CAM photosynthesis. Plants with this adaptation keep their leaf pores, or stomata, closed during the day when it's hot and open them only at night to exchange gasses—they essentially hold their breath all day. CAM photosynthesis enables these plants to retain precious moisture during the day and store carbon dioxide as malic acid at night. So if you want more of the sharp taste of malic acid in your purslane, collect it early in the morning.

How to Spot Them

Look for purslane growing in sunny, disturbed spots such as garden beds, sidewalk cracks, and patches of bare soil. It likes warm weather. You can see it from late spring until early autumn, but after the first cold snap, it immediately withers and dies.

Redstem Stork's-Bill

Erodium cicutarium

Redstem stork's-bill takes its name from its long, pointed seed capsules that resemble sharp bird beaks. They grow straight up in the air, often in clusters on larger plants, like a spiky punk hairdo. As cool as the seed capsules look, what the seeds do when the capsules explode is even more amazing.

Exploding Capsules and Crawling Seeds

Each seed capsule is made of five seeds with long tails that are fused together. (The tail is the part that looks like a stork's bill.) As the capsule dries, stress builds inside, because the dried tails want to spiral rather than remain straight. Eventually, the tails spring into a spiral shape, the capsule explodes, and the seeds are flung up to eighteen inches from the plant—which is pretty far for a tiny plant.

Once it hits the ground, a seed "crawls" a short way along the surface until it reaches a crevice and then drills into the soil with the help of its tail. Moisture in the environment causes the tail to straighten out, while drying causes it to twist again. Depending on conditions, the

Small pink flowers with five petals

Long, pointed seed resembles a stork's bill

Feathery, fernlike leaves

tail can curl and uncurl repeatedly. You can find videos of this humidity-powered "drill" online.

In early spring, before its seed capsules appear, look for the plants' small, pink-purple flowers and fernlike leaves. Each leaf is composed of small, deeply lobed leaflets covered with tiny hairs. A new plant starts as a ring of leaves on the ground, and stems grow from there. Some reach upward, but many keep a low profile, creating a dense carpet along the ground.

Redstem stork's-bill is a nutritious part of the diet of threatened Mojave Desert tortoises in southern Utah. It's also good forage for livestock and big game, including pronghorn, mule deer, and elk.

Western Heritage

Redstem stork's-bill may have been one of the first European plants to spread to what is now the western United States. Most botanists believe it arrived with Spaniards in the 1700s as a stowaway in the ballast of ships or in bags of seeds. A few botanists argue that it may have already been growing in California when the Spanish arrived, since adobe bricks from the earliest Spanish missions contain the plant's seeds. Either way, stork's-bill has been flinging seeds around the West for a long time.

How to Spot Them

Once you learn to recognize redstem stork's-bill, you'll see it everywhere along the Wasatch Front—in lawns, sidewalk cracks, gardens, vacant lots, pastures, meadows, and the foothills. It blooms most profusely from March through May, but you can spot a few blossoms year-round if it's not too cold. In the winter, plant leaves may turn red.

Rubber Rabbitbrush

Ericameria nauseosa

Rubber rabbitbrush is glorious in the fall when its brilliant yellow flowers set whole meadows aglow. Navajo weavers preserve some of this ephemeral brilliance by making a yellow dye from the flowers. The tiny, tubular blossoms grow in dense clusters at the ends of the shrub's branches. If you look closely, you'll see that each tube opens into a five-pointed star. The papery texture of the flowers and their long, protruding styles—part of the female pistils—give the flower heads a delicate, wispy appearance.

Sneeze-Free

A late bloomer, rubber rabbitbrush flowers from August through October, and sometimes through November at lower elevations. Some people blame their fall allergies on its profusion of yellow blossoms, but its pollen is too large to float on the wind. It's transported by pollinators instead. Many bees and butterflies take advantage of the plant's largesse at a time when few other plants are in bloom.

This brushy shrub usually grows to two to five feet tall. Its thin, up-sweeping branches bear numerous slender leaves. Both the stems and leaves are covered in soft, feltlike hairs that give the plant a gray-green hue. Stems often have small swellings, or galls, created by insect larvae. The larvae inject the plant with hormones that cause it to grow these small, edible shelters, where the larvae can develop. The gall remains behind once the insect emerges.

A Stretchy Goal

Rubber rabbitbrush has a rubbery latex in its sap. When rubber was in short supply during World War II, scientists investigated the plant as a new source of natural rubber but couldn't determine an efficient way to extract it. In the 1980s, a botanist at Brigham Young University looked into developing a viable extraction process. More recently, researchers at the University of Nevada, Reno, studied whether rabbitbrush could be grown as a commercial crop for rubber and biofuels.

Dense clusters of
tubular yellow flowers

Thin leaves covered
in soft hairs

Thin, whitish branches

How to Spot Them

Look for rubber rabbitbrush in sunny, dry locations. It thrives in the foothills, lower canyons,
many open spaces, around Utah Lake, and
along roads and trails. You may see it planted
in xeriscaped yards because it needs very little
water to survive. Watch for its yellow flowers
starting in August. Dry, puffy seeds remain on
the plant all winter and are popular with birds.

Indigenous people in the West
have used rubber rabbitbrush
for healing medicines and
ceremonies. The plant has the
power to heal landscapes too.
Land managers often plant it
to reclaim mining sites, restore
degraded rangelands, and provide erosion control.

Russian Olive

Elaeagnus angustifolia

▲ Russian olives grow in twisting, crooked shapes and can have multiple trunks. You'll find many birds flitting among the branches of these Russian olives along the Jordan River.

The Russian olive's distinctive leaves—green-gray on top and gray-white underneath—give the tree a silvery look. The tiny star-shaped hairs on each leaf's surface are the source of this silvery effect. New leaves are completely silver because of the dense coating of hairs on both sides. As the hairs on the top surface of a leaf wear away with time, the leaf becomes greener.

Russians olives grow in twisting, crooked shapes and can have multiple trunks. They are not usually big enough to climb, which is probably best since their smooth, reddish brown branches can have large thorns. Small, yellow, intensely fragrant flowers cover the trees starting in May. Later in the summer, they develop small fruits that start off looking like silvery, hairy olives. As they mature, they become brown and shiny.

Rugged Workhorses

First cultivated as an ornamental tree, the Russian olive became popular in the Great Plains and the West for its resilience. Whatever environmental stresses they faced—extreme temperatures, poor soils, high salt levels, varying water levels—the hardy trees endured. In the first half of the twentieth century, many government agencies widely promoted and planted Russian olives for windbreaks, erosion control, and wildlife habitat.

They became common in many Utah cities as an ornamental tree in the early twentieth century, and in the 1930s, they were planted as part of conservation projects. The perception of Russian olives in Utah changed from "useful tools" to "dangerous invaders" when the trees began spreading along river corridors in southern Utah and outcompeting other plants.

Conservation groups now invest significant resources in removing them, but they are extremely difficult to eradicate.

Different Contexts, Different Decisions

The ecological impacts of Russian olives on Utah's river corridors are significant, variable, and complicated, which sometimes makes management decisions difficult. As the authors of one study noted, areas dominated by Russian olives don't support as many different bird species as those with a mix of vegetation, but removing all the Russian olives in these locations would be worse for birds.

Russian olives are very common in open spaces in cities and suburbs along the Wasatch Front. What is the role of wild Russian olives in urban areas? One way to approach this question is to think about all the ecological services they provide to cities, with little or no support from people—shade and cooling, erosion control, slowing stormwater, food and shelter for wildlife, and a shimmer of silvery green.

How to Spot Them

Because they tolerate a wide range of conditions, Russian olives grow in many locations along the Wasatch Front. Look for them in wet areas along rivers and streams or the shores of Utah Lake. They are also common in parks, open spaces, vacant lots, roadsides, and in the foothills. You'll often see many birds flitting among the branches of these trees along the Jordan River.

Smooth, reddish brown branches

Small, fragrant yellow flowers

Silvery green-gray leaves

The fruit of the Russian olive is edible and has a sweet flavor, but it's rather dry and mealy. Although people don't usually find them tasty, more than fifty species of birds and mammals do.

Showy Milkweed

Asclepias speciosa

Showy milkweed definitely lives up to the "showy" part of its name. Standing three to four feet tall, the plant is crowned with baseball-size heads of fragrant pink flowers. Each individual flower is a star within a star. Bunched together on spherical flower heads, they look like exploding fireworks.

A Nectar Quid Pro Quo

Milkweeds have some of the most complex flowers in the plant kingdom. Their dark pink petals bend backward, creating the outer star. The inner pale-pink star is actually the plant's highly modified reproductive parts. Similar to orchids, these structures shape the behaviors of visiting insects. A luscious pool of nectar awaits pollinators at the base of each "arm" of the inner star, but its waxy, slippery surface is hard to grasp. As it struggles to hold on, a pollinator may slip a leg into a special slit that's cleverly designed to attach a pollen sac when the insect pulls its leg out.

   If a pollinator successfully delivers its pollen sac to another milkweed flower, the plant will start forming its iconic fruit. These seed capsules, which resemble bumpy, green squash, grow up to five inches long. In fall and winter, they turn brown and split open to release hundreds of papery brown seeds attached to silky hairs that float away in the wind.

Monarch Mainstay

If you're a monarch butterfly caterpillar, you care most about showy milkweed leaves. Milkweeds are the only plants monarch caterpillars feed on. Their leaves contain toxins that prevent most caterpillars from munching on them, but monarch caterpillars have co-opted this defense system and made it their own. The caterpillars not only tolerate milkweed toxins, but they store the toxins in their own bodies, which makes them—and their future butterfly selves—taste terrible to predators.

Leathery, veiny, gray-green, lance-shaped leaves

Spherical flower heads

Pink, star-shaped flowers

Break a milkweed's leaf in half and watch the "milk" ooze out, but take care not to get this irritating latex sap on your skin. The sap helps seal the plant's wounds, but it also contains toxins that are harmful to the skin.

The decline in milkweed populations as a result of herbicide use in agriculture and habitat loss is one key cause of recent dramatic declines in monarch butterfly populations. Programs nationwide are encouraging people to plant local milkweed species to support monarchs. There are lots of great monarch projects in Utah and many ways to get involved, from planting milkweed in your yard to monitoring butterfly populations.

How to Spot Them

Showy milkweed isn't fussy about where it sprouts as long as it has full sun. It usually grows in colonies and prefers disturbed areas, such as pastures and roadsides. Watch for it on dry slopes in the foothills, along the Jordan River, and in many parks and open spaces. It blooms from May to September. You can see the dead stalks with remnants of seedpods year-round.

Speedwells

Bird's-Eye Speedwell

Veronica persica

Round leaves with many large teeth

One petal is lighter and smaller than the other three

Striped flowers

Ivy-Leaved Speedwell

Veronica hederifolia

Lobed, ivy-shaped leaves

Smaller, often paler flowers

Fringe of delicate hairs on leaves

Tiny speedwell plants with delicate flowers start popping up in lawns, flowerbeds, and sidewalk cracks on sunny days in late winter. They bring a sprinkling of cheerful blue to neighborhoods across the Wasatch Front. At least a dozen different species grow wild in Utah—some local and some introduced. The two you're most likely to meet are bird's-eye and ivy-leaved speedwell, both imports from Eurasia.

These two species can be challenging to tell apart at first, in part because they are so small. To get to know them, you'll need to get down low. Both plants grow close to the ground and spread in loose mats. Sometimes, they even grow tangled together. The key to distinguishing between them is paying attention to their leaves.

Round and Toothy or Lobed and Lashed?

Bird's-eye speedwell's leaves are roundish with many deep, coarse teeth along their edges. Their toothy margins contrast with ivy-leaved speedwell's smooth-edged leaves. As its name advertises, ivy-leaved speedwell's leaves look a bit like lobed ivy leaves. They have one large, rounded lobe in the center with either one or two smaller lobes on each side. Its leaves are a bit plumper than bird's-eye speedwell's and definitely fuzzier. A fringe of delicate hairs surrounds each leaf, like eyelashes.

There are also subtle differences between the plants' flowers. Bird's-eye flowers are usually larger, up to a whopping third of an inch across. They range from pale blue to bright

223

blue-violet, fading to white in the center. Fine, dark blue lines radiate out from the middle as if fairies painted pinstripes on each flower. If you look closely, you'll see that one of the four petals is smaller, and sometimes lighter colored, than the other three.

Ivy-leaved flowers are the same general shape but only about an eighth of an inch wide. They tend to be paler, ranging from light blue or purple to white with pastel pinstripes. If you confuse the two species at first, don't worry. Just enjoy their miniature blue beauty.

How to Spot Them

Bird's-eye and ivy-leaved speedwells start flowering in February. You may see them blooming as late as June in moist areas, but they don't tolerate heat very well. Look for them filling in bare spots in lawns and growing anywhere they can find a bit of moisture, such as in gardens and in cracks and crevices at the base of a wall. You can also find them in many parks and open spaces.

Tall Whitetop

Lepidium draba

Like many common plants, tall whitetop has many descriptive common names. The bunches of small white flowers clustered at the top of the plant definitely give it a white top. Each flower has four petals arranged in the shape of a cross. This distinctive flower shape is a hallmark of plants in the mustard family (Brassicaceae). If you see other plants with cross-shaped flowers, you can be pretty sure you've found one of the more than 4000 species of mustards.

A Tasty Defense System

Tall whitetop is sometimes called a pepperweed—the common name for plants in the genus *Lepidium*. Like most mustards, they have a pungent, peppery taste thanks to chemical compounds called glucosinolates. If you enjoy the sinus-clearing properties of horseradish or the bitterness of Brussels sprouts, thank glucosinolates. Mustards didn't evolve these compounds to please our

Clusters of white, four-petaled flowers

Often grows in dense stands

Leaves clasp directly to stem

palettes, but rather as a natural insecticide. Whitetop's young, tender leaves and prebloom flower heads resembling broccoli (another mustard) are edible and taste quite spicy.

Another common name for pepperweed is hoary cress. "Hoary," an old-fashioned word for something gone gray or white with age, refers to the gray-green cast of the plant's leaves. A sprinkling of tiny white hairs gives them a soft appearance. The leaves are oblong with pointed tips and often have wavy edges. They clasp directly to the plant's stem on alternating sides as they ascend.

A Hearty Plant

The best way to tell different hoary cresses apart is by the shape of their fruit. In fact, it can be difficult to tell what hoary cress you're looking at until its fruit appears. Whitetop is also known as heart-podded hoary cress because its tiny fruits look like upside-down hearts. There are also lens-podded (*Lepidium chalepense*) and globe-podded (*Lepidium appelianum*) hoary cresses, but they aren't common along the Wasatch Front.

Each whitetop plant produces more than 1000 fruits, but they are more likely to spread via rhizomes, which are underground stems. As new plants sprout from the rhizomes, they

Tall whitetop may have first arrived in the eastern United States from Europe as a garden plant. It first showed up in the western United States in the early 1900s as a stowaway in alfalfa seeds from Central Asia.

can form dense stands that shine bright white when they bloom in early spring. Like other mustards, whitetop excels at taking advantage of the disturbed sites human activities create.

How to Spot Them

Look for tall whitetop in sunny, disturbed meadows and vacant lots, along roads and trails, and in yards and parking strips. They thrive with a bit of moisture along streams, but plants can survive in drier locations as well. They bloom in late April through May and then produce heart-shaped fruit.

Yellow Salsify

Tragopogon dubius

Yellow salsify seed heads look like dandelions on steroids. Each individual seed with its feathery parachute is more than an inch long. Together, the seeds form puffy globes that can be four inches across. They practically beg to be waved in the air to send a flurry of fluffy parachutes floating on the wind.

Before they become giant puffballs, salsify flowers look like exploding yellow starbursts. Each petal in the starburst is a separate ray flower, with the outer ray flowers growing much longer than the inner ones. Spiky green bracts extend beyond the longest ray flowers, enhancing the explosion effect.

You can also spot salsify with purple flowers along the Wasatch Front. Though yellow

Many black anthers

Thin, green, leaflike bracts extend beyond the flower head

A starburst of yellow ray flowers

and purple salsify look nearly identical except for flower color, purple salsify is actually a different species, *Tragopogon porrifolius*.

Retiring Early

If you go looking for salsify flowers late in the day, you'll find what look like slender green pods atop its stems instead. Flowers open with the rising sun each morning and close in the early afternoon. This daily schedule earned them one of their many common names—Jack-go-to-bed-at-noon.

Salsify's long, thin leaves look a lot like grass. During its first year, the plant grows only a cluster of leaves, saving up energy in its roots to flower the following summer. In its second year, a branching stalk grows up to three feet tall. Small leaves clasp onto the stalk on alternate sides, and each branch is crowned by a single starburst flower.

Root Vegetable

Originally from Eurasia, salsify probably arrived in the United States as a garden flower in the early 1900s. Its long, fleshy taproot resembles a parsnip and can be eaten raw or cooked. In fact, purple salsify was cultivated in Europe

Salsify's fluffy seed heads remind some people of the silky hair under a goat's chin. Goat's beard is one of the plant's common names and is the meaning of its genus name, *Tragopogon*, in Greek.

and North America for many years as a root vegetable commonly known as oyster root. It occasionally appears on the menus of restaurants that serve local, seasonal foods today.

How to Spot Them

Salsify plants like sun but can tolerate a bit of shade. They are very common in the foothills and along the Jordan River. You can find them in open meadows and vacant lots, along roads and trails, and in the canyons. They start blooming in May and continue through July, though you may spot a few flowers as late as September. Leaves and stems die back with a fall frost.

Yellow Sweetclover

Melilotus officinalis

Bees flock to yellow sweetclover to sip its sweet-scented nectar. Beekeepers in ancient Greece recognized it as a fantastic honey plant—which bees probably already knew—and it's been a favorite of beekeepers ever since. In fact, sweetclover's genus name, *Melilotus*, means "honey lotus" in Greek.

Its bee-attracting flowers grow in loose clusters on spikes branching off long stems. Each small flower has a banner, one petal that stands above the other four grouped together below it in a cup shape. While not a true clover, sweetclover does have clover-like leaves made up of three slender leaflets with toothed

edges. When the plants get tall, their many stems and flower spikes make them seem a bit like lanky teenagers not quite accustomed to their long limbs.

DIY Nitrogen

Sweetclovers perform the nifty trick of fixing nitrogen from the soil—a skill shared by most fellow members of the legume family. With the help of bacteria living in special nodules on their roots, legumes convert nitrogen from the air into a form the plant can use. Because plants need nitrogen to grow, being able to make their own is a huge advantage.

Flowers tend to droop

Many spikes of
yellow flowers

Leaves divided into
three slender leaflets

In the early 1900s, farmers began taking advantage of sweetclover's nitrogen-fixing skills. They planted it in fallow fields as a "green manure" crop. Plowing it under in the fall returned nitrogen and all the other nutrients it had gathered over the summer into the soil. Once widely cultivated, its popularity declined after chemical fertilizers became common in the 1950s.

Healing Habitats

Yellow sweetclover has been a useful tool in habitat restoration projects to stabilize road cuts, help mining sites and fire scars recover, and provide forage for deer, elk, and antelope. It may also benefit wildlife in unexpected ways. A 2008 study in Capitol Reef National Park found many local wild bees foraging yellow sweetclover. Because it flowers in midsummer when other local plants aren't in bloom, sweetclover is likely increasing wild bee populations in the park.

How to Spot Them

Yellow sweetclover is very common beside roads and trails along the Wasatch Front. It doesn't compete well with other plants, so look for it on sunny sites with lots of disturbance. You can spot its yellow flowers from mid-May through October.

Sweetclover flowers can be yellow or white. The two plants are very similar—so similar that scientists have gone back and forth on whether they are the same or separate species. The current thinking is that white sweetclover is its own species, *Melilotus albus*.

NEARBY NATURE FIELD TRIPS

You can find lots of nature in your own neighborhood, but it's also exciting to explore different areas and expand the circle of plants and animals you know. Dozens of places along the Wasatch Front have been set aside as open spaces in or near cities, where you can enjoy time outside and meet new species. The field trips in this guide are just a sampling of the many nearby nature adventures that await you.

Most of these field trips are family-friendly. Almost all start at locations with restrooms, and many offer a park with a playground and picnic pavilion. The trails tend to be paved or packed gravel and not too steep. That said, a few trips may be challenging for young children or kids who haven't hiked much.

A bit of planning and packing will make your adventure more enjoyable. The season and time of day of your journey will impact what wildlife you see. For example, you won't see many animals in the middle of a hot summer day because they'll be taking shelter from the heat. For any adventure, be sure to pack the items you'll need for comfort and safety: water, snacks, sunscreen, a hat, and extra clothes for changing weather conditions.

You don't need a lot of equipment for your adventures. A pair of binoculars will come in handy for spotting birds. Consider downloading free apps, such as iNaturalist or Merlin, which can help you identify species you encounter. Take time to look closely, turn over a few leaves and rocks, or sit quietly and listen. Open eyes and alert ears tuned to the environment around you are the most important tools you can bring along.

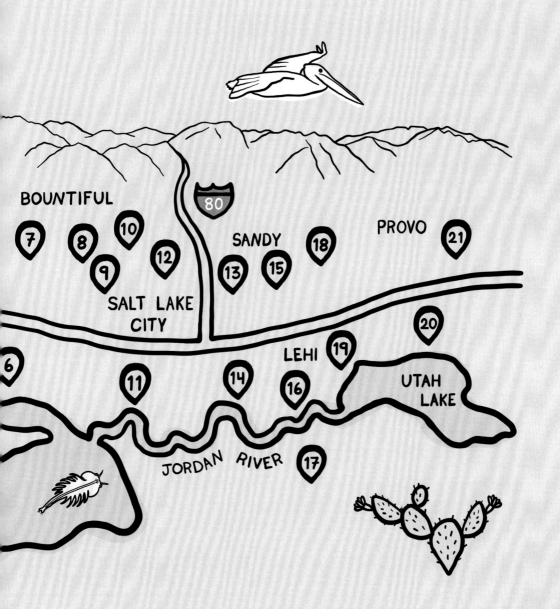

BOUNTIFUL

80

SANDY

PROVO

7

8

10

9

12

13

15

18

21

SALT LAKE
CITY

20

6

LEHI

19

11

14

16

UTAH
LAKE

JORDAN RIVER

17

Ogden River Parkway

A journey along the eastern third of the Ogden
River Parkway path offers a delightful mix of opportunities to explore the
natural world—pedal along the forested path, explore carefully cultivated
gardens, or wade into the river to fish. The entire Ogden River Parkway runs
4.4 miles along the river, from the mouth of Ogden Canyon, through downtown Ogden, to the 21st Street Pond. This broad, paved path is accessible for
strollers and wheelchairs and perfect for a leisurely family bike ride.

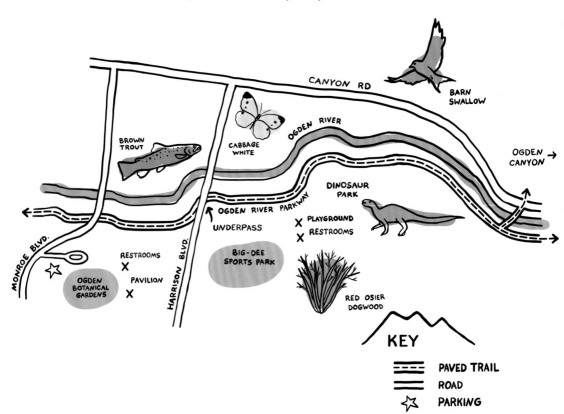

CANYON RD

BARN
SWALLOW

BROWN
TROUT

CABBAGE
WHITE

Ogden River

OGDEN
CANYON →

DINOSAUR
PARK

Ogden River Parkway

← UNDERPASS

X PLAYGROUND
X RESTROOMS

MONROE BLVD.

RESTROOMS
X

PAVILION
X

HARRISON BLVD.

BIG-DEE
SPORTS PARK

OGDEN
BOTANICAL
GARDENS

RED OSIER
DOGWOOD

KEY

≡≡≡ PAVED TRAIL

=== ROAD

☆ PARKING

► Towering cottonwoods line a section of the Ogden River Parkway, casting dappled shade on the cyclists, walkers, and runners who flock to the trail.

◄ The paths of the Ogden Botanical Gardens connect to the Ogden River Parkway.

Garden Paths

Hop on the Ogden River Parkway from the parking lot at Ogden Botanical Gardens. The parkway runs alongside some of the garden's beautiful displays and connects to other paths throughout the garden. You can explore the botanical gardens' paths, park, and pavilion free of charge daily from dawn to dusk—just one of the terrific community amenities along the Ogden River Parkway.

As you follow the path past the botanical gardens, look for a row of trees with plaques on the north side. This is the Powerline Arboretum, an exhibit of trees that are safe to plant under powerlines because they don't grow taller than twenty-five feet. You may recognize some street trees that grow in your neighborhood.

WHERE: Ogden Botanical Gardens, 1750 Monroe Boulevard, Ogden
DIFFICULTY, DISTANCE: Easy. Out-and-back walk of about 3 miles on a paved path. Many options for longer walks.
FACILITIES: Restrooms, playground, picnic pavilions
SPECIAL NOTES: Dogs allowed on leash. Often busy on weekends with both walkers and cyclists.

River Paths

Continuing to the east, the parkway offers views of the Ogden River as it flows through meadows and in and out of a riparian forest. Occasionally, unmaintained dirt paths lead down to the river or parallel the paved parkway. Some of these paths are steep and eroded. Some dead-end in a tangle of brush. But some lead to discoveries, such as a beaver dam, a jumping fish, a quiet pool, or a hidden wildflower. Following any of them will add a sense of adventure to your trip.

Watch for dense stands of coyote willow (*Salix exigua*) along this section of the parkway. It's the most common willow growing at low elevations in Utah, often along rivers or in wet meadows. Because of its slender, pointed leaves, it's also known as narrowleaf willow.

Willow thickets provide valuable food and cover for butterflies, bees, birds, and beavers along the river. In fact, the combination of willows, which serve as host plants for many different caterpillars, and the diversity of flowering plants along the river and in the botanical gardens makes the parkway a great place to look for butterflies.

After about half a mile, where the parkway dips beneath Harrison Boulevard and emerges into Big-Dee Sports Park, look for the mud nests of cliff swallows clinging to the beams of the underpass. You'll see a patch of showy milkweed (more butterfly habitat!) growing along the north side of the path. If you need a restroom or a playground at this point in your walk, you can find both on the east end of the sports park's wide lawn.

▼ Coyote willows, like these near the underpass, grow in sunny spots along the river.

▲ Views to the Wasatch Mountains open as the trail enters Big-Dee Sports Park. The open lawn is a great spot for having a picnic or flying a kite.

◀ Cottonwood leaves glow along the parkway on fall afternoons. Look for narrowleaf, Fremont, and hybrid cotton-woods along the path.

Forest Path

After crossing and quickly recrossing Park Boulevard, the parkway path runs through a dense section of riparian forest shaded by large cottonwoods, box elders, and Siberian elms. Take this opportunity to practice identifying some common Utah trees and shrubs. Look for red osier dogwood (*Cornus sericea*) with its distinctive red branches. Chokecherry (*Prunus virginiana*) sports long clusters of white flowers, followed by red fruits that ripen to dark purple. The narrowleaf cottonwood (*Populus angustifolia*) has long, slender leaves that resemble those of its cousins, the willows, and turn brilliant yellow in the fall.

On the south side of the path, you'll catch a glimpse of something few urban nature walks offer—dinosaurs! The parkway runs behind Ogden's George S. Eccles Dinosaur Park, where sculptures of more than a hundred dinosaurs are spread across the grounds. You can see and hear quite a few of the full-size, realistically painted replicas through the chain-link fence. Paleontology fans will enjoy identifying them.

Connected Paths

After emerging from behind the dinosaur park, the parkway continues another third of a mile next to Park Boulevard before reaching the junction with Ogden Canyon and Valley Drive. The section of river near the footbridge just before the junction is a popular fishing spot, but it's not the only one. A restoration project completed in 2012 transformed a neglected, debris-filled section of Ogden River west of downtown into a Utah Blue Ribbon fishery known for its brown and cutthroat trout.

The junction is a good turnaround point, but you'll have plenty of other options if you're looking for a longer walk. Weber County's extensive trail system connects urban areas with the surrounding foothills and canyons. Cross the footbridge to connect to the Canyon Trailhead or cross Valley Drive to the south to access the Birdsong and Rainbow trails. If you're ready to head home, you can save these trails for another day.

▲ There are several popular fishing spots on the Ogden River as it flows through the city, along with many places to wade.

TRIP 2
Gib's Loop

WHERE: 29th Street Trailhead, 29th Street and Buchanan Avenue, Ogden
DIFFICULTY, DISTANCE: Moderate. A 3-mile loop on well-maintained dirt trails and city streets. Many options to connect with other trails.
FACILITIES: Restrooms
SPECIAL NOTES: Dogs must be leashed. Can be muddy in the spring. Bring plenty of water in the summer.

Gib's Loop has an "edgy" feel. The first half of the loop is in the foothills along the edge of the Mount Ogden Golf Course. As it loops back north, the trail forms the boundary between the golf course and neighborhood backyards. It's an enjoyable walk any time of year. The trail has quite a bit of shade on summer days and the added bonus of Strong's Creek—a lovely spot to cool your feet. In the winter, the western exposure and bare trees allow the sun to warm you.

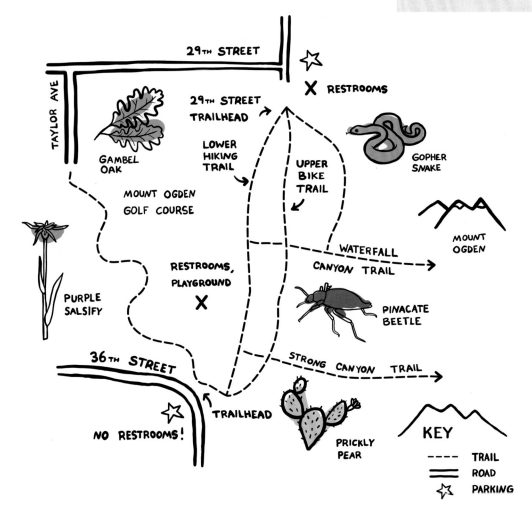

29TH STREET

TAYLOR AVE

RESTROOMS

29TH STREET TRAILHEAD

GAMBEL OAK

LOWER HIKING TRAIL

GOPHER SNAKE

MOUNT OGDEN GOLF COURSE

UPPER BIKE TRAIL

MOUNT OGDEN

PURPLE SALSIFY

RESTROOMS, PLAYGROUND

WATERFALL CANYON TRAIL

PINACATE BEETLE

36TH STREET

STRONG CANYON TRAIL

TRAILHEAD

NO RESTROOMS!

PRICKLY PEAR

KEY

- - - - TRAIL
===== ROAD
☆ PARKING

Away from the Crowds

Don't be discouraged if you see lots of cars at the 29th Street Trailhead parking lot when you arrive. Most hikers will be headed to the popular Waterfall Canyon Trail. After you pass through the small trailhead pavilion, look for a wooden post with signage for Gib's Loop. (There is a separate Gib's Loop trail for bikes.) From here, you'll be traveling on a different trail than the Waterfall Canyon crowd. Similar signposts will help you stay on the trail at junctions along the way.

▲ Gib's Loop follows the edge of the Mount Ogden Golf Course, where breaks in the forest of Gambel oaks offer both mountain and valley views

◄ The first section of Gib's Loop passes through open meadows.

► Listen for spotted towhees doing a two-footed, backwards hop to turn over leaf litter under the Gambel oaks along the trail.

The trail begins by passing through a sunny meadow inhabited by common foothill residents, including big sagebrush, rubber rabbitbrush, yellow salsify, and evening primrose. Cottonwood trees grow in a small ravine that parallels the trail. (The bike path runs along the bottom of the ravine.) After about a quarter mile, the edge of the golf course comes into view and the trail enters a forest of tall Gambel oaks.

Deceptive Borders

Walking along Gib's Loop at the edge of the golf course, the boundaries between the city and the foothills seem sharp. The green lawn of the golf course ends and the Gambel oaks begin. This is a common experience along the Wasatch Front, where changes in ownership—such as where U.S. Forest Service lands meet neighborhoods—create abrupt changes in land use.

Human impacts in the foothills, however, don't end at backyard fences, and many animals use resources in both habitats. It's more interesting to think of cities and the surrounding foothills as parts of an interconnected system rather than separate and distinct.

Spotted towhees (*Pipilo maculatus*) are a good example of an animal that moves between the valleys and the foothills of the Wasatch Front. You might hear a spotted towhee scratching in the leaf litter in search of seeds or bugs along the trail. Because they feed on the ground, towhees spend their winters on the valley floors where there is less snow. However, many prefer to nest at a bit higher elevation in the foothills. Mule deer also make seasonal migrations that connect the valleys with the foothills, canyons, and mountains.

Cold-Weather Cacti

After another quarter mile, the trail makes a small switchback and then merges briefly with the paved path through the golf course. Look for patches of plains prickly pear (*Opuntia polyacantha*) in the open, drier terrain here. We usually think of cacti as desert dwellers, but you'll find plains prickly pear throughout Utah and the western United States. Not only are they adapted to hot, arid conditions, but they are also incredibly cold tolerant, surviving at temperatures below –30 degrees Fahrenheit in northern Canada.

The trail ducks back into the oaks before arriving at Strong's Creek. In another third of a mile, the trail reaches the 36th Street Trailhead. Sometimes gopher snakes hang out along this section of the trail. Look for a patch of purple salsify on the zig-zag down to the small parking area. From here, you have lots of options: You can go back the way you came for a round trip of 2.6 miles. You can go back to Strong's Creek or another junction and explore other trails. Or you can complete Gib's Loop.

The second half of Gib's Loop follows a small dirt road heading north from the 36th Street Trailhead. You'll pass along backyard fences on your left and follow the curve of the golf course on your right, though it's hidden behind trees. Look for Strong's Creek again as it flows into a small retention pond before spilling down into the neighborhood. The trail narrows from a road to a path as it enters the oaks again before arriving at Marquardt Park. The last mile back to the trailhead is along Taylor Street and 29th Street. Enjoy a walk through Mount Ogden Park along the way.

⬆ An engraved bench provides both helpful signage and a lovely place to rest on the bridge over Strong's Creek.

⬇ Take your pick—from Gib's Loop you can connect to a variety of other foothill trails.

▲ Plains prickly pears along the trail produce showy, lemon-yellow flowers that contrast with the rather stark, reserved nature of the rest of the plant.

TRIP 3

Beus Pond

WHERE: 4240 Country Hills Drive, Ogden
DIFFICULTY, DISTANCE: Easy. The 0.4-mile flat, paved path loops around the pond. An informal dirt path with steep sections makes a half-mile loop.
FACILITIES: Restrooms. Playground and picnic pavilion at the adjacent park.
SPECIAL NOTES: Dogs must be leashed.

On one hand, Beus Pond is your typical neighborhood duck pond. You'll see a crowd of the regular duck-pond denizens eagerly looking for handouts—mallards, Canada geese, Muscovy ducks, swan geese, and graylag geese. But the pond also often attracts some water-loving birds that are less common in urban areas, plus one that is relatively rare in Utah. With patience, luck, and a pair of binoculars, you can spot some cool birds here. And if you're not a bird person, you'll find plenty of other reasons to visit Beus Pond.

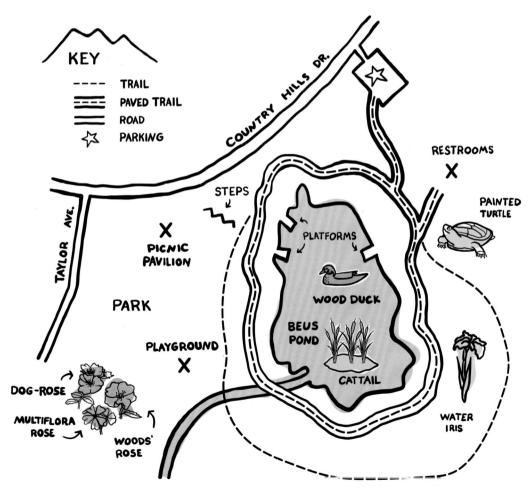

KEY

- - - - TRAIL
═══ PAVED TRAIL
──── ROAD
☆ PARKING

COUNTRY HILLS DR.

TAYLOR AVE.

STEPS

PICNIC PAVILION

PARK

PLAYGROUND

DOG-ROSE

MULTIFLORA ROSE

WOODS' ROSE

PLATFORMS

WOOD DUCK

BEUS POND

CATTAIL

RESTROOMS

PAINTED TURTLE

WATER IRIS

Local Celebrities

Wood ducks *(Aix sponsa)* are the stars of Beus Pond. These stunning birds are common in the eastern United States, but not in Utah. They prefer to live in wetlands bordered by large trees, and we don't have much of this habitat in our state. Wood ducks need trees because they nest in tree cavities. Unlike most waterfowl, they are at home high in the branches. Their webbed feet are tipped with strong claws that help them perch in trees and grip bark.

Wood ducks live at the pond year-round, but the best time to look for them is from fall to early summer when the males are decked out in their spectacular breeding plumage. The males have an iconic iridescent-green head with a crest that swoops to a point behind the neck. Their chests are a radiant chestnut-brown flecked with white.

The elegant females have a warm-brown body and gray-brown head adorned with a crest and a white teardrop shape around the eye. In late summer, the males look similar to the females, but without the teardrop, and their eyes and beaks remain bright red throughout the year. The wood ducks at Beus Pond are fairly accustomed to people, so they may be willing to let you get close to take some good photos.

You may spot lots of other interesting plants and animals while strolling around the pond—perhaps a belted kingfisher, a black-capped night heron, or an American white pelican fishing for dinner. Look for red-eared sliders and painted turtles basking on a log. A bramble of wild blackberries growing near the path at the south end of the pond makes for tasty summer snacking. In the spring, a lovely stand of yellow irises blooms in the water at this end of the pond.

▲ Flotillas of ducks patrol the waters of Beus Pond, which attracts a variety of other water-loving birds too.

► In the fall, fruit capsules filled with shiny seeds that look like little coins droop from the stems of the yellow irises at the edge of the pond.

►► This wood duck couple in the tall trees around Beus Pond could be looking for a nesting cavity.

►► The broad, shady path around Beus Pond is full of charms—little bridges, peaceful benches, and piers that project into the water.

Into the Woods

If you feel like getting off the pavement for a bit of an adventure, take the informal dirt path that starts at the restroom and makes a slightly larger loop around the pond. Be aware that a few steep, eroded spots on the path may be tough for young children or people uncomfortable with a little scrambling. The route can be confusing at the pond's south end, where a variety of paths intersect and diverge, but you can't get seriously lost with the pond visible on one side and backyards on the other. Kids will love the opportunity to explore.

Even though it's only a few yards from the paved path, the dirt path has the feel of a secluded forest. You might startle a mule deer taking cover in groves of Gambel oaks or hear the scolding chitter of a red squirrel. In spring and early summer, the groves are carpeted with bright green undergrowth. Luxuriant fronds of bracken ferns and segmented stems of rough horsetails make the forest feel unusually lush for our dry state.

A Trio of Roses

Following the dirt path around to the west, you parallel a little stream that flows into the pond. An enchanting set of wood-post stepping stones across the stream leads to a playground at the adjacent Forest Green Park. You can also access the playground from a dirt path immediately north of the bridge across the stream on the paved path. As you complete the loop to

the north, you'll pass three different species of rose: dog-rose *(Rosa canina)* and Woods' rose *(Rosa woodsii)* have individual blooms of white and pink, respectively, and the white flowers of the less-common multiflora rose *(Rosa multiflora)* grow in clusters.

You can also enjoy a fascinating bit of history at Beus Pond. The farmhouse of Italian immigrants Michael Beus and Marianne Combe Beus once stood near here. Michael and his son built the dam that created the pond. You can find evidence of Marianne's skill and hard work as well. She planted an acre of mulberry trees, fed their leaves to silkworms, and harvested an impressive amount of silk thread—nearly enough for two dresses. You can still find the occasional mulberry tree growing near the pond today.

▼ Multiflora roses bloom in a tumbling cascade on large, tangled shrubs.

▲ A shady canopy of Gambel oaks and abundant bracken ferns beckon explorers on the dirt path around the pond.

TRIP 4

Kays Creek Parkway

WHERE: Adam J. Welker Trailhead, 2721 North 2125 East, Layton

DIFFICULTY, DISTANCE: Easy. Paved trail is 2.25 miles long and mostly flat with a short, steep climb to the reservoir.

FACILITIES: No restrooms. One picnic table at the far east end of the canyon.

SPECIAL NOTES: Fishing is permitted in the reservoir. Swimming is not. Dogs must be leashed.

FIELD TRIP 4

Kays Creek Parkway runs through a canyon
tucked away in a residential neighborhood on the east side of the city of Layton. Though not very long, the canyon has a lot to offer: open meadows, a forest, wetlands, the tumbling north fork of Kays Creek, and a trout-filled reservoir. The broad, paved path through the canyon is popular with walkers and runners year-round. If you go in the winter, keep an eye out for ice in shady spots on the trail.

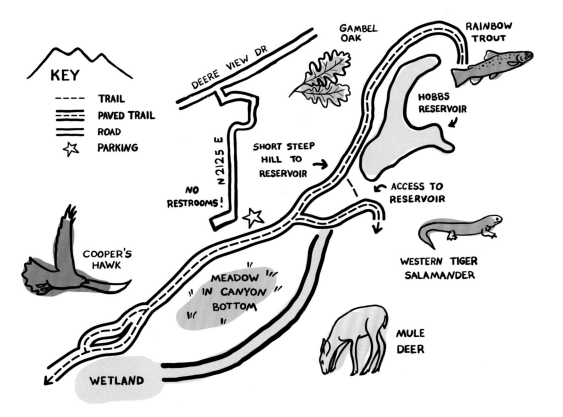

KEY

- - - - TRAIL
≡≡≡≡ PAVED TRAIL
──── ROAD
☆ PARKING

DEERE VIEW DR

GAMBEL OAK

RAINBOW TROUT

HOBBS RESERVOIR

N 2125 E

SHORT STEEP HILL TO RESERVOIR

NO RESTROOMS!

ACCESS TO RESERVOIR

COOPER'S HAWK

WESTERN TIGER SALAMANDER

MEADOW IN CANYON BOTTOM

MULE DEER

WETLAND

The Adam J. Welker Trailhead, located at the end of a curving road that traverses the north side of the canyon, is the best place to access the parkway. The trailhead is roughly in the middle of the 2.25-mile-long path running east to west in the canyon. If you want an easy walk or a warm-up before you climb to the reservoir, start by heading west.

Meadow Meanderings

The canyon is broad and open here. The trail passes through a meadow dotted with groves of cottonwoods and Russian olives. In the summer, it ripples with tall grasses, such as smooth brome and rye. Keep an eye out for curly dock, great mullein, yarrow, and salsify. Mule deer frequent the meadow to feed at dawn and dusk, seeking cover in the trees on the hillsides during the day. Red foxes have also been spotted here. Watch for raptors such as Cooper's hawks circling over the meadow looking for a meal. You won't see much of Kays Creek on this section of the trail; it flows through an eroded channel on the south side of the ravine.

Soon the trail passes through groves of black hawthorns, wild cherry trees, and even a few wild pears entwined with pink Woods' roses and white dog-roses. On summer mornings, watch for birds darting in and out of these tangled trees. The trail then opens to a large wetland filled with phragmites and cattails. After descending slightly 0.7 mile from the parking lot, the trail ends at a street. For a different perspective, walk back toward the trailhead on the path that loops around the south side of the wetland. Enjoy the beautiful views of the Wasatch Mountains as you head east.

To the east of the trailhead, the canyon narrows a bit as you travel through a riparian forest of cottonwood and box elder trees along Kays Creek. Look for stands of tall Gambel oaks growing on the hillside to the north. After 0.3 mile, you'll arrive at a junction near the foot of the earthen Hobbs Reservoir dam. Both paths climb sharply to the reservoir, though the path to the left (north) is shorter and not quite as steep.

▼ Tall cottonwood trees dot the meadow at the trailhead for Kays Creek Parkway.

▲ A black-headed grosbeak perches among the willows on the lower section of Kays Creek, where the canyon's combination of tall trees, rich understory, and easy access to water is ideal grosbeak habitat.

▲ A wetland in the old floodplain of Kays Creek at the west end of the canyon is filled with phragmites and cattails.

◀ Hobbs Reservoir offers fishing, kayaking, and a wonderful place to spend a languid summer afternoon.

Cast a Line

Hobbs Reservoir is surrounded by a chain-link fence, but you can enter through openings on both sides near the dam. The Kays Creek Irrigation Company completed the dam in 1920 to provide water for local farmers and still owns and operates the site today. Thanks to a collaboration between the irrigation company, Layton City, and the Utah Division of Wildlife Resources (DWR), the reservoir is open to the public as a community fishery.

The reservoir is sufficiently deep and shaded to support cold-water-loving trout. DWR stocks it regularly and requires that anglers throw back all fish larger than fifteen inches, creating an opportunity for more people to catch large rainbow and cutthroat trout—in a suburban neighborhood! Green sunfish and bluegill also swim in the reservoir. Fishing requires a free "Walk-in Access" permit, which you can obtain by scanning the QR code on the sign posted on the fence. If you decide to cast a line, follow all the posted regulations, especially "No bait fishing."

▶ Rainbow trout are regularly stocked at Hobbs Reservoir. One could end up in your net.

◄ The paved path around the reservoir offers plenty of shade and opportunities to practice your plant identification skills with the iNaturalist app.

More Water Lovers

Fish aren't the only animals that call the reservoir home. Look for bullfrogs basking in shallow water along the shore during the summer and fall. Western terrestrial garter snakes—which love to swim—also hang out near the reservoir. You might spot a barred tiger salamander near the water's edge or under nearby logs and rocks, though they're mostly nocturnal as adults.

The paved trail continues another mile along the north side of the reservoir through a shady forest of box elders, Russian olives, and Gambel oaks. Wild cherries lining parts of the path create a bower of pale blossoms in the early spring. At the east end of the canyon, the trail crosses a small footbridge over Kays Creek before turning west again. Shortly thereafter, it dead-ends rather abruptly.

From the trail's end, you can enjoy the walk back to the trailhead, or, if you're feeling adventurous, take a dirt path leading back to the dam along the south side of the reservoir. The dirt path begins at a set of steps headed downhill into the canyon. It's steep in spots and has some drop-offs, so it may not be suitable for young children. Winding through the forest, the path has the feel of a hike in a mountain canyon and offers great views of the reservoir.

TRIP 5

Great Salt Lake Shorelands Preserve

Venturing into the heart of Great Salt Lake's wetlands would usually require rubber boots and possibly a machete. The boardwalk at the Great Salt Lake Shorelands Preserve lets you explore the wonders of the marsh, surrounded by cattails, ponds, and mudflats—all while keeping your feet dry. Beautiful interpretive signs along the boardwalk describe the plants and animals you may see and hear on your visit. You can also listen to stories about the preserve on a free audio guide by scanning the QR code on the sign at the trailhead.

WHERE: 1002 South 3200 West, Layton
DIFFICULTY, DISTANCE: Easy. The mile-long boardwalk loop in the wetlands is wheelchair accessible and stroller friendly.
FACILITIES: Restrooms, interpretive exhibits
SPECIAL NOTES: Bring binoculars if you have them. In the summer, bring water and perhaps mosquito repellant. No dogs or bikes allowed.

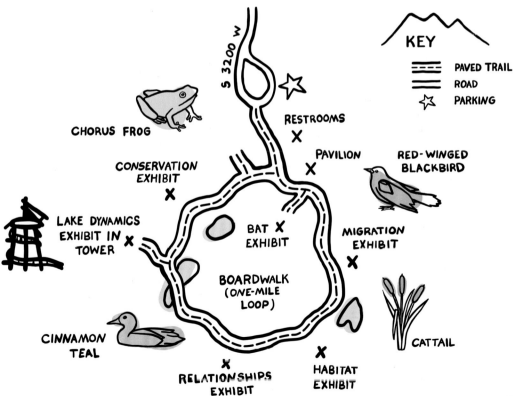

S 3200 W

KEY
=== PAVED TRAIL
=== ROAD
☆ PARKING

CHORUS FROG

RESTROOMS
✕

PAVILION
✕

RED-WINGED
BLACKBIRD

CONSERVATION
EXHIBIT
✕

LAKE DYNAMICS
EXHIBIT IN ✕
TOWER

BAT ✕
EXHIBIT

MIGRATION
EXHIBIT
✕

BOARDWALK
(ONE-MILE
LOOP)

CINNAMON
TEAL

CATTAIL

RELATIONSHIPS
EXHIBIT
✕

HABITAT
EXHIBIT
✕

Spanning 4400 acres, the preserve is protected and owned by The Nature Conservancy. You won't see Great Salt Lake from the boardwalk, but its waters help sustain the preserve's unique system of saltwater and freshwater marshes. The lake and its habitats support about ten million migratory shorebirds and waterfowl each year. A vital sanctuary along the lake's eastern shore, the wetlands and uplands of this preserve draw more than 250 different bird species to nest, rest, or feed.

Inspired Design

From the parking lot, the boardwalk crosses over a small pond on its way to a graceful open-air pavilion. (Listen for chorus frogs calling from the pond in the spring!) Take a moment to explore the exhibits in the pavilion and enjoy its unique architecture. The pavilion, boardwalk, and viewing tower are all made of wood recycled from the twelve-mile-long Lucin Cutoff railroad trestle that crossed Great Salt Lake from 1904 until the late 1950s. The swooping canvas sails that shade the pavilion were designed to resemble bird wings.

◄ The boardwalk at the Great Salt Lake Shorelands Preserve winds through a sea of cattails and a variety of wetland habitats.

▶ The shade pavilion's materials and distinctive design were selected to complement its beautiful setting.

You can begin a one-mile loop on the boardwalk going either east or west from the pavilion, but heading east will save the viewing tower as a treat for the second half of the walk. As you leave the pavilion, look for plaques embedded in the boardwalk that give you a glimpse into the remarkable journeys made by the migratory birds that travel here. Some fly up to 5000 miles each year, connecting habitats across the hemisphere.

Wings over the Wetland

On the first spur of the boardwalk you'll find an exhibit about another flying creature—the bat. The Great Salt Lake Shorelands Preserve provides key habitat for bats along the Wasatch Front, especially a colony of Mexican free-tailed bats. The colony's numbers have been dwindling as other wetlands in Davis County are impacted by encroaching development. The bats spend the summer evenings zipping through the marshes, dining on insects.

Although bats may be more challenging to spot, you can easily encounter a wide variety of birds during different seasons at the preserve. Northern harriers *(Circus hudsonius)*—also known as marsh hawks—are common year-round residents of the wetlands. Watch for them gliding low and slow over the marsh with their wings held in a V-shape. Unlike other hawks, harriers both look and listen for their prey—mostly rodents and small birds hidden in dense vegetation. The distinctive large white band across its rump and its owlish face make the northern harrier easy to identify.

Look for migratory cinnamon teals *(Spatula cyanoptera)* nesting along the boardwalk. Males are a rich, rusty brown with red eyes, while females are a more camouflaged mottled brown. Both have surprising powder-blue patches on their shoulders, visible when they take flight. These little ducks startle easily, so if you want to see them, be a quiet observer. They prefer areas with open water, cattails, or hardstem bulrushes at the preserve.

As you make your way around to the viewing tower, keep an eye out for the aerial acrobatics of swallows hunting insects on the wing. Six swallow species use the preserve: barn, bank, northern rough-winged, cliff, violet-green, and tree. Barn swallows build little cup-shaped mud nests on the tower. Sometimes a group of swallows gather in a sociable line on the tower's wire railing.

▼ A northern harrier's dish-shaped face directs the sound of scurrying prey to its ears.

◄ Look for a splash of blue on the shoulders of both female and male cinnamon teals.

Bird's-Eye View

Climb to the top of the tower for a bird's-eye view of the preserve. This is a great spot to take out your binoculars to scan for birds and other wildlife. You can also see how close development is approaching the preserve on the east and how far from the marsh the lake is on the west. Today Great Salt Lake covers only 40 percent of the area and holds less than a third of the water it did historically. Diverting water from rivers that feed the lake for agriculture, lawns, and homes caused this dramatic drop. Groups such as The Nature Conservancy are working to reverse the lake's decline. As you approach the tower, look for a plaque marking Great Salt Lake's historic high-water peak of 4212 feet.

On your way back to the pavilion, you'll see a short set of steps descending to a pond. They invite you to look closely at the tiny plants and animals thriving here, such as bright-green speckles of duckweed and graceful, gliding water striders. Just be careful not to become so absorbed in the life of the pond that you slip in and get your feet wet.

▲ The top of the viewing tower provides a glimpse of the preserve's broader context on the Wasatch Front.

TRIP 6

Eccles Wildlife Education Center at Farmington Bay

WHERE: 1157 South Waterfowl Way (approximately 1700 West Glovers Lane), Farmington

DIFFICULTY, DISTANCE: Easy. The 1.2-mile nature walk explores the wetland along a smooth gravel path and sections of boardwalk. A number of dirt roads offer other bird-viewing options.

FACILITIES: Nature center and restrooms

SPECIAL NOTES: Bring binoculars if you have them. Some roads are closed during nesting season, March 1 to September 15. The nature walk is open year-round. The center is open Tuesday through Saturday, 9:30 a.m. to 4:30 p.m.

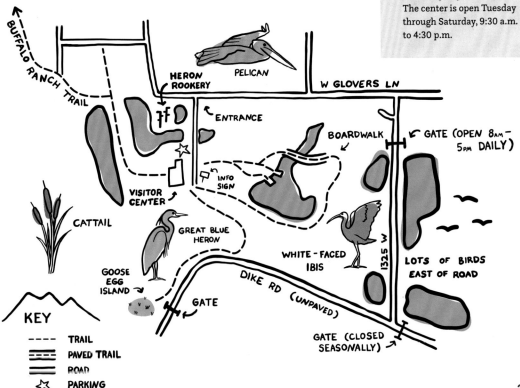

BUFFALO RANCH TRAIL

HERON ROOKERY

PELICAN

W GLOVERS LN

ENTRANCE

BOARDWALK

GATE (OPEN 8AM – 5PM DAILY)

VISITOR CENTER

INFO SIGN

CATTAIL

GREAT BLUE HERON

WHITE-FACED IBIS

1325 W

LOTS OF BIRDS EAST OF ROAD

GOOSE EGG ISLAND

GATE

DIKE RD (UNPAVED)

GATE (CLOSED SEASONALLY)

KEY

---- TRAIL
≡≡≡ PAVED TRAIL
— ROAD
☆ PARKING

Even if you've never been a bird-watcher before, you

can't help becoming one at Great Salt Lake's Farmington Bay. The number and variety of birds wading, soaring, dabbling, and nesting around the wetlands in this nature preserve is astonishing. Each year, the lake provides essential habitat for more than 10 million migrating birds representing 338 different species. More than 250 of these species visit Farmington Bay. It's a world-class location for spotting and photographing birds on the doorstep of the rapidly growing Wasatch Front.

The George S. and Dolores Doré Eccles Wildlife Education Center is a great place to start your visit. The center's exhibits highlight many of the birds you're likely to encounter. The staff and volunteers are happy to answer your questions and help you practice using spotting scopes or binoculars. You can also pick up a map, a kid-friendly scavenger hunt, and a checklist of birds—essentially an adult scavenger hunt. Though the birds are the stars at Farmington Bay, you can also spot plenty of other wildlife here: coyotes, red foxes, chorus frogs, bullfrogs, garter snakes, turtles, dragonflies, and more.

▲ American white pelicans are among the hundreds of bird species that can be spotted at Farmington Bay. During the breeding season, both male and female pelicans develop a pronounced bump on their upper beak.

Heron High-Rise

Before you even enter the education center, you'll see one of the coolest features at Farmington Bay. Six telephone poles with platforms jutting out like random, horizontal branches rise from the wetland near the northwest corner of the parking lot. It's not a land art installation, but rather a great blue heron rookery. Herons like nesting in groups, preferably off the ground where their chicks are safe from land-based predators. This artificial rookery provides visitors a front-row seat as these large, elegant birds raise their families each spring.

Wander the Wetlands

Near the opposite corner of the parking lot is the start of the 1.2-mile nature trail loop. You can travel the loop in either direction, but going counterclockwise will save the boardwalk for the second half as an enticement for young hikers. The broad gravel path starts by following a canal lined with cattails. Look for great mullein, tall whitetop, wild teasel, and bittersweet nightshade growing along the path. You might spot a muskrat swimming in the canal along with a variety of water birds.

The second half of the trail takes you into the marsh. Watch for the ubiquitous red-winged blackbirds perched among the cattails. Large Asian carp cruise the water around the base of the cattails. In the late spring, you might see them roiling in shallow spots as they spawn. Eventually the path becomes a boardwalk and then a bridge crossing open water to the other side of the pond. Check out the views across the pond to the Wasatch Mountains from the two pavilions.

▶ Herons build their stick nests on platforms attached to telephone poles

◀ The surrounding landscape becomes more liquid than solid as you travel on the boardwalk through the marsh and over the pond.

Behind a red-winged blackbird singing on the bridge, you can catch a glimpse of the city of Farmington.

A bald eagle appears to walk on water as it crosses the ice at Farmington Bay in the winter.

Birds for All Seasons

The kaleidoscope of birds at Farmington Bay shifts with the seasons. Spring brings flocks of migrating birds headed north and is a great time to see waterfowl, waders, shorebirds, and raptors. Spring is also breeding and nesting season. Songbirds are setting up territories and singing their hearts out. The long list of birds that commonly nest in the wetlands includes Canada geese, mallards, western grebes, white pelicans, black-necked stilts, and several species of gulls and terns. In the fall, the wetlands become a staging area where thousands of waterfowl and shorebirds rest and refuel before flying south for the winter.

▲ The nature trail runs along one of the canals that biologists use to manage the water in the wetlands at Farmington Bay.

Farmington Bay is famous for its winter residents too. More than a hundred bald eagles arrive in November to spend the winter in the marsh dining on carp. You can spot them sitting in trees or resting on the ice. (Be sure to bring binoculars.) In February and March, the whistling calls of large flocks of tundra swans fill the wetlands as these beautiful birds stop to refuel on sago pondweed during their journey north. The Eccles Wildlife Education Center hosts annual events to celebrate the eagles and the swans. Check the center's website for dates.

Managed and Unmanageable Water

You can learn about the history of the wetlands on Goose Egg Island—a short walk or drive from the education center. The island is actually a heap of dirt transported to the wetlands from Farmington after torrential rains caused landslides in the city during the infamously wet spring of 1983. Because the wetlands were flooded by the runoff that spring, the island became one of the few locations where birds could nest.

Interpretive signage on the island—now a peninsula—explains how the Civilian Conservation Corps built the complex set of ponds, dikes, islands, and water-control structures that created a framework for the wetlands in the 1930s. Biologists at the Utah Division of Wildlife Resources manage the flow of fresh water from the Jordan River and Farmington Creek through this system today to maintain the habitats that millions of birds depend on.

TRIP 7

Freedom Hills Trail

The panoramic views of Great Salt Lake's

Farmington Bay, Antelope Island, and beyond are your reward for climbing the Freedom Hills Trail's seventeen switchbacks. Relax on a comfortable bench at the top as you contemplate the vistas. The views are beautiful any time of day but are particularly spectacular at sunset. Don't be intimidated by all the switchbacks; they are laid out to create a reasonably gentle climb, and there are plenty of benches along the way for rest stops.

WHERE: Just north of intersection of Old Haul Road and Park Hills Drive, Centerville

DIFFICULTY, DISTANCE: Moderate. A smooth gravel trail ascends 365 feet over a half mile. Create a 2-mile loop using the rocky Bonneville Shoreline Trail and a connector path.

FACILITIES: Restrooms, picnic pavilion, playground, and disc golf course

SPECIAL NOTES: The trail has very little shade, so avoid hot days and bring plenty of water. Bikes and leashed dogs allowed.

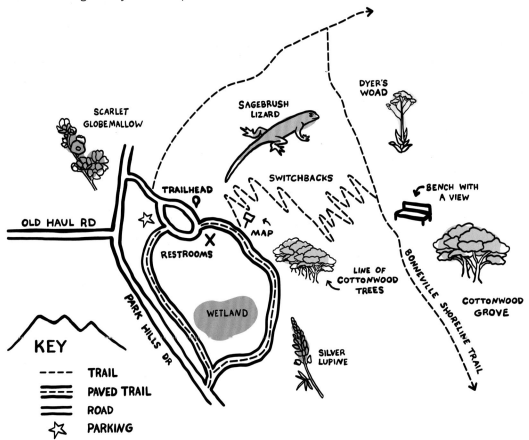

SCARLET GLOBEMALLOW

SAGEBRUSH LIZARD

DYER'S WOAD

TRAILHEAD

SWITCHBACKS

BENCH WITH A VIEW

OLD HAUL RD

MAP

RESTROOMS

LINE OF COTTONWOOD TREES

COTTONWOOD GROVE

BONNEVILLE SHORELINE TRAIL

PARK HILLS DR

WETLAND

SILVER LUPINE

KEY

- - - - TRAIL

═══ PAVED TRAIL

──── ROAD

☆ PARKING

The views from the Freedom Hills Trail get more and more spectacular as you climb.

The gently graded, snaking switchbacks lead you to the top without stealing all your breath.

The hillside and Freedom Hills Park below were once a gravel pit that supplied materials for the construction of Interstate 15 during the 1970s. The City of Centerville purchased the gravel pit in about 2005 and transformed it into a place where people can enjoy a foothill stroll or play a round of disc golf. The park is also designed to be a buffer between natural disturbances in the foothills and the neighborhood to the west. A berm along the west side of the park protects the neighborhood from landslides and floods. Fire hydrants around the open lawn enable it to double as a helicopter landing and refilling site for foothills firefighting.

Hidden Water

A short, paved path from the parking lot leads to a map kiosk marking the start of the gravel switchbacks. They wind through a dry Wasatch-foothills habitat filled with plants adapted to hot, arid conditions. You might spot a sagebrush lizard scurrying among the rocks. As you climb, keep an eye out for a row of fast-growing cottonwood trees along the side of the longest switchback. Cottonwoods aren't typical foothills inhabitants—they like to keep their feet wet. A grove of cottonwoods is usually a tip-off that a source of water is nearby.

When you reach the top of the switchbacks, you'll find the source of the water in a grove of cottonwoods just south of the bench. A couple of mountain springs collect into a tiny stream running down the hillside. Enjoy this shady oasis filled with other water-loving plants sustained by this small, but dependable, trickle. Springs also feed the marshy spots filled with phragmites and cattails in Freedom Hills Park at the base of the hill.

Explore the Shore(line)

The groomed gravel switchbacks end at the Bonneville Shoreline Trail, which doubles as a fire break road in this part of Davis County. You can explore along the trail in either direction, gaining different perspectives on the magnificent views. The trail is wide, but rocky and uneven. Keep an eye out for off-highway vehicles (OHVs) and other vehicles that use it as a road.

Descending the switchbacks is the easiest way to return to the parking lot. If you feel like a longer walk, create a two-mile loop by following the Bonneville Shoreline Trail to the north. After nearly a mile, you'll see a rocky

▲ Enjoy the deep, cool shade of the cottonwood grove at the top of the Freedom Hills Trail—it's hard to believe you're in the Wasatch foothills.

▲ As rye dries, its blue-green leaves turn golden yellow, and its long, bristly seed heads tend to droop.

two-track road heading down the hill and angling south, just before the Bonneville Shoreline Trail begins to bend to the east. Follow the two-track until you see a small footpath leading to the parking lot on your right.

Foothill Newcomers

The Freedom Hills Trail is a great place to get to know some of the common plants that grow in the Wasatch foothills. Like Freedom Hills, most of the foothills have been impacted by human activities, though a gravel pit is at the extreme end of the spectrum. These disturbances have resulted in a mix of plants that have lived in the foothills for a long time, such as big sagebrush, silvery lupine, and Utah milkvetch, growing alongside relative newcomers like rye, Balkan toadflax, and dyer's woad.

Like many introduced species, rye, Balkan toadflax, and dyer's woad have long and interesting relationships with humans that eventually brought them to Utah. Rye *(Secale cereale)*, for example, is a hardy crop that grows with little water and survives extreme cold. By 1876, farmers had planted hundreds of acres of rye in northern Utah. About the same time, gardeners began planting Balkan toadflax *(Linaria dalmatica)* in the western United States. Its bright yellow blossoms resembling snapdragons had been blooming in European gardens for hundreds of years. Both plants have found a home in disturbed habitats along the Wasatch Front outside the gardens and fields where they were first planted.

Dyer's woad *(Isatis tinctoria)* has clusters of small, bright yellow flowers and is famous for the bright blue dye produced by its leaves. They yield the same indigo dye as true indigo *(Indigofera tinctoria)*, just at lower

◄ The yellow flowers of dyer's woad bloom early in the spring; by mid-June, its dangling seedpods are turning from green to black at lower elevations.

concentrations. For centuries, woad was highly valued as the main source of blue dye in Europe. Early North American colonists grew woad for dye, and some sources indicate that it was brought to Utah to use for dye too. Others say it arrived in Utah mixed with seeds imported from Europe.

When these plants sprout in rangelands or grow uninvited in croplands, they may cause problems for ranchers and farmers. But what about when they grow in the dynamic Wasatch foothills that have long been impacted by human activities? Here they are part of a novel ecosystem—a new combination of plants and animals that live together in and around cities. The species that thrive in novel ecosystems are often resilient and adapted to rapidly changing environments. Their resiliency may be key to providing ecosystem services, such as retaining water and preventing erosion, in the future.

TRIP 8

Creekside Park

Creekside Park is a nature-play nirvana for kids. A broad, shallow spot in Mill Creek welcomes wading and splashing. Tunnels of Gambel oaks invite exploration and imagination. The short, paved path along the stream is a perfect walk for little legs. The lure of a shady picnic table and another stream access point at the end of the path provide extra motivation. The only potential drawback of this park is the super-cool playground, which is designed to be accessible for people of all abilities—it could be difficult to convince kids to leave.

WHERE: 600 Mill Street, Bountiful
DIFFICULTY, DISTANCE: Easy. Paved path is about a tenth of a mile long along Mill Creek. Stroller and wheelchair accessible.
FACILITIES: Restrooms, picnic pavilions, and an amazing playground
SPECIAL NOTES: Water levels can be too high for safe stream play in the spring and after rain storms. Dogs are allowed on leash.

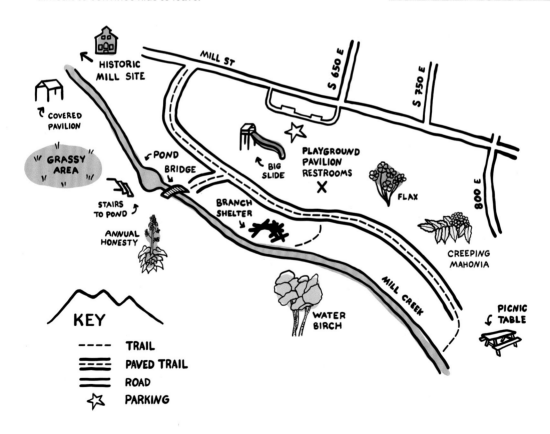

HISTORIC MILL SITE

MILL ST

S 650 E

S 750 E

COVERED PAVILION

GRASSY AREA

POND BRIDGE

BIG SLIDE

PLAYGROUND PAVILION RESTROOMS

FLAX

800 E

STAIRS TO POND

BRANCH SHELTER

ANNUAL HONESTY

CREEPING MAHONIA

WATER BIRCH

MILL CREEK

PICNIC TABLE

KEY

---- TRAIL
=== PAVED TRAIL
— ROAD
☆ PARKING

◄ The paved path along Mill Creek is a great beginner expedition—short and shady, with the goal of the stream at the end.

◄ Kids can make discoveries in a Woods' rose— jagged leaves, pink petals, spiky stamens, and maybe even some bonus beetles.

Nature Play

Nature play is pretty much what it sounds like—play directed by kids that engages them with nature and its elements. Collecting leaves and rocks, digging in the dirt for buried treasure, chasing butterflies, and lying in the tall grass are all forms of nature play. Putting your ping-pong table in the backyard—not so much.

Research has documented the many benefits of nature play for children's physical, social, and mental health. In fact, there is a growing movement among pediatricians to encourage—or even prescribe—unstructured play-time outside for kids. Salt Lake City has adopted a children's outdoor bill of rights and the State of Utah created the Every Kid Outdoors initiative to offer caregivers ideas for a wide range of fun local outdoor activities.

Water and Forest Adventures

You might start a nature-play visit to Creekside Park by following the steps leading from the west side of the playground down to the beautiful suspension bridge over Mill Creek. There's a winding, wheelchair-accessible path too. On the far side of the bridge is a lawn with a small wooden gazebo nestled among the trees along the creek. Two sets of stone steps make it easy to get into the shallow creek from the lawn. It's the perfect spot for wading, floating sticks, looking for water bugs under rocks, and spotting dragonflies. Water shoes would be a good idea for stream adventurers.

Creekside Park also offers forest adventures. The paved path heading east from the bridge passes through large blue spruces and Gambel oaks as it parallels Mill Creek. The ivy engulfing some of the oaks gives the path

► Tall blue spruces stand along the path leading from Creekside Park to the suspension bridge over Mill Creek.

◄ A broad, shallow spot in the creek with stone steps leading into the water from both banks was designed for playing in the stream.

an enchanted feeling. Watch for dirt paths leading to shelters built with branches in the oak thicket that make a great home base for all kinds of imaginative nature play. The thicket is also a wonderful place to collect leaves and rocks, search for roly-polies and garden snails, and watch for birds and squirrels. The streambank is eroded in places here—watch for drop-offs.

Budding Botanists

Continuing east along the path, young naturalists can meet and learn to recognize some common wild urban plants. Creeping mahonia (*Beberis repens*), also known as creeping Oregon grape, is a great beginner plant. It's easy to identify year-round and fun to investigate, and there's plenty of it along the trail. This low-growing shrub has matte-green leaves rimmed with spines

that resemble holly leaves. Encourage kids to feel their leathery texture and trace their curvy shape. The leaves turn gorgeous shades of red, orange, and purple in the fall and stay on the plant through the winter.

In the spring, kids can smell creeping mahonia's small and fragrant yellow flowers that grow in clusters like grapes. By midsummer, the flowers turn into clusters of dusty blue berries. The berries are edible, but not very tasty raw. Kids can also compare creeping mahonia to its close cousin, Oregon grape *(Berberis aquifolium)*. This plant has shiny leaves instead of matte leaves and tends to grow more upright rather than creeping low to the ground.

Some History and a Mystery

If you'd like to add a historical component to your Creekside adventure, visit the site of the Heber C. Kimball Gristmill on the southeast corner of Mill Street and Orchard Drive. It's a quarter-mile walk west along Mill Street from the Creekside Park parking lot. Like many urban streams, Mill Creek has an industrial past. Its water turned the Kimball Gristmill's large stones for grinding flour from 1853 to 1892. You can see the original millstones, the stone foundation of the three-story mill, and a 1:3 scale replica of the mill at the site.

One of the site's interpretive markers shows a photo of a black bear with a length of sturdy chain looped around its neck. The man holding the other end of the chain, George Quinn McNeil, captured bears in the Wasatch Mountains and trained them to "do work around the mill." He planned to take them on tour performing a circus act, but the bears had other plans. According to the marker, they "misbehaved" a short distance from Bountiful and McNeil canceled the tour. You're left to wonder how the bears misbehaved and what became of them.

▼ Kids will find all kinds of uses for the branch shelters located along the trail—a home in the forest, a construction opportunity, or a quiet place to think.

▲ With its distinctive leaves, creeping mahonia is an easy plant for kids to recognize and fun to explore as it changes throughout the year.

Memory Grove Park and Lower City Creek Canyon

WHERE: 300 North Canyon Road, Salt Lake City

DIFFICULTY, DISTANCE: Easy to moderate. 2.4 miles out-and-back on a paved road closed to traffic. There is a dirt path to explore too.

FACILITIES: Restrooms, benches

SPECIAL NOTES: Limited street parking on Canyon Road. More parking is available on East Capitol Boulevard across from the state capitol.

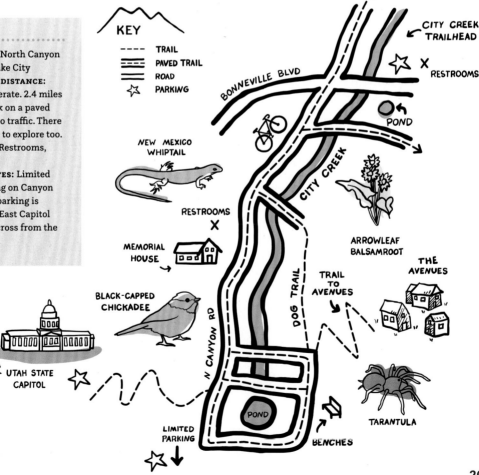

KEY

---- TRAIL

▬ PAVED TRAIL

── ROAD

☆ PARKING

CITY CREEK TRAILHEAD

BONNEVILLE BLVD

X RESTROOMS

POND

NEW MEXICO WHIPTAIL

CITY CREEK

ARROWLEAF BALSAMROOT

RESTROOMS X

MEMORIAL HOUSE

THE AVENUES

TRAIL TO AVENUES

DOG TRAIL

N CANYON RD

BLACK-CAPPED CHICKADEE

UTAH STATE CAPITOL

TARANTULA

POND

LIMITED PARKING

BENCHES

◄ The dome of the Utah State Capitol peeking through the trees in Lower City Creek Canyon is a reminder that Salt Lake City's history is intimately connected to City Creek.

▶ City Creek flows past Meditation Chapel, with its pink marble walls and green copper roof, one of many monuments in Memory Grove.

No other stream flows through Salt Lake City's history like City Creek. In arid Utah, rivers often provided the water that made building cities possible, sustaining people and crops. Streams also powered cities' early industries. A walk through Memory Grove and Lower City Creek Canyon is full of reminders of the connections between Salt Lake City's human history and its natural history.

Passing through the gate to Memory Grove, you'll see a landscape filled with monuments to fallen soldiers who fought in conflicts from World War I through the Korean War. Follow Canyon Road—which is closed to traffic beyond the gate—or walk among the monuments toward the north end of the open lawn. City Creek runs down the center of the lawn through a constructed rock-lined channel into a pond before being routed underground.

Sustaining Cities for Centuries

The first city in the Salt Lake Valley sustained by City Creek's waters dates to the Fremont period. Between 950 and 1150 generations of Fremont people lived in a large village near the creek, where they grew fields of maize (corn)

► Crews prepare to bury City Creek in an underground culvert at the south end of Memory Grove. Behind them is the stable that later became Memorial House.

and beans. They also harvested wild plants, hunted game, and collected fish, frogs, and turtles from the nearby waterways. Archaeologists excavated a small portion of the village in consultation with Utah's tribal nations after a backhoe encountered human remains in 1998 during the construction of the TRAX light rail along South Temple at 300 West.

Later Salt Lake Valley residents depended on and managed the creek's water from the moment of their arrival. On July 22, 1847, two days before Brigham Young famously reached the valley, an advance party of settlers camped along City Creek's south branch near where the Salt Lake City and County Building stands today. The next day they dammed and diverted water from the creek, and by the time Young arrived, City Creek was irrigating five acres of potatoes. Soon the new city's residents channeled the creek's north branch into a canal that ran west along North Temple for their main culinary water supply.

An Industrious Creek

The city acquired what is now Memory Grove in 1902, but it didn't become a park until the 1920s. If you had visited the area in the first decade of the twentieth century, you would have seen a dusty industrial zone. The P. J. Moran Asphalt Company excavated gravel from the east side of the canyon just behind where Memorial House stands today. In fact, Memorial House was originally built as a stable for the asphalt plant.

One of P. J. Moran's other business ventures had an even greater impact on City Creek. His construction company was the contractor for the City Creek "aqueduct"—the project that buried City Creek in a huge culvert through most of Salt Lake City. After 1910, the creek disappeared from view south of Memory Grove for eighty-five years.

Just across the creek from Memorial House, you'll see the beginning of the Freedom Trail. This half-mile dirt trail enters a cool riparian forest and is a great place to look for wild plants and animals. Plenty of paths lead down to the stream for wading or racing stick boats. Off-leash dogs enjoy romping on the trail and in the water. If you'd prefer not to meet wet dogs or plan on pushing a stroller, just stick to Canyon Road. There are great opportunities to spot many plants, birds, and insects from the road as it exits the park and enters Lower City Creek Canyon.

If you take the Freedom Trail, look for an old stone foundation next to the path. In the 1970s, this ruin was rumored to be a witch's house, haunted by disembodied voices and lights. A closer examination of the historical record reveals it to be the remnants of a miller's house, which stood next to the three-story Empire Grist Mill. The waters of City Creek turned the mill's massive thirty-foot-diameter waterwheel to grind wheat. Walking along City Creek today, the gurgling stream hardly seems like an industrial power source, but two sawmills, another grist mill, and a turning mill also stood on its banks in the late 1800s.

▲ The Freedom Trail runs through the trees on the east side of City Creek. You can catch a glimpse of Canyon Road paralleling the creek to the west.

Interwoven Worlds

The Freedom Trail rejoins Canyon Road at a footbridge. Keep an eye out for patches of bearded iris along the road. You might spot an apple or cherry tree too. It's not always clear what plants were cultivated and which sprouted on their own in City Creek Canyon. Some are likely the wild descendants of plants people once tended.

▲ You can still see the foundation of the miller's house, which stood next to the Empire Grist Mill in Lower City Creek Canyon. It's the smaller of the two main buildings in this photo.

▶ Northern pygmy owls live in mountain forests in the summer but move to lower elevation habitats such as City Creek Canyon in the winter.

Because City Creek Canyon is a corridor that connects the city to surrounding mountain habitats, you can sometimes catch a glimpse of mountain residents here. For example, northern pygmy owls (*Glaucidium gnoma*) perch in Lower City Creek. Not much bigger than a house sparrow, these tiny, fierce owls hunt during the day. Although they usually target small songbirds, they can take down birds that are quite a bit larger than themselves, including American robins and northern flickers.

Where Canyon Road meets Bonneville Boulevard, follow the dirt path down to the shore of a small retention pond, where you might meet an angler casting a line or a garter snake going for a swim. From here, cross Bonneville Boulevard and continue up City Creek Canyon, or head back the way you came. A variety of trails in Lower City Creek connect to the canyon's rim.

Upon returning to the gate at Memory Grove, follow City Creek into the city it nourished. This portion of the creek was "daylighted," or returned to the surface, in 1995. Look for a series of tiles embedded in the sidewalk with the tracks and names of animals that live in the canyon. The tile closest to the city is a human footprint.

▲ The last in a series of tiles engraved with the tracks and names of animals that live in the canyon represents the human connection to City Creek.

TRIP 10

Red Butte Loop

Abundant wild plants and animals, spectacular views, fascinating history, and a glimpse of a Wasatch Front treasure. The Red Butte Loop packs all this into a 3.25-mile foothill hike that follows the perimeter of Red Butte Garden and passes right in front of the Natural History Museum of Utah. A walk on this trail is especially magical in the spring, when a riot of wildflowers blooms on the hillsides, but it will reward you with discoveries throughout the seasons.

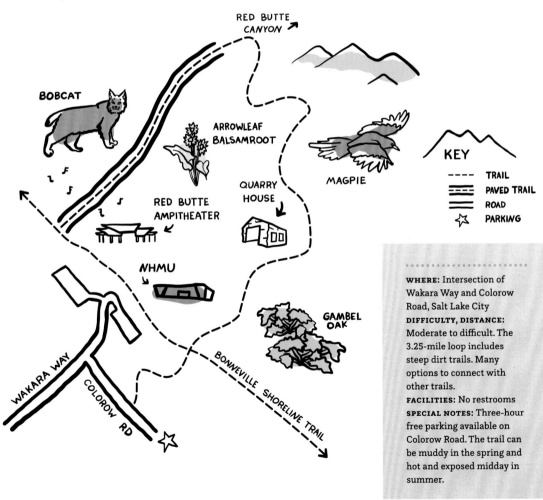

RED BUTTE CANYON

BOBCAT

ARROWLEAF BALSAMROOT

MAGPIE

KEY
- - - - TRAIL
═══ PAVED TRAIL
═══ ROAD
☆ PARKING

QUARRY HOUSE

RED BUTTE AMPITHEATER

NHMU

GAMBEL OAK

WAKARA WAY

COLOROW RD

BONNEVILLE SHORELINE TRAIL

WHERE: Intersection of Wakara Way and Colorow Road, Salt Lake City

DIFFICULTY, DISTANCE: Moderate to difficult. The 3.25-mile loop includes steep dirt trails. Many options to connect with other trails.

FACILITIES: No restrooms

SPECIAL NOTES: Three-hour free parking available on Colorow Road. The trail can be muddy in the spring and hot and exposed midday in summer.

Plants Aplenty

The trail begins on the east side of Colorow Road, about 300 feet south of the corner with Wakara Way. It meanders to the east through a shady grove of tall Gambel oaks with an understory of creeping mahonia, Woods' rose, and honeysuckle to the broad Bonneville Shoreline Trail. Cross the Shoreline Trail and continue heading up the hillside on the trail across from the Poetry Path marker.

The trail switchbacks through a community of plants adapted to the dry, sunny hillside, including big sagebrush, rye, and antelope bitterbrush. In the spring, patches of yellow arrowleaf balsamroot, bright pink redstem stork's-bill, purple Utah milkvetch, and pale pink longleaf phlox flowers will be in bloom. Listen for magpies clacking among the Gambel oaks. If you're very lucky, in the fall you may come across a male desert tarantula slowly wandering in search of a mate. You'll have a good view of the museum's outdoor terraces as you climb. The exhibits on the terraces are open to the public and accessible from the Bonneville Shoreline Trail.

After about half a mile, the trail comes to another junction by a bench. Take the path to the left to follow the fence around Red Butte Garden. The next half mile is the steepest section of the trail. Pause to enjoy the views of the valley or get a closer look at one of the many different plants growing among the oaks. In the spring, you can see western waterleaf, spotted stick-seed, and two types of bluebells—shortstyle and sagebrush.

▲ Friendly sunflowers greet hikers in the fall as the Red Butte Loop climbs into the foothills past the Natural History Museum of Utah.

Sandstone Foundation

There's a break in the climb after a quarter mile, where the trail makes a hairpin turn through a gully. You'll see the remnants of a stone wall here. As you round the bend, look back across the gully at the ruins of the Quarry House inside the Red Butte Garden fence. A sandstone quarry in Red Butte Canyon

▲ Pink Woods' roses, yellow arrowleaf balsamroot flowers, and starbursts of ternate desert parsley bloom among the Gambel oaks and antelope bitterbrush along the trail.

supplied the Nugget Sandstone used in the construction of many Salt Lake City buildings between 1848 and the early 1900s.

Despite its name, the Quarry House wasn't part of the main quarry's operations. It was actually built by young men in the Civilian Conservation Corps (CCC) based at Fort Douglas in the 1930s during the Great Depression. The CCC crews did a lot of stone construction around the fort. The Quarry House was associated with a small quarry, where the crews obtained sandstone after the larger quarry up the canyon closed.

A Living Museum

The final climb after the Quarry House leads to the highest point on the trail. The lovely meadow is awash with yellow arrowleaf balsamroot and northern mule's ears flowers in the spring. From here, you can look down into metropolitan Salt Lake Valley and turn around to see the place with the least human impacts along the Wasatch Front—Red Butte Canyon.

Aside from the quarry, Fort Douglas limited most other uses of the canyon to protect the source of its water. Today the canyon is a natural area set aside for scientific research. Scientists and students can apply for a permit to study the area. A U.S. Forest Service report proposing this designation described the canyon as "a living museum and a biological library of a size that exists nowhere else in the Great Basin."

Red Butte Canyon is critical habitat for many species, including large mammals such as moose, mountain lions, elk, deer, bobcats, and coyotes.

Sometimes these animals make their way from the canyon onto foothill trails or even into neighborhoods. It's thrilling when our daily lives intersect with theirs in a wondrous encounter. Knowing how to share space with wild creatures is critical to coexisting safely and keeping them wild. The actions you take—or don't take—will make a big difference to them. Be sure to follow several "wild aware" rules on your foothill expeditions to keep you and the wildlife safe in the foothills.

- Make noise to alert wildlife to your presence.

- Hike, jog, or bike with a companion.

- Observe wildlife from a safe distance. Never approach or feed wildlife.

- Keep dogs on leash and on trails, and don't let pets interact with wildlife.

Closing the Loop

The descent toward the road and Red Butte Creek is steep, and there is loose rock on the trail in places. It can be easy to lose your footing if you're distracted by a swallowtail butterfly flitting among the flowers or trying to spot the lazuli bunting you heard calling. After crossing the creek, the trail joins Red Butte Canyon Road. Follow the road down to the canyon through a riparian forest of box elders, Gambel oaks, and a few big Siberian elms.

When the road reaches the end of the canyon, look for the signs for Bonneville Shoreline Trail. The trail turns south, hugging the perimeter of Red Butte Garden, and crosses Red Butte Creek again. Follow the trail in front of the museum until you reach the path that leads back through the oak grove to Colorow Road. Enjoy the engraved stones of the museum's Poetry Path along the way.

▲ It's easy to miss the Quarry House hidden in the Gambel oaks if you aren't watching for it. Though many people assume the structure dates to the mid-1800s, it was actually built in the 1930s.

◀ From the highpoint of the trail, you can look into Red Butte Canyon, the least-developed canyon on the Wasatch Front.

▲ The refreshing water of Red Butte Creek and shade of the riparian forest offer a cool respite from the sunny foothills in the summer.

◄ This bobcat visited the terraces at the Natural History Museum of Utah.

Fred and Ila Rose Fife Wetland Preserve

WHERE: 9th South River Park, approximately 1000 West Genesee Avenue, Salt Lake City

DIFFICULTY, DISTANCE: Easy. About a mile of paved and packed gravel paths. Connections to many other trails.

FACILITIES: Restrooms and picnic tables at 9th South River Park

SPECIAL NOTES: The shallow, warm pond is usually covered in algae in the summer, but there's still plenty to see. Dogs aren't allowed in the preserve but are permitted on leash on connecting trails.

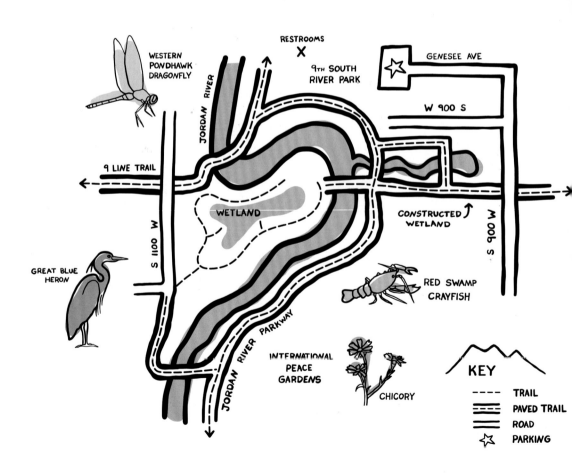

▲ Trains once rumbled over this bridge across the Jordan River on the rail line that crossed the preserve.

The Jordan River makes a big, lazy oxbow bend

around the Fred and Ila Rose Fife Wetland Preserve. It's one of the few places in Salt Lake City where you can still see the river in its original meandering course. The small pond in the center of the oxbow is relatively new. The city completed the pond in 2014 as part of its efforts to create more habitat where wild plants and animals—and humans—can thrive in the city. Those efforts are definitely paying off.

The preserve sits at the junction of two important trails—the north-south Jordan River Parkway and the east-west 9 Line Trail. You can take either trail to reach the wetland or explore them for longer adventures after a wetland walk. If you're driving, the 9th South River Park on Genesee Avenue is a convenient place to start.

Wet, Dry, and Wet Again

The 9 Line Trail is built along an old railroad line that ran right through the oxbow. If you enter the preserve from the east, you'll walk across the old railroad bridge. Before the rail line was constructed in 1910, the land around the oxbow would have flooded seasonally and shifted shapes. Because a shifting landscape isn't conducive to building a rail line, the Oregon Short Line Railroad reinforced the river's banks at the oxbow, constraining the river and reducing the seasonal wetlands.

When Salt Lake City purchased the site in 2010, it was dry and flat as a pancake. Creating the wetland required carting off tons of fill and sculpting the landscape to create wetland, riparian, and upland habitats. Then the city planted a variety of native plants and waited to see what wildlife would show up.

▲ The city used huge earth movers to transform a flat meadow into a wetland that improves water quality and creates habitat for diverse wildlife.

Neighborhood Naturalists

Some people wondered whether many species would really use the wetland. To find out, the city's Trails and Natural Lands Division teamed up with the Natural History Museum of Utah and Hartland Community 4 Youth and

▼ The seasonal wetlands in the oxbow at Fife Wetland Preserve had been filled and flattened for a hundred years when Salt Lake City purchased the site.

▲ Citizen scientists at a Neighborhood Naturalists event document the plants and animals at the Fife Wetland Preserve to create a record of how the site changes over time.

Families (a community organization based in the neighborhood around the wetland) to launch the Neighborhood Naturalists project.

Neighborhood Naturalists citizen scientists have been recording the plants and animals they encounter at the preserve since 2016 by taking photos using the iNaturalist app. The project will document how the community of plants and animals at the preserve changes over time. Participating in the project is easy. Any observations made on iNaturalist at the preserve become part of the dataset.

Citizen scientists have recorded more than 400 species in and around the small preserve! One amazing citizen scientist, Rebecca Ray, recorded a couple of rarely seen species that haven't been documented anywhere else in Utah. They both have memorable names: Crotch's lady beetle *(Hippodamia sinuata crotchi)*, named after nineteenth-century entomologist George Crotch, and violaceous globetail *(Sphaerophoria pyrrhina)*, a hover fly with a small violet stripe on its face.

Data Made a Difference

The data gathered by Neighborhood Naturalists volunteers led Salt Lake City to change the way it manages the site. Their observations confirmed that at least 110 species of insects and spiders, including several uncommon species, reside at the wetland. In response, the city dramatically reduced chemical and mechanical weed treatments and focused on "solarizing" and hand-pulling weeds, which is much less disruptive to insect populations.

Fife Wetland Preserve attracts a variety of water birds that aren't as unusual but are fun to see. Mallards and Canada geese nest around the wetland. You may spot them in the river or the pond with a line of fluffy ducklings or goslings paddling behind. Stately great blue herons often stride the wetland's shallow water. Big, black double-crested cormorants *(Nannopterum auritum)* frequently stand on tiny islands in the pond with their wings outstretched. They look a bit like they are practicing yoga, but they're actually drying their feathers.

The main mammals that use the wetland—aside from humans—are muskrats *(Ondatra zibethicus)*. They are very common here and active during the day, so you're likely to spot one. Look for them swimming purposefully in the pond or the river, possibly dragging tasty cattails or grasses behind them. They live with their families in burrows in the banks with secret underwater entrances.

Water Purifier

Just west of the Fife wetland, you can see another type of constructed wetland. Look for viewing platforms that extend over a narrow band of water flowing into the Jordan River. The water comes from storm drains that gather runoff from many neighborhoods along Red Butte and Emigration creeks.

The water—along with the trash and pollutants it picked up in the neighborhoods—used to flow straight into the Jordan River. This wetland was built to filter out some of those harmful materials. If you see trash floating in the water, it means the wetland is doing its job. And even though it wasn't built as wildlife habitat, muskrats, mallards, and red-winged blackbirds have moved in.

A short walk along the banks of the river through the International Peace Gardens makes a nice pairing with a visit to Fife Wetland Preserve. The trails leading south on either end of Fife connect to the path that runs along the riverbank through a shady forest of large cottonwoods, box elders, and willows. You'll get a different view of the river and opportunities to go down to the water. Plus, you'll catch glimpses of a miniature Japanese pagoda, a tiny Matterhorn, and other architecture from around the world in the Peace Gardens.

▾ Deploying her extensive knowledge of insects and the power of close observation, citizen scientist Rebecca Ray has documented several uncommon species at the wetland.

▲ You can often spot double-crested cormorants at Fife Wetland Preserve along with the ubiquitous mallards and Canada geese.

TRIP 12

Salt Lake City Streamside Preserves

Tucked within Salt Lake City neighborhoods, Miller Bird Refuge and Nature Park, Hidden Hollow Preserve, and Wasatch Hollow Preserve are three hidden gems along three urban streams that offer bite-size nature experiences. You could easily visit all of them in a day, but why rush? Each shady oasis offers a stream to explore, paths to stroll, and plenty of beauty to savor. Each preserve also contains a story about renewal and people who nurture their neighborhood nature.

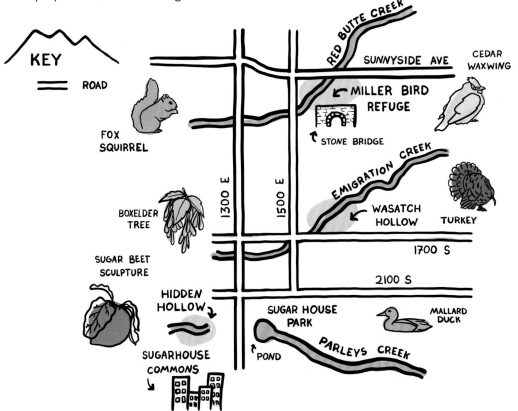

KEY

ROAD

FOX SQUIRREL

RED BUTTE CREEK

SUNNYSIDE AVE

CEDAR WAXWING

MILLER BIRD REFUGE

STONE BRIDGE

EMIGRATION CREEK

1300 E

1500 E

BOXELDER TREE

WASATCH HOLLOW

TURKEY

1700 S

SUGAR BEET SCULPTURE

2100 S

HIDDEN HOLLOW

SUGAR HOUSE PARK

MALLARD DUCK

SUGARHOUSE COMMONS

POND

PARLEYS CREEK

MILLER BIRD REFUGE AND NATURE PARK	WASATCH HOLLOW	HIDDEN HOLLOW
WHERE. 1708 East 900 South, Salt Lake City **DIFFICULTY, DISTANCE:** Easy. Broad dirt path makes a 0.8-mile loop. Suitable for strollers. **FACILITIES:** No restrooms, interpretive signs **SPECIAL NOTES:** Park on the street. Dogs must be leashed.	**WHERE:** Wasatch Hollow Park, 1631 East 1700 South, Salt Lake City **DIFFICULTY, DISTANCE:** Easy. About 1 mile of dirt and gravel paths. **FACILITIES:** Playground and restrooms at the adjacent park **SPECIAL NOTES:** Dogs allowed only on a small section of trail. Better to leave them at home.	**WHERE:** Approximately 1166 East 2100 South in Sugar House Commons, Salt Lake City **DIFFICULTY, DISTANCE:** Easy. Half-mile paved path. You can also explore a dirt path. Suitable for wheelchairs and strollers. **FACILITIES:** Restrooms and picnic pavilions at Sugar House Park **SPECIAL NOTES:** Park at Sugar House Commons. Dogs allowed on leash.

The urban creeks flowing through the three preserves are treasures. Only 1.2 percent of Salt Lake City's total land area is riparian, or streamside, habitat, and just 0.4 percent of arid Utah is riparian. Despite their scarcity, riparian habitats play an outsize role in sustaining wildlife. Many animals, including 75 percent of Utah's bird species, depend on the rich resources they provide. Visiting these nature preserves offers a glimpse of the diverse plant communities that thrive along streams and the wildlife that use them.

You can also get a sense of the challenges faced by urban streams in the preserves. Sometimes the streams stop flowing in the summer as upstream water users claim their rights. Or you may see the streams raging after a rainstorm, when runoff from pavement, roofs, and other hard surfaces is channeled down storm drains that dump into streams. Culverts along a stream's course can accelerate the stormwater into scouring flash floods.

For the Birds

Miller Bird Refuge and Nature Park is the oldest of these three riparian gems. Minnie Miller—a dynamic entrepreneur and renowned cattle breeder—donated property along Red Butte Creek to Salt Lake City in 1935 to honor her late husband and his love of birds. The stone bridge and other rockwork in the refuge were built soon thereafter by crews employed by the Works Program Administration that provided jobs for millions of Americans during the Great Depression.

In 2010, a Chevron pipeline near the Bonneville Shoreline Trail ruptured, releasing 16,000 gallons of oil into Red Butte Creek. The spill was devastating for the stream's aquatic life and the surrounding neighborhood. The immense cleanup effort that followed included measures to improve the stream's ecology, such as creating a more meandering streambed to help reduce erosion.

Walking along Red Butte Creek in the refuge, you'll pass through a typical Wasatch Front riparian forest. Its multistory layers create excellent habitat

▶ Red Butte Creek flows beneath a stone bridge in Miller Bird Refuge. Built in the 1930s, the scenic bridge is a great place to take photos.

▲ Little downy woodpeckers frequent the riparian forests in all three preserves. You may hear them drumming on trees before you see them.

for a variety of birds. The tallest members of the forest are trees, such as box elders and cottonwoods. Shrubs, including common hawthorn, golden currant, Woods' rose, and creeping mahonia, populate the middle level. The understory is home to a mix of grasses and wildflowers—some local and some newcomers. In Miller Bird Refuge, you'll also often see plants that have "escaped" from backyards bordering the path, such as annual honesty, oriental poppies, and tulips.

Kid Power

The short stretch of Parleys Creek that runs through Hidden Hollow Preserve was filled with debris and slated to be buried under a parking lot when students from Hawthorne Elementary School discovered it in 1990. The kids researched the forgotten history of the site—the block was once a thriving community park with a swimming pool—and discovered that many wild plants and animals continued to live along the creek despite its degraded condition. Joining forces with other students, they successfully lobbied the Salt Lake City Council to rezone the area as open space.

Tucked away between commercial buildings, Hidden Hollow provides a cool respite on a hot day—a stark contrast to the asphalt and concrete around it. The preserve is a great place to talk with kids about the impact they can have on their community. Several demonstration gardens offer kids a chance to explore the plants that live in different habitats along the Wasatch Front. You can combine an adventure in Hidden Hollow with a visit to Sugar House Park thanks to the tunnel connecting them beneath 1300 East.

▼ Surrounded by commercial development, Hidden Hollow lives up to its name.

▲ Golden currant (*Ribes aureum*), with yellow flowers that smell like vanilla or cloves, grows in all three preserves and in many other habitats along the Wasatch Front.

Community Collaboration

Wasatch Hollow Preserve protects about a half mile of Emigration Creek. In the mid-2000s, a series of developers proposed building homes in a core portion of the site. Though development seemed imminent, a group of neighborhood residents, city and county open-space programs, and Utah Open Lands joined forces to make sure the eleven-acre site remained a community open space.

The larger north loop of the trail at Wasatch Hollow passes through a special area set aside for protecting urban wildlife. Dogs are not permitted here because their presence—even their scent—stresses many animals and makes them less likely to use the area. Mule deer frequent the preserve, using the stream as a corridor to move between habitats in the city. If you're lucky, you might spot wild turkeys.

▶ A trail camera placed by a Wasatch Wildlife Watch citizen scientist captured this mule deer along Emigration Creek in Wasatch Hollow.

▲ This bridge over Emigration Creek leads to an area of Wasatch Hollow Preserve designated as habitat for urban wildlife. The preserve is one of the few places below Emigration Canyon where the creek flows above ground and is still relatively undisturbed.

As you cross over Emigration Creek into the wildlife zone, look for Hodgson's Spring seeping up from the ground, forming a small pond. The spring's water was once piped to the Utah State Penitentiary located in what is now Sugar House Park. After the prison closed in 1951, the spring was filled in. During the rehabilitation of the preserve in 2015–2016, Salt Lake City removed the fill. The spring soon returned, along with a stand of cattails, adding to the richness of the preserve's habitat.

Big Cottonwood Regional Park Holladay Lions Area

WHERE: 4650 South 1590 East, Millcreek

DIFFICULTY, DISTANCE: Easy. About 1 mile of packed gravel and dirt paths. Packed gravel suitable for strollers and wheelchairs.

FACILITIES: Restrooms, playground, picnic tables

SPECIAL NOTES: Dogs allowed on leash. Exposed in the summer. Bring water.

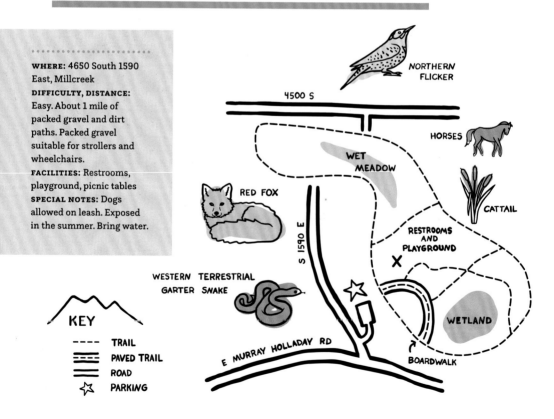

▲ The boardwalk near the playground takes you close to the open water section of the wetland. Keep your eyes and ears open for birds in the water and among the plants.

The Holladay Lions Area of Big Cottonwood Regional Park sits between two major streets, but most drivers zipping along 4500 South and Murray Holladay Road don't realize this urban nature hot spot exists. The park offers wetlands, meadows, and thickets of Russian olive to explore. It's a great place to practice your naturalist skills. One single dedicated naturalist has documented a hundred different species here over the years. He comes back in different seasons to see what new discoveries await.

On and Off the Beaten Path

A network of paths runs through the park. One gravel path makes a loop around the wetland at the south end. A boardwalk overlooks a small area of open water. A longer loop heads to the north through stands of Russian olive trees, sprinkled with patches of marsh and meadow. The gravel path emerges into a large area of manicured lawn with a wet meadow in the center. A dirt path encircles the lawn, passing by horse corrals on the east.

You can spot many species from these formal paths, but the observation opportunities get even more interesting when you start exploring the numerous informal dirt paths. On the north side of the park, be sure to walk across the manicured lawn to the cattails and hardstem bulrushes growing in the wet meadow. In the summer, you'll often see dragonflies and damselflies hovering above or perched on their tall stems. Six different species of these insects have been observed here and there are likely more to be found.

◄ Follow the informal dirt paths at Big Cottonwood Regional Park to encounter species hiding in meadows, thickets, and wetlands.

▲ A red fox basks in the warm sun of a Wasatch Front fall afternoon. You can spot foxes and their dens year-round at this park.

Fabulous Foxes

If you see what appears to be a super-size rodent burrow on your exploration, it's probably a fox den. Families of red foxes have been raising their kits in this park for years (and photographers have been taking gorgeous photos of them). Beyond the large opening, a typical fox den has several chambers and a tunnel that leads to other openings. Foxes use their dens as nurseries and shelters in bad weather, but they usually prefer sleeping under the stars.

Female foxes give birth inside the den in early spring. The blue-eyed kits begin to emerge four to five weeks later, often lured by tasty morsels their parents leave just outside the den. With some patience, you might spot kits tumbling, tussling, and learning to hunt. Foxes are active most of the year at the park, although they avoid the heat of the day in the summer. You're more likely to see them if there aren't too many off-leash dogs around.

▲ An American kestrel keeps a sharp eye on the meadows at the park.

◄ Showy milkweed's bumpy green pods explode into mounds of seeds with fluffy white parachutes in the fall. Patches of milkweed are planted for monarch butterfly caterpillars in many Wasatch Front parks.

Grab Your Binoculars

The Holladay Lions Area of Big Cottonwood Regional Park also attracts many birds and lots of birders looking to add interesting species to their observation lists. The three habitats in the park provide resources for birds with different needs. In the wetlands, you'll see common marsh birds such as mallards and red-winged blackbirds, but harder-to-spot birds such as Virginia rail and sora have also been documented here. The Russian olive trees provide food and cover for diverse perching birds, including cedar waxwings, white-crowned sparrows, lesser goldfinches, yellow warblers, and evening grosbeaks.

The open meadows are hunting grounds for raptors, including Cooper's hawks, red-tailed hawks, and a surprising number of American kestrels (*Falco sparverius*). Kestrels are tiny falcons about the size of a mourning dove. Look for them sitting on high perches scanning for tiny prey—mostly insects, rodents, and small birds. Or listen for their high-pitched call—a series of quick, excited "klee" or "killy" notes. They are quite colorful for raptors: males have slate-blue heads and wings, and both sexes have warm reddish-brown backs and tails.

Kestrel Watch

Kestrel populations are in decline, especially in the eastern United States. They appear to be holding steady in Utah for now and are making use of open spaces in urban areas. HawkWatch International is working with citizen scientists along the Wasatch Front to understand the factors that cause kestrel populations to decline. You can get involved in their American Kestrel Study in a variety of ways, including monitoring nest boxes, reporting banded birds, and building your own nest box.

Many of the plants featured in this guide grow in the park, along with a variety of other common urban flora. Dense clumps of purple deadnettle mingle with blue-flowered madwort in the spring. Chicory, lamb's quarters, showy milkweed, and curly dock bloom throughout the summer. Plant observations are a great way to boost your Big Cottonwood Regional Park species tally.

Jordan River Parkway: Millrace Park to Arrowhead Park

WHERE: Millrace Park, 1150 West 5400 South, Taylorsville

DIFFICULTY, DISTANCE, ACCESS: Easy to moderate. A 3.2-mile out-and-back, packed gravel and dirt trail.

FACILITIES: Restrooms, picnic pavilions, dog park

SPECIAL NOTES: Dogs allowed on leash.

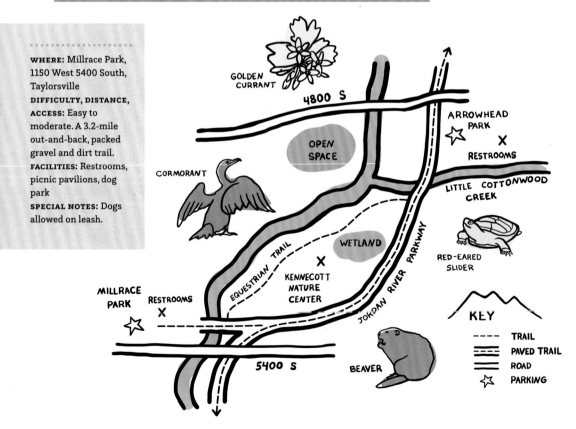

▶ Paddling is a wonderful way to experience the wildlife and beauty of the Jordan, with boating access points all along the river, including at Millrace and Arrowhead parks. Check the Jordan River Commission website for info on the water trail.

There are many beautiful places to walk along the Jordan River, but the trail between Millrace Park and Arrowhead Trailhead ranks near the top. If you've never visited the Jordan River before, this is the place to start. The river is particularly picturesque here; you can see some of the extensive work that's gone into improving the river habitat, and there's plenty of wildlife to observe.

From Trashed to Treasured

The Jordan River flows down the center of the urban Salt Lake Valley, a ribbon of blue connecting Utah Lake to Great Salt Lake. Like most urban rivers, it has a history of abuse and neglect. As the valley developed, people channelized the meandering river, diverted its water, and used it as a dumping ground. The recent history of the river is much more hopeful. Communities all along its fifty-mile corridor are investing in the river as a valuable asset, a place for people to connect with nature and recreate close to home.

The Jordan River Parkway is just one example of these investments. At more than sixty miles, if you include the various connector trails, it is the longest paved urban trail in the United States. It weaves through fifteen cities along the river, in and out of parks, neighborhoods, marshes, meadows, and riparian forest. To begin this field trip, hop onto the parkway at Millrace Park by crossing the bridge south of the playground.

At the end of the bridge, take the gravel path, which is technically the equestrian trail and not the main Jordan River Parkway. This path runs right along the riverbank, where you'll typically spot the most wildlife. There are lots of places to wade in the river. As you travel, scan the west bank of the river for slider turtles basking on logs. A pair of binoculars will help you spot them. You may see a muskrat or even a beaver cruising in the river.

River Serenades

The river provides important habitat for many birds, including some of the migratory birds that visit Great Salt Lake and Utah Lake each year. More than 150 species have been documented on the eBird app on this short stretch of river. In addition to the ubiquitous mallards and Canada geese, you're likely to see and hear red-winged blackbirds and belted kingfishers. Both have distinctive calls that will help you identify them.

Red-winged blackbirds (*Agelaius phoeniceus*) are famous for their "conk-a-lee" song that's part of the soundtracks of marshes across North America. Males aggressively defend their territories in the spring, belting out their songs all day long. You'll often see them swaying on cattails or reeds, but they also perch in trees. As their name advertises, males are glossy black with a scarlet shoulder patch bordered by a yellow stripe. Females are streaked in brown and white and look a bit like sparrows.

Belted kingfishers (*Megaceryle alcyon*) are also loud and bold. They announce any disturbance with a loud, rattling, almost mechanical call. You'll often hear them before you see them. These bluish gray-and-white birds perch on branches near the water, where they can keep an eye out for fish. Their large, crested heads and long bills give them a top-heavy appearance, but they are perfectly suited for diving into the water to grab dinner when it swims past.

The Path Less Traveled

After about a mile, leave the gravel equestrian trail and take the dirt footpath that follows the river. Sometimes the path branches, so you can choose your own adventure. If one branch looks like too much of a scramble for your taste, you can always find another route. There are delightful surprises to

▲ Signs like this one, just across the bridge from the beginning of this walk in Millrace Park, are posted all along the Jordan River Parkway to help you navigate the trail and its many connector paths.

▶ There are plenty of spots to get down to the water along this stretch of the river, though you may have to share them with Canada geese or mallards.

▲ Belted kingfishers, like this watchful male, are common along this section of the Jordan River. A female kingfisher has an additional splash of color—a band of chestnut color across her belly and flanks.

discover along the way—a secret grove of elms, a small footbridge, a tunnel through a wall of matrimony vine.

You'll also have a chance to help Salt Lake County monitor some of the restoration work on this section of the river. Watch for stations where you can place your mobile device in a bracket that positions it to take a photo of a particular project. The stations are usually near an interpretive sign with details about the natural channel design and bioengineering techniques being deployed. After you take a photo, post it to Twitter with the hashtag listed on the photo station. It will become part of a record of the changes at the site over time.

The dirt path leads past the Kennecott Nature Center, a special classroom where thousands of fourth graders come for hands-on nature experiences. Just beyond the nature center, a marsh thick with cattails extends to

▲ A boardwalk provides a stroller- and bike-friendly alternative to the dirt path along the river near Arrowhead Park.

◄ Your photos can contribute to restoration efforts along the river by helping Salt Lake County monitor the status of a variety of projects, such as this one aimed at controlling erosion.

the east. It's one of the largest wetlands on the Jordan River. After another half mile, you'll cross a bridge where Little Cottonwood Creek flows into the Jordan River just before the trail enters Arrowhead Park. You'll find picnic tables and restrooms at the park.

Arrowhead Park makes a good turnaround point, but if you want a little more adventure before you head back, cross the Jordan River on the street at 4800 South to visit the Little Confluence Open Space. Explore a quiet nature trail amid hundreds of cottonwoods and willows planted by the county's Million Trees program and TreeUtah. You can't get back to Millrace Park on this side of the river, so be sure to cross back to the east side for your return journey. On your way back, you'll see the river from different angles and can explore the paths you didn't take.

Dimple Dell

Plan to spend some time getting to know Dimple Dell. With more than fifteen miles of trail winding through 630 acres, there's a lot to explore. Dimple Dell is a long ravine that starts near the mouth of Bell Canyon and runs west to about 300 East through the neighborhoods of Sandy and White City. You can stay high on the rim to enjoy the views or descend to the tree-lined watercourse at the bottom of the ravine. Whatever route you choose, there will be fascinating plants and animals to meet.

WHERE: Granite Park, 2725 East Grouse Creek Circle (10000 South), Sandy
DIFFICULTY, DISTANCE: Easy to difficult. Fifteen miles of trail vary from flat and firm to steep and sandy.
FACILITIES: Restrooms, picnic pavilion, and playground at Granite Park
SPECIAL NOTES: Trails are open to horses and bikes. Dogs allowed on leash. Depending on your route, there may not be much shade.

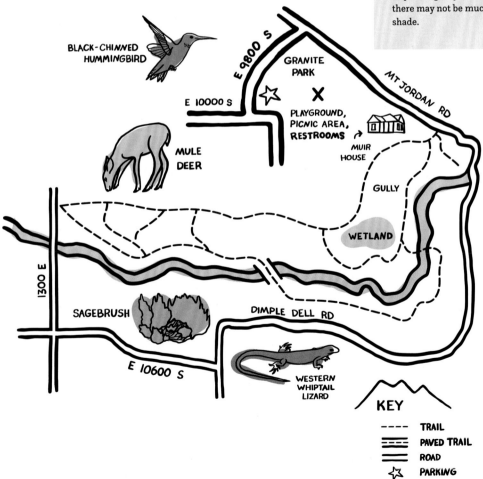

BLACK-CHINNED HUMMINGBIRD

E 9800 S

GRANITE PARK

E 10000 S

X

PLAYGROUND, PICNIC AREA, RESTROOMS

MT JORDAN RD

MUIR HOUSE

MULE DEER

GULLY

WETLAND

1300 E

SAGEBRUSH

DIMPLE DELL RD

E 10600 S

WESTERN WHIPTAIL LIZARD

KEY

- - - - TRAIL
===== PAVED TRAIL
===== ROAD
☆ PARKING

You can access the trail system from numerous places along both sides of the ravine. Granite Park on the northeast end of Dimple Dell is a good launchpad for your first visit. From here you can make a roughly three-mile loop that includes a stop at a historic site, a stroll along Dry Creek, and a walk along the rim.

History Underfoot

Look for the bark-covered path taking off from the east side of the park near a sign about trail etiquette. As you walk to the east, you'll pass through fields that James and Janet Muir farmed in the early twentieth century. Their house lies just half a mile ahead. Built in 1897, it was listed on the National Register of Historic Places for its unusual building material—granite blocks that may have come from the famous Temple Quarry in Little Cottonwood Canyon. This quarry was the source of the granite for the Church of Jesus Christ of Latter-day Saints Temple in downtown Salt Lake City.

Just south of the house, you'll see a grove of black locust *(Robinia pseudoacacia)* trees and a few old fruit trees. Black locusts were among the first and most popular trees planted by European-American settlers in the Salt Lake Valley. These trees are a little more recent—a tree-ring study dated them to the 1930s. Other remnants of the working farm are scattered amid the sagebrush and grass to the west of the house—irrigation systems, fencing, and out-building foundations.

▲ The Muir Family once farmed these open fields on the north rim of Dimple Dell. The granite block house they built and a few old trees still stand near the trail.

From the Muir House, travel south for about a quarter mile to take in the view over Dimple Dell at Sunset Point, or skip this side trip and head back west to the junction with the Sleepy Hollow Trail. (The trails are marked with posts.) The descent to Dry Creek at the bottom of the ravine is a bit steep and sandy, but it's only about a quarter mile long.

A Home and a Highway

As you probably guessed, Dry Creek doesn't run year-round. The water that flows in the spring and early summer is enough to sustain some water-loving plants, such as cottonwoods and willows, along its banks. It's also a draw for wildlife. In fact, Dimple Dell provides both habitat for wild animals and an important corridor they can use to travel safely.

Citizen scientists from the Wasatch Wildlife Watch project have been placing trail cameras in Dimple Dell each summer since 2018 to document

▶ A Wasatch Wildlife Watch trail camera captured this coyote along Dry Creek in Dimple Dell. The ravine is critical habitat for urban wildlife.

▲ Compared to its dry rim, the bottom of Dimple Dell seems lush, as trails pass by patches of marsh and through groves of cottonwoods.

CAM17   78F 25C ●   05-27-2020   19:16:5

the mammals that use the area. The motion-triggered cameras have snapped thousands of images of mule deer, red foxes, striped skunks, raccoons, coyotes, and mountain cottontails. The data shows that Dimple Dell is more heavily used by these animals than any other open space in the Salt Lake Valley. The ravine is also likely a core habitat for urban-adapted species such as foxes and raccoons.

Dimple Dell is just one of more than 200 sites studied by Wasatch Wildlife Watch. Citizen scientists place and monitor trail cameras from City Creek to Little Cottonwood canyons and in many Salt Lake County open spaces. One important goal of the project is to identify critical wildlife habitats and the corridors that connect them so that future development can best serve wildlife and people.

From the intersection with Dry Creek, follow the bark-covered trail along the bottom of the ravine until you come to a fork in the trail. Take the left fork to cross to the south side of the creek and explore the trails running west along the watercourse. Alternatively, you can take the right fork to begin the climb back to the rim.

Watch Where You Step

Traveling along the rim offers some great opportunities to spot invertebrates. During the warmer months, you're likely to encounter a black pinacate beetle (*Eleodes* spp.) sauntering down the trail. These beetles never seem in much of a rush because they have a chemical defense that makes many predators think twice before attacking. A pinacate doing a headstand is getting ready to spray a stinky liquid from its abdomen. As long as your face isn't within a few inches of the acrobatic beetle, you have nothing to fear.

Keep an eye out for the conical nests of hardworking western harvester ants (*Pogonomyrmex occidentalis*) along the rim trail. These incredible structures and the colonies that live in them can persist for up to forty years! Harvester ants can sting, so tread carefully around their homes for your safety and theirs.

As you travel the nearly mile-long trail along the rim back to the park, enjoy spectacular views of the contorted geology of the Wasatch Mountains, and be sure to note the trails you want to investigate another day.

▼ Pinacate beetles are very common in the Wasatch foothills. Known for their smelly defense system, you'll most likely see them busily searching for decaying matter to munch.

▲ Climb back to the rim for a view down the length of Dimple Dell. Look for plants that have adapted to this arid environment, such as antelope bitterbrush and big sagebrush, on the hillside.

TRIP 16

Galena Soo'nkahni Preserve

FIELD TRIP 16

WHERE: Jordan River Rotary Park, 958 West 12300 South, Draper
DIFFICULTY, DISTANCE: Easy to moderate. Paved, 3.6-mile out-and-back path. Option for a bark path too.
FACILITIES: Restrooms, picnic pavilions, playground
SPECIAL NOTES: Travel off the paved trail or bark equestrian trail is not allowed in the preserve.

Covering 252 acres, the Galena Soo'nkahni Preserve is the largest open space on the Jordan River. *Soo'nkahni* means "many homes" in the Shoshone language. This name refers to the extraordinary archaeological site on the preserve and reflects the enduring connection of Utah's Indigenous people to the land here and all along the Wasatch Front. A sundial-shaped marker built of local stone at the southern end of this walk honors this ongoing relationship.

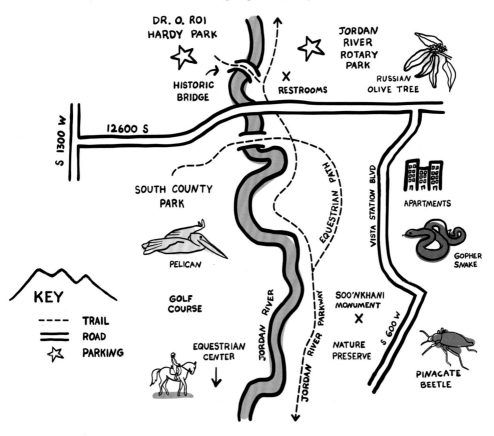

DR. O. ROI HARDY PARK

JORDAN RIVER ROTARY PARK

HISTORIC BRIDGE

X RESTROOMS

RUSSIAN OLIVE TREE

S 1300 W

12600 S

SOUTH COUNTY PARK

APARTMENTS

PELICAN

GOPHER SNAKE

KEY

GOLF COURSE

SOO'NKAHNI MONUMENT X

VISTA STATION BLVD

- - - - TRAIL
===== ROAD
☆ PARKING

EQUESTRIAN CENTER

JORDAN RIVER

JORDAN RIVER PARKWAY

EQUESTRIAN PATH

NATURE PRESERVE

S 600 W

PINACATE BEETLE

Bridges and Once-Troubled Water

A piece of more recent history lies at the beginning of your walk. Look for the historic bridge over the Jordan River just north of the parking lot at the Jordan River Rotary Park. A bridge has stood at this location since 1865. For many years, it was the only way to cross the Jordan River at the south end of the Salt Lake Valley. The current steel truss bridge was built in 1909 and restored as a pedestrian bridge in 2001.

As you head south, you'll be traveling along a section of the Jordan River Parkway that nearly eroded away in 2011. Rivers are naturally dynamic, their banks shaped and reshaped by erosion. But in urban areas, a river's shifting course can threaten trails, roads, and buildings. Keeping structures away from a river's banks and floodplain is the best approach but often not the reality. An interpretive sign near the top of the boat ramp shows how Salt Lake County deployed natural channel design to reduce erosion along this riverbank.

As the trail dips beneath the underpass at 12600 South, look for the gourd-shaped nests of cliff swallows clinging to the beams overhead. Busy flocks of cliff swallows flit through the underpass in the summer. You can see the nests of another swallow in the bank of the west side of the river just south of the underpass. True to their name, bank swallows nest in large colonies burrowed into riverbanks and sandy cliffs. More recently, they've taken to nesting in sand and gravel piles at construction sites.

▲ The rich wetlands around the Jordan River supported people for thousands of years. The Galena Soo'nkahni Preserve includes an ancient and significant archaeological site on the bluffs above the wetlands.

▲ This steel truss bridge carried traffic across the Jordan River from 1909 until 1981. The cities of Draper and Riverton restored it as a pedestrian bridge on the Jordan River Parkway in 2001.

► Cliff swallows build their intricate mud nests in sociable groups on the 12600 South underpass. If a swallow is home, you can see the white patch on its forehead glowing from the dim entrance.

An interpretive sign near the underpass shows photos of both swallows and several of the many other birds you're likely to spot along this section of the trail. For the next three quarters of a mile, the trail passes by groves of Russian olives and stands of coyote willow. The thick vegetation often obscures the river but provides great habitat for birds.

Life on the Bluffs

The vistas change as you enter the Galena Soo'nkahni Preserve. The river meanders through a broad wetland bordered by wet meadows. The trail swings to the east along the base of a low bluff. On top of the bluffs a little further south, archaeologists encountered a remarkable site that contains some of the earliest evidence of people living in the Salt Lake Valley. Charcoal taken from a hearth at the site has been dated to more than 3000 years ago.

Even more surprising—and still a bit mysterious—are the residues of corn dating to 2500 to 3000 years ago. That's 500 to 1000 years earlier than previous evidence of corn in northern Utah. More research is needed to determine whether people grew the corn at the site or elsewhere. The people living on the bluffs had many other rich resources on their doorstep. The wetlands were filled with abundant birds, fish, mammals, and a variety of edible plants. More species of plants and animals were available nearby in the foothills and canyons.

In the small section of the thirty-acre site they excavated, archaeologists found two pit houses dating to about 2400 years ago and thousands of artifacts reflecting people's daily lives—sharp blades for butchering, stones for

▲ Look for birds perched in the Russian olives and willows lining the riverbank. American robins, western kingbirds, Bullock's orioles, cedar waxwings, and song sparrows frequent this area.

▲ Archaeologists carefully explore and record one of the pit houses people lived in 2400 years ago above the Jordan River wetlands at Galena Soo'nkahni Preserve.

◀ Natural History Museum of Utah archaeologist Anne Lawlor points out a tiny stone bead among grinding stones, scrapers, and awls from the site. NHMU is the steward of the thousands of artifacts collected at Galena Soo'nkahni.

grinding seeds, pottery for storage and cooking, scrapers for cleaning hides, bone awls for sewing, and tons of stone flakes from making a variety of tools. A few items speak to the people's desire for beauty—a tiny stone bead and fragments of red ochre that could be used to decorate many surfaces, including skin.

The wetlands sustained Indigenous peoples for thousands of years. The archaeological evidence of life on the bluffs spans from 3000 years ago to about 1500 years ago. Later, bands of Ute people lived along Utah Lake, Jordan River, and Great Salt Lake. Shoshone, Goshute, and Paiute peoples also relied on the area's many resources.

Honoring Ancestors and Land

When the Utah Transit Authority announced plans to construct a FrontRunner train station over the archaeological site in 2009, leaders of Utah's tribal nations spoke out to oppose the disruption of the ancient homes and the land. Their efforts were critical to halting the plan and preserving the site.

Unfortunately, workers building the FrontRunner rail line accidentally trenched and dumped fill dirt on a section of the site. Part of the funding to mitigate this disturbance went into constructing the stone monument you'll encounter about two miles from your starting point. Each pillar in the circle represents one of Utah's eight federally recognized tribal nations. At the dedication of the monument in 2015, Jason Walker, former chairman of the Northwestern Band of the Shoshone Nation, explained, "This is sacred land to us. This is something we would like to stay pristine forever."

Galena Soo'nkahni Preserve is now owned by the Utah Division of Forestry, Fire, and State Lands and is protected by a conservation easement with Utah Open Lands. Please respect the sacred nature of the preserve and remain on the paved trail or the bark equestrian trail during your visit.

The preserve runs for three quarters of a mile beyond the monument, to where 14600 South crosses the river. The monument makes a good turn-around point, but it's well worth continuing your explorations if you have time and energy. On your way back, consider taking the bark equestrian trail that begins near the north end of the preserve. It's much less traveled than the paved trail and offers great bird-watching.

▲ The stone pillars in this monument honor Utah's Indigenous peoples, past and present, and their enduring connection to this place.

TRIP 17
Blackridge Trail

WHERE: 15000 South Ashland Ridge Drive (5390 West), Herriman
DIFFICULTY, DISTANCE: Moderate to difficult. A 3.4-mile loop on a dirt trail that climbs about 400 feet.
FACILITIES: Restrooms, picnic pavilion, sandy beach
SPECIAL NOTES: Popular mountain biking trail on the weekends. Follow trail etiquette and move aside for cyclists. No shade on this trail.

The Blackridge Loop winds over a small ridge projecting from the southern end of the Oquirrh Mountains on the west side of the Salt Lake Valley. As you climb, stunning views of the Wasatch and the Oquirrhs unfold. Compared to the showy views, the landscape itself is understated. At first glance, it's easy to assume there isn't much living here. Green is not the dominant color of these dry foothills, even in the spring. But if you challenge yourself to look closely, you'll encounter many species at home in this harsh environment and many stories embedded in the landscape.

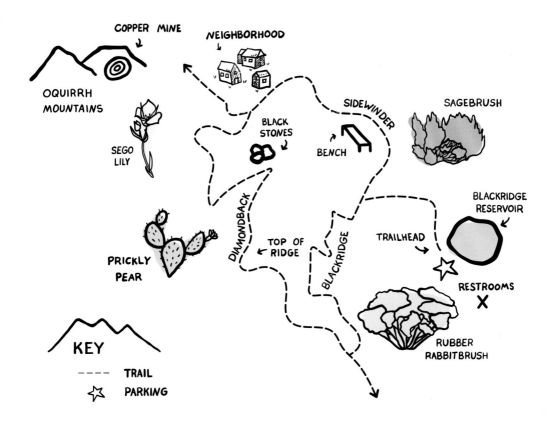

COPPER MINE

NEIGHBORHOOD

OQUIRRH MOUNTAINS

SEGO LILY

BLACK STONES

SIDEWINDER

SAGEBRUSH

BENCH

BLACKRIDGE RESERVOIR

DIAMONDBACK

TOP OF RIDGE

BLACKRIDGE

TRAILHEAD

PRICKLY PEAR

RESTROOMS
X

RUBBER RABBITBRUSH

KEY

- - - - TRAIL
☆ PARKING

Fed by Fire

The trail takes off from the south end of the parking lot for Blackridge Reservoir, curving along a gap between two neighborhoods. As you round the corner and start up the switchbacks, keep an eye out for clumps of small Gambel oaks. Pale, bare trunks protrude from many clumps. Some of the dead trunks have blackened sections too. The skeletal trunks and the dense new growth around them are a record of the fire that swept across these foothills in 2010.

Fire is common in this ecosystem—occurring roughly every few decades—and important to its health. Gambel oaks are adapted to rise from the ashes. Their ligno-tuber, a swelling at the base of an oak's trunk, stores starch and dormant buds. If a fire destroys the tree's branches and trunk, the ligno-tuber sends out new growth. More than a decade after the fire, the new trees are still quite small, because oaks grow slowly—especially in the challenging conditions here. It may take a Gambel oak a hundred years to reach a diameter of four or five inches.

▼ The pale, bare trunks protruding from small clumps of Gambel oaks are evidence of the fire that scorched these foothills and destroyed three nearby homes in 2010.

◄ Desert paintbrush is adapted to dry, rocky soils, so it's right at home in this ecosystem. One of its survival tricks is tapping into the roots of other plants, such as sagebrush, to siphon off water and nutrients.

▲ A bench, a colorful rock garden, and spectacular view of the Oquirrhs make a great spot to rest.

Tiny but Tough

After about four small switchbacks, you'll come to a trail junction. Take the Sidewinder Trail that swings east around the shoulder of the ridge. In the spring, if you can pry your eyes away from the views, you'll find an exuberant display of diminutive, desert-adapted wildflowers around your feet. Many of the plants here grow low to the ground to conserve water. Their warm tones seem to reflect the warm, dry landscape—the vibrant red of desert paintbrush, the coppery orange of scarlet globemallow, and various shades of yellow of ternate desert parsley and foothill deathcamas.

As the trail continues around the shoulder, views open to the north and west. Look for a bench next to a little "garden" of whimsical painted stones, where you can pause to enjoy the vistas. After about a mile, you'll reach a trail junction. Stay left on the Sidewinder Trail toward the ravine filled with oaks. Stay left at the next junction too, and continue your climb toward the ridge. The trails here are designed for mountain bikes, so the grades are never super-steep.

An Explosive Past

Keep an eye out for rounded, rough-textured rocks along the trail. Some are black and others are reddish. When you get to the saddle, you'll see large black stones tumbled all across the ridgeline. Bands of black stone also run along the ridge of South Mountain to the west. These rocks are evidence of a different fiery event in this area's history.

South Mountain is one of the youngest volcanoes to have erupted along the Wasatch Front. Geologists date it to a bit more than thirty million years

◀ One of the youngest, or most recent, volcanoes to erupt around the Salt Lake Valley produced this huge black boulder and many smaller black stones along the trail.

▲ From the high point on the ridge, enjoy spectacular views of the Wasatch Mountains and look for your starting point and next objective— Blackridge Reservoir.

ago, long after dinosaurs went extinct sixty-five million years ago. A column of lava likely erupted from the north end of South Mountain. As it cooled, it created bands of volcanic rocks cemented together by ash up to 300 feet thick. The ridge the trail crosses is part of this same formation. Over time, erosion has broken off sections of the formation, rounded the rock fragments, and spilled them across the foothills below the ridge.

Survival Experts

On your way back to the reservoir, the trail passes a grove of about a dozen Utah junipers (*Juniperus osteosperma*) that were spared by the wildfire. Depending on fuel loads and topography, fires can burn in mosaic patterns that leave unburned patches surrounded by blackened vegetation.

▲ A high school mountain bike team outlines the many switchbacks that the trail traverses on the way down from the ridge. You can see junipers spared by the fire above them.

Maybe these junipers were in one of those unburned patches. More likely, the grasses on the hillside didn't burn hot enough to ignite the junipers' crowns—other isolated junipers survived the fire too.

Having escaped a brush with death in the fire, these junipers could live for centuries. The oldest known Utah juniper is more than 1200 years old. Even an average juniper lifespan is 350 to 700 years. These trees are specialists at enduring extreme heat and drought. Their massive root systems can search out water up to twenty-five feet beneath the surface. Junipers can also send out roots up to a hundred feet horizontally to find water closer to the surface. Imagine the stories of fire and rain their growth rings tell.

The last section of the trail zigzags through switchbacks that lengthen the route but make the descent easier for bikes and your knees. Resist the urge to take shortcuts—any paths you create will accelerate erosion in this fragile landscape. Staying on the trail will also help you avoid a surprise encounter with a rattlesnake. Two sections of the trail, Diamondback and Sidewinder, are probably named for western color, but Great Basin rattlesnakes do live here. Following good trail etiquette will help keep you and the snakes safe.

TRIP 18

Highland Glen Park

Some urban ponds can seem a bit unfriendly. Property managers may not be eager for people to explore around a pond, much less get into it. The Highland Glen Pond is at the other end of the spectrum—a welcoming, hands-on pond with many recreational amenities. Although the pond is certainly the centerpiece of Highland Glen, the park also offers lots of other opportunities to explore nature.

WHERE: 4800 Knight Avenue, Highland
DIFFICULTY, DISTANCE: Easy. About a mile of ADA-accessible paved and packed gravel paths as well as dirt paths to explore.
FACILITIES: Restrooms, playground, beach, picnic sites
SPECIAL NOTES: The water in the pond can have high levels of harmful bacteria in the summer. The pond is monitored regularly. Look for posted warning signs before you get in the water.

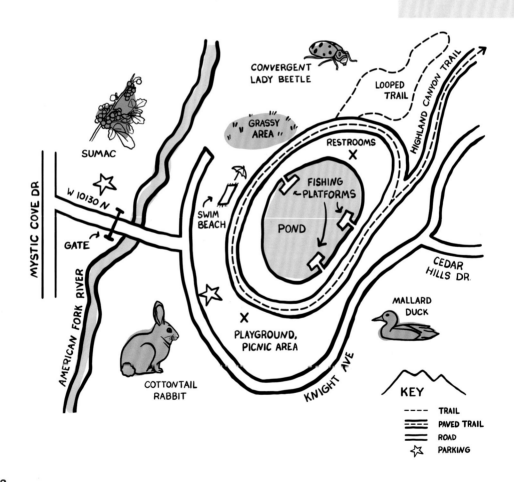

CONVERGENT LADY BEETLE

LOOPED TRAIL

HIGHLAND CANYON TRAIL

GRASSY AREA

RESTROOMS

SUMAC

W 10130 N

FISHING PLATFORMS

SWIM BEACH

POND

MYSTIC COVE DR

GATE

CEDAR HILLS DR.

AMERICAN FORK RIVER

MALLARD DUCK

PLAYGROUND, PICNIC AREA

KNIGHT AVE

COTTONTAIL RABBIT

KEY

- - - TRAIL
=== PAVED TRAIL
=== ROAD
☆ PARKING

▶ Family-friendly Highland Glen Park offers a pond, numerous picnic sites, a volleyball court, and many paths to explore against the spectacular backdrop of American Fork Canyon.

▲ The pond at Highland Glen welcomes water-lovers with a beach and a life jacket loaner station.

Come on In!

Highland Glen Park offers a buffet of water-focused activities. The pond has a beach for waders and swimmers and a life jacket loaner station where you can borrow an orange life preserver for your aquatic adventures. If you'd rather float than swim, bring your kayak, paddleboard, or floaty toys to the pond. Be aware, however, that there's no lifeguard on duty, so keep water safety top of mind.

The three platforms extending into the pond are popular with anglers. The Utah Division of Wildlife Resources (DWR) regularly stocks the pond with rainbow trout, so fish are plentiful. You can also catch largemouth bass, bluegill, and channel catfish here. The DWR has developed community fisheries like this one all along the Wasatch Front to provide places where

people can cast a line close to home and new anglers can learn the basics of fishing. Be sure to check the current rules for community fisheries before you try your luck at the pond.

Locals and Long-Distance Travelers

The platforms are also great places to observe the waterfowl that gather at the pond. You're all but guaranteed to spot a flotilla of mallards cruising the water or waddling on the shore. If you like feeding ducks, consider bringing them corn, lettuce, or halved grapes—something other than bread. A bread-heavy diet can prevent ducks from getting all the nutrients they need to stay healthy.

Though the pond isn't very large, migrating waterfowl occasionally use it as a rest stop during their spring and fall journeys. Red-breasted mergansers are particularly fun to spot. The distinctive crests on their heads appear messy and ragged—like they just received an electric shock. Their sleek bodies are built for diving to feed on small fish. They breed in northern Canada in the summer and spend winter on the coasts, but you may see one passing through Utah at Highland Glen.

Song-Filled Forest

If you need a break from water activities, follow the paved path to the east side of the pond where it connects to a short loop trail through a grove of Gambel oaks. As you stroll through the shady grove, listen and look for a variety of birds—American robins, black-capped chickadees, Woodhouse's scrub-jays, black-chinned hummingbirds, western tanagers, ruby-crowned kinglets, and more. Shrubs such as fragrant sumac and golden currant twining through the grove provide bird cover and food. In the fall, look for

► Look for migrating red-breasted mergansers that stop to feed on fish at the pond. Females aren't as brightly colored as this male, but they have the same spiky "hairdo."

▲ The sign for the Looped Trail stands amid a patch of fragrant sumac, one of the shrubs that provide great bird habitat along the trail.

sumac's slightly fuzzy red berries, golden currant's shiny red and orange berries, and deep purple blackberries.

In the spring, water from the American Fork River (via an irrigation canal) rushes down a slope on the east side of the grove next to a charming set of stone steps. It continues along a stone-lined channel crossed by footbridges before entering the pond. In dry years, the water disappears in the summer as demands for irrigation increase. The grove remains a cool respite on hot summer days, and dirt paths through the shrubs invite exploration. If you venture off the main path, keep an eye out for poison ivy.

The paved paths that wind through the many picnic tables west and south of the pond are also good places for observing birds and plants. If you want a bit more adventure, follow the path that leads west from the south end of the pond across the road to the floodplain of the American Fork River. From the small parking lot, you'll see a short social trail heading north. Follow the trail or simply venture out into the brush to explore. You may encounter mule deer and cottontail rabbits in this unmaintained space. Prickly pear cacti live here too, so watch your step.

TRIP 19

North Utah Lake Shoreline Trail

WHERE: Northlake Park, 500 West 2000 South, Lehi

DIFFICULTY, DISTANCE: Easy to moderate. Out-and-back trip of 3.5 miles on a paved path with options to follow dirt trails.

FACILITIES: Restrooms

SPECIAL NOTES: Bring binoculars for spotting birds.

Like its salty sister to the north, Utah Lake is a key link in the Pacific Flyway traveled by millions of migratory birds each year. From the paved trail along the north end of Utah Lake, you can see and hear more than 200 species of birds—both those stopping by and year-round local residents. The flat, paved trail between Northlake Park and Saratoga Road is stroller-friendly and makes for a great family bike ride. Along the way, you can stroll around a duck pond and explore shady groves of trees. Numerous dirt side trails lead to the lakeshore.

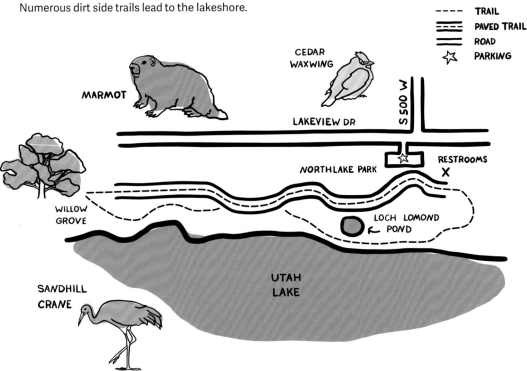

KEY

- - - - TRAIL
≡≡≡ PAVED TRAIL
═══ ROAD
☆ PARKING

MARMOT

CEDAR WAXWING

LAKEVIEW DR

S 500 W

NORTHLAKE PARK

RESTROOMS X

WILLOW GROVE

LOCH LOMOND POND

SANDHILL CRANE

UTAH LAKE

► The paved trail along the north shore of Utah Lake passes through meadows, wetlands, and groves of trees filled with birds.

▲ Follow the dirt path closer to the lakeshore on one leg of your out-and-back journey to see even more birds.

For the best bird-spotting and a bit of an adventure, take one of the paths toward the shore from Northlake Park and follow the informal dirt path along the shoreline west for about a mile to where the trail ends in a large grove of willow and cottonwood trees. You'll need to reconnect with the paved trail for a bit in the middle. The shore path will likely include negotiating marshy spots, crossing small creeks, and a bit of route-finding. It's best when the wetland vegetation hasn't grown too tall.

◄ Caspian terns often hang out with other shorebirds. Their large, red bills make them stand out in a crowd.

Think Like a Bird

As you explore, think of the habitat around the lake as a variety of zones where you can look for different birds. The first zone is the lake itself. Depending on the time of year, you can see American white pelicans, three species of grebes (western, Clark's, and eared), Canada geese, and a variety of ducks paddling on the lake. Binoculars or a spotting scope make identifying birds on the water much easier.

The lakeshore is the next habitat. Here you may see migrating shorebirds, such as marbled godwits, black-necked stilts, and American avocets, scurrying on long legs at the water's edge. Caspian terns also congregate along the shore. Their bright red bills, black caps, and hefty size make these summer residents easy to recognize. Look for them soaring over the water, hunting for fish.

In some areas, wetlands begin a few steps from the shore. Watch for red-winged and yellow-headed blackbirds swaying on the cattails and reeds, loudly defending their territories. The marsh wrens and song sparrows are more likely to be hiding among the tall plants. Listen for their songs—a buzzy trill for the marsh wren and a series of clear, bright notes ending in a trill for the song sparrow.

In other areas, the shore gives way to meadows. In spring, pairs of sandhill cranes (*Grus canadensis*) stride through these meadows. These cranes are always an impressive sight—tall and stately, with slate-gray plumes and red crowns. They mate for life, and couples stay together year-round. You may also spot killdeers skittering through a meadow, famous for their shrill, high call that sounds like their name.

Scattered throughout the meadows are shrubby patches and brush piles that provide cover for birds that hop along the ground foraging for seeds or bugs, such as white-crowned sparrows and spotted towhees. In the winter, rarer species, such as Harris's sparrows, mingle with the flocks. Yellow-bellied marmots have taken up residence in the largest branch piles

► The extensive wetlands around Utah Lake are recognized nationally for their importance to wildlife and are easy to access along the North Utah Lake Shoreline Trail.

▲ Sandhill cranes arrive in northern Utah in March and stay for the breeding season in the summer.

Name That Tune!

Many large trees grow along sections of the paved trail—a dense stand of Russian olives at the east end and groves of tall cottonwoods and willows farther west. As you pass the trees, you'll hear a bonanza of bird songs from cedar waxwings, western kingbirds, western wood-pewees, American gold-finches, yellow warblers, and many more. After a big storm in the spring, you may spot some migrating warblers taking shelter here.

Try using the Sound ID function on the free Merlin bird identification app as you stop in one of the groves on a spring morning. This amazing app identifies birds by "listening" to their songs. It also enables you to compare

◄ Though yellow-bellied marmots tend to prefer living in rocky areas at higher elevations, they are a common sight among the branch piles that dot the north shore of Utah Lake.

▲ The grove of large willows near the west end of the trail offers cover for birds and deep shade for hikers. People have built some impressive branch shelters in its depths.

Utah Lake's PR Problem

Many people think Utah Lake is polluted and are reluctant to visit. The lake was certainly mistreated in the past, but its water quality improved significantly after many polluting practices ceased in the 1970s. Agreements to increase the water flowing into the lake and improvements in wastewater treatment have helped reduce harmful algal blooms in the summer. Numerous projects to help threatened species recover and rehabilitate habitat are succeeding.

Despite all the ways Utah Lake is improving, inaccurate ideas about it being dirty or irredeemable persist. Researchers studying Utah Lake identify a lack of community connection as a significant threat to the lake's future. People won't care about what happens to a place they don't know about or value. One of the most important ways to help Utah Lake is to visit and share your stories and photos with friends.

the song of the bird you heard to the songs of species the app identifies as possible matches. It seems magical when photos of a half-dozen birds appear on your screen as the app picks out their voices from the chorus of a spring morning.

Near the west end of the trail, you'll see signs for a wildlife study area. The Hutchings Museum Institute in Lehi is operating the Utah Lake Field Station in partnership with the State of Utah. With the help of citizen scientists, the museum is gathering data about the plants and animals living on the site to plan for future habitat improvements. The museum also offers opportunities to get involved in monitoring kestrel boxes or creating habitat for monarch butterflies on the site. Contact the Hutchings Museum to arrange a visit to the field station or to volunteer for a project.

TRIP 20

Provo River Delta

This field trip differs from others in this book because, as of June 2022, key features of the Provo River Delta didn't exist yet. Giant excavators were still reshaping 260 acres of pasture into braided channels and ponds. Crews had just finished digging the first of four openings in the Skipper Bay Dike that will connect the river delta to Utah Lake. Slated for completion in 2024, the Provo River Delta Restoration Project will create a rare habitat on the urban Wasatch Front—a broad floodplain where river, lake, and land merge and constantly shift.

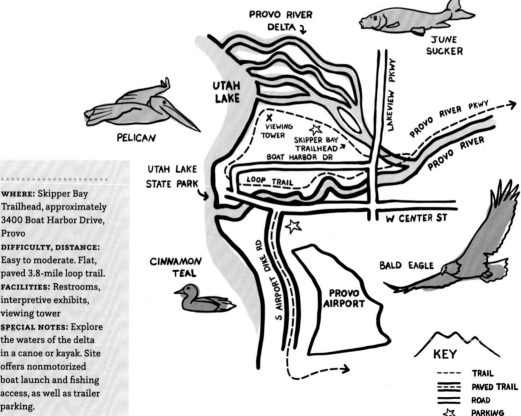

WHERE: Skipper Bay Trailhead, approximately 3400 Boat Harbor Drive, Provo

DIFFICULTY, DISTANCE: Easy to moderate. Flat, paved 3.8-mile loop trail.

FACILITIES: Restrooms, interpretive exhibits, viewing tower

SPECIAL NOTES: Explore the waters of the delta in a canoe or kayak. Site offers nonmotorized boat launch and fishing access, as well as trailer parking.

KEY

- - - - - TRAIL
≡≡≡ PAVED TRAIL
=== ROAD
☆ PARKING

▲ Excavators sculpt a maze of ponds and channels to re-create the Provo River Delta in a pasture. Terraces of coconut fiber "soil lifts" reinforce the new banks.

► June suckers actually don't suck. Unlike most suckers, they're not bottom-feeders. They dine on zooplankton in the water.

A Uniquely Utah Fish

The impetus for this restoration project is a uniquely Utah fish—the June sucker (*Chasmistes liorus*). Utah Lake is the only place in the world where this fish lives naturally. In 1986, June suckers were placed on the endangered species list after their population declined to about 400 adults and virtually none of their young were able to survive. The baby fish either became dinner for predators or starved to death in the first few weeks of their lives.

June suckers were abundant in the past when Utah's Indigenous people and early European-American settlers could depend on plentiful catches. So what happened? Over the years, people built dikes across Skipper Bay and

other lakeshore areas, draining the Provo River's historic floodplain to create more land for farming and development. They moved the river itself into a single leveed channel. These changes destroyed the "nursery" in the warm, slow-moving waters of the Provo River Delta, where baby June suckers could hide and feed until they were big enough to survive in the lake.

The goal of the Provo River Delta Restoration Project is to re-create the historic delta in the north half of Skipper Bay as key habitat for baby June suckers. Hatchery programs have successfully increased the population of adult June suckers living in Utah Lake. In fact, the species was downlisted from endangered to threatened status in February 2021. The nursery for baby June suckers in the delta will give the species a shot at becoming self-sustaining.

Amphibious Adventures

The delta restoration project creates a new place for people to hike, paddle, and fish. You can walk a loop trail that runs along the south side of the new river delta, connects to the remaining portion of Skipper Bay Dike, and then joins Provo River Parkway beside the banks of the old channelized river. This fascinating stroll passes through the various transformations the river and lake have gone through over time. Be sure to climb the observation tower for a view of the delta. You can also cross the diversion structure at the southeast part of the loop to explore the nature-themed playground at Provo River Delta Gateway Park.

Given the delta's watery nature, you'll need a boat to explore most of it. A boat launch provides convenient access for kayakers, canoeists, and paddleboarders who want to glide through marshy channels and ponds. Anglers can reel in bluegill, channel catfish, largemouth bass, and white bass. The

▶ Crews made the first of four openings in the Skipper Bay Dike in June 2022—a big moment in the project. The connection between the delta and Utah Lake is vital to the June sucker's survival.

▲ Cattails grow in a pond dubbed "Gumby" by project designers for its iconic shape.

▶ Ute ladies'-tresses have spiraling stalks of flowers said to resemble braided hair, or tresses. This little orchid's range overlaps with the traditional homeland of the Ute people.

◀ The delta's braided channels offer tranquil paddling and fishing in a rich wetland habitat.

complexity of the new delta provides much greater habitat diversity for these fish than the channelized river.

In May and June, you can see adult June suckers spawn in the swifter flowing waters where the Provo River enters the southeast corner of the delta. Watch for males defending their spawning sites in the riffles of the river. You might see hundreds of fish congregating in deeper pools. June suckers are especially vulnerable during spawning, so give them plenty of space.

Orchids that Love a Good Flood

If you're out in the delta in midsummer, you may catch a glimpse of a different threatened species on the shore as you float by— Ute ladies'-tresses *(Spiranthes diluvialis)*. These little orchids have delicate, white flowers that grow in spirals around the upper part of the plant's stem. They live in wet habitats, which are vulnerable to being developed or drained. For their long-term survival, they need regular disturbances, such as floods, which tend to be frowned upon in areas developed for agriculture or housing. (Their species name, *diluvialis*, means "of the flood.") The floodplain in the delta offers great habitat for a population of orchids that had been hanging on in the wet pasture.

As many other species find homes in the restored delta, it will be exciting to see who moves in and how the river delta changes over the years. There will certainly be surprises the project planners didn't anticipate. Even after it settles in a bit, the delta will continue to be a dynamic place as water levels change with the seasons.

It's a Bird! It's a Plane!

On one of your trips to the Provo River Delta, make time to check out a nearby birding hot spot—the Airport Dike Road. Access this road from Center Street, just east of the bridge over the Provo River near the entrance to the Utah Lake State Park. You can park on either side of Center Street by the collection of historic gas station signs. The Airport Dike Road starts on the south side of Center Street near a historic marker about the resorts at Utah Lake.

The road is a liminal space—a narrow, raised strip that separates Utah Lake from the former lakebed that was drained to create the airport. From this little ribbon of road, people have spotted more than 250 species of birds, including some rare spring and fall migrants. You may see herons and egrets wading in the canal on the airport side of the road. You may also meet a marmot, rock squirrel, garter snake, or gopher snake. The road continues south along the lake a little more than two miles before turning east. This jog in the road makes a good turnaround point for a bird-watching walk.

▲ Sandwiched between the airport and Utah Lake, Airport Dike Road offers great year-round birding.

Bicentennial Park

WHERE: 1440 South 1600 East, Provo
DIFFICULTY, DISTANCE: Easy. Quarter-mile loop on a wetland boardwalk, plus a park to explore.
FACILITIES: Restrooms, playground, picnic pavilion, disc golf, dog park
SPECIAL NOTES: Wetland can be buggy in late spring. You might bring mosquito repellant or wear long sleeves.

At first glance, Bicentennial Park seems like a regular neighborhood park, with large shade trees, wide lawns, a playground, and a duck pond. But just south of the duck pond, a boardwalk heads into a wetland with a marsh and a dense grove of peachleaf willows. Surrounded by Provo neighborhoods, this small wetland provides a bit of urban habitat for small, water-loving animals and plants. It's a great place for making close observations. The interpretive signage along the boardwalk will help you identify the species you see and discover the story of how the wetland came to be.

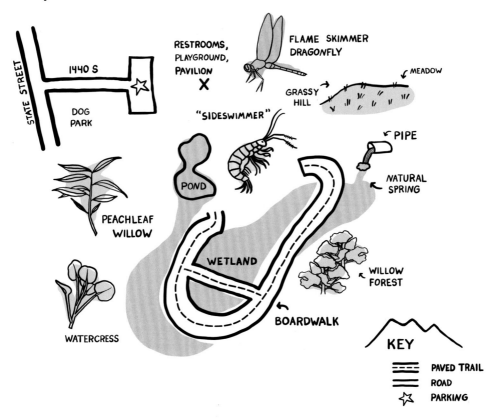

◄ Nuttall Spring
flows out of a
concrete basin
that was part of
the Nuttall family's
water system. A
pipe took the water
from the spring to a
small pump house
that pumped it
up the hill to their
home.

Spring-Fed

The wetland at Bicentennial Park relies, in part, on water from Nuttall Spring.
You can see the spring as it emerges from a pipe in the side of the slope near
the northeast entrance to the boardwalk loop. The slope is part of an escarpment—a place where the elevation changes sharply as a result of erosion or
faulting—that roughly parallels the Wasatch Fault. If you stand in the center
of the park, you can see the escarpment starting on its south end by the wetland and then swinging north along its east edge. It's this change in geology
that brings groundwater to the surface at Nuttall Spring.

   The spring water flows out of the pipe into a concrete basin that was part
of a water system built by dairy farmers William and Margaret Nuttall. They
piped the spring water up to their house, which stood on top of the escarpment at the northeast corner of the park. The Nuttall family eventually sold
this land—once their orchard and pasture—to Provo City for the creation of
Bicentennial Park.

Under the Rocks

A small pool forms where the spring water flows out of the concrete basin. If you turn over rocks in the pool, you can find tiny freshwater crustaceans that resemble shrimp. They belong to the large genus *Gammarus* but are commonly known as sideswimmers or scuds. They make a living as part of the cleanup crew in ponds and streams, munching on decaying plants and animals. Their presence is often a sign of a healthy pond or stream.

As you search for sideswimmers, you'll probably find other cool underwater invertebrates. Place your discoveries in a small, clear container filled with water and use a magnifier to see them up close. (The macro lens on your phone camera can work as a magnifier too.) Be sure to release your invertebrate friends gently when you're done examining them.

Thirsty Willows

The water of Nuttall Spring and other seeps from the escarpment sustains a lush grove dominated by large peachleaf willows. Like many willow species, these trees need moist conditions to survive. They thrive in river floodplains, marshes, and other places that are seasonally wet. Without the springs, they wouldn't be growing here next to the dry foothills.

As you follow the boardwalk into the dense willow grove, you'll pass through a tangle of shrubs on either side—lots of Woods' roses and black hawthorns, but some red osier dogwoods, golden currants, and sandbar willows too. The combined shade from the willows and shrubs makes it difficult for much else to grow in the understory. The rich leaf litter on the forest floor

▼ Huge peachleaf willow trees lean over the boardwalk and shade the wet forest floor.

The boardwalk crosses a small, open-water marsh that was constructed in 1997 as a mitigation project.

Watercress grows in the wetland throughout the year. It's a great source of food for aquatic insects, birds, mammals, and fish.

▲ One huge Fremont cottonwood near the pond predates the park. Perhaps the Nuttall family planted it here.

is a wonderful habitat for invertebrates—insects, spiders, millipedes, worms, and snails—that sustain birds. The raised boardwalk keeps your feet dry and prevents them from disturbing the life in the litter.

Wetland Tally

On the west side of the wetland, you'll find a marsh with standing water where cattails and hardstem bulrushes grow. Duckweed and algae spread across the marsh's surface in the summer. You can often spot watercress growing near the outlet to the ponds. Damselflies and dragonflies patrol the skies over the marsh, hunting for their next meal.

This marshy section of the wetland was created in 1997 as mitigation for the destruction of another wetland where the Provo Towne Centre Mall now stands. People often drain wetlands for both agricultural and urban development, but sometimes we construct, enhance, and restore wetlands too. Overall, however, wetlands are on the decline. According to the U.S. Fish and Wildlife Service, Utah lost 30 percent of its wetlands between the 1780s and 1980s. As an arid state, we didn't have that many to begin with.

The wetland isn't the only spot at Bicentennial Park for making nature observations. A grassy hill on the southeast side of the park leads to an open meadow. (The hill is great for winter sledding!) If the meadow hasn't been mowed, you can find lots of different urban plants here. Spring in the meadow is a pastel patchwork of speedwell, crossflower, redstem stork's-bill, and tall whitetop. On your way back to the parking lot, be sure to give a nod to the stately old Fremont cottonwood near the pond. It was growing here long before the park was created.

ACKNOWLEDGMENTS

This book was truly a collaborative effort. Dozens of people from along the Wasatch Front and beyond contributed their knowledge of the myriad ways cities and nature are intertwined, the great number of species that share our communities, and the many wonder-filled places to explore neighborhood nature. This project would not have been possible without their contributions of expertise and time. Our heartfelt thanks to all the people listed here. Our deepest apologies to anyone we missed.

ESSAYS

Accomplished community experts contributed essays to this book. We also asked several writers to share their insights on urban nature. You can read more about them in the bios at the end of their essays: Riley Black, Julia Corbett, Ellen Eiriksson, Tony Gliot, Sarah Jack Hinners, Lewis Kogan, Emma Marris, Amy Sibul, and Brian Tonetti.

SPECIES ACCOUNTS

A whole crew of passionate local scientists and expert naturalists contributed to the writing of the species accounts. They advised on species selection, compiled research, reviewed drafts of text, and provided insightful comments all along the way.

BIRDS

Cooper Farr, Director of Conservation at Tracy Aviary, recruited an amazing team of local bird experts to compile research on birds and reviewed the draft species accounts. The crack research team included Jeanne LeBer, Cooper Farr, Janice Gardner, Charles Hurd, Keeli Marvel, John Middleton, John Neill, Bryant Olsen, Teri Pope, and Anne Terry.

FUNGI AND A LICHEN

Bryn Dentinger, Curator of Mycology at the Natural History Museum of Utah (NHMU), along with students Kendra Autumn, Talia Backman, and Karrin Tennant, compiled research on fungi and lichen. Ellen Eiriksson, NHMU Citizen Science Manager, composed the wonderful first drafts of the text.

INVERTEBRATES (INSECTS, SPIDERS, AND FRIENDS)

Christy Bills, NHMU Entomology and Malacology Collections Manager, researched and composed lovely, lively drafts. She reviewed subsequent drafts along with NHMU Executive Director Jason Cryan. Professor Jack Longino of the School of Biological Sciences at the University of Utah reviewed the ant description and connected us to researcher and ant photographer Toby Hays.

MAMMALS

Austin Green, biologist and founder of Wasatch Wildlife Watch, compiled research and reviewed all the draft mammal accounts. Eric Rickart, Curator of Vertebrate Zoology at NHMU, advised on species selection and reviewed text as well. Kody Wallace shared her tremendous expertise on bats. George Oliver of the Utah Division of Wildlife Resources answered tricky historical questions. Denise Peterson of Utah Mountain Lion Conservation and Kirk Robinson of Western Wildlife Conservancy contributed their mountain lion knowledge.

REPTILES AND AMPHIBIANS

Alison Whiting, Curator of Herpetology at the Monte L. Bean Life Science Museum, and Jonny González, biologist, herp fan, and informal science educator at Red Butte Garden, both compiled research and provided comments on draft text. Jack Sites Jr., professor emeritus at Brigham Young University, advised on species selection.

STREET TREES

Tony Gliot, Salt Lake City's urban forester, and Jeran Farley, the State of Utah's Urban & Community Forest Coordinator, generously reviewed draft descriptions.

WILD PLANTS AND TREES

Alison Izaksonas, Herbarium Collections Manager at NHMU, compiled research for many of the plants. She and Daniel Murphy, Collections Manager at the Idaho Botanical Garden and author of the "Awkward Botany" blog, reviewed the draft accounts. Professor Mark Brunson of the Environment and Society Department at Utah State University reviewed and provided guidance on some of the less-beloved species. Biology Professor Emeritus William Gray at the University of Utah answered questions about several local plants.

FIELD TRIPS

Many people provided suggestions of possible field trip locations to feature in this book, including Julie Peck-Dabling, Bryan Fox, Aimee Horman, Lewis Kogan, Andrea Nelson, Heather McEntire, Suzie Middleton, Soren Simonsen, Chad Welch, Stefanie Zwygart, and the staff of many local city parks departments.

Others helped with research and reviewed draft descriptions, including Bruce Cox of Centerville City, Erin Haycock, Mark Jasumbak, Lewis Kogan, Cevan LeSieur, Keeli Marvel, NHMU Assistant Anthropology Collections Manager Anne Lawlor, Larisa Bowen and Andrea Nelson of The Nature Conservancy of Utah, Keith Hambrecht of the Utah Division of Forestry Fire and State Lands, Wendy Fisher of Utah Open Lands, Christopher Merritt and Elizabeth Hora of the Utah State Historic Preservation Office, Hayley Pace of Utah State Parks, and Diane Simmons, Melissa Stamp, and Paula Trater of the U.S. Bureau of Reclamation.

PHOTO AND ILLUSTATION CREDITS

Photographers shared wonderful images of species and places, including Dirk V. Baker, Colby Bryson, City Journals, Casey Clifford, Bryn Dentinger, Katrina Derieg, Jeran Farley, Robert Fischer, Austin Green, Toby Hays, Sarah Jack Hinners, Sean Hoover, Mark Johnston, Lewis Kogan, Jeff Langford, Tim Lee, Alec Lyons, Jack McEntire, Heather McEntire, Mary Miller, Matthew Mulvey, BJ Nichols, Celestin Philippe, Dawn Renee Farkas Prasad, Amy O'Connor, Eric Olsen, Rebecca Ray, Beach Ries, RiverRestoration, Brian Tonetti, Utah Division of Wildlife Resources, Wasatch Wildlife Watch, Ray Wheeler, and Alyson Wilkins. Sam Nelson advised on tree photography. And thanks to freelance photographer Kirstin Roper, who worked on this book and on the "Nature All Around Us" exhibit.

All illustrations by Casey Clifford

Amy O'Connor and Ray Wheeler, page 67 (top)
Beach Ries, page 9 (top)
BJ Nichols, pages 30, 137 (right)
Casey Clifford, page 33
Celestin Philippe, page 22
Dawn Renee Farkas Prasad, pages 206, 286 (right)
Dirk V. Baker, page 325 (bottom)
Eric Olsen, page 45
Jake McEntire, page 39
Jason Carey, pages 60, 61
Jeran Farley, page 189 (bottom)
Katrina Derieg, page 73 (right)
Mary Miller, page 73 (left)
NASA/Marshall Space Flight Center, page 49 (bottom)
NPS/Zion National Park, page 85
Robert Fischer, page 11 (top right)
Ron Stewart, Utah Division of Wildlife Resources, page 247 (bottom)
Russell, A. J. & O'Sullivan, T. H., photographer. (1869) Salt Lake City and Wahsatch Mountains / T. H. O'Sullivan, phot., 1869. [Photograph] Retrieved from the Library of Congress, page 47
Salt Lake City Public Lands Department, pages 53, 280

Scott Root, Utah Division of Wildlife Resources, page 323 (bottom)
Sean Hoover, page 153
Stuart Ruckman, pages 250, 252
Toby Hays, page 133 (top)
Tsu Dho Nimh/wikimedia, page 142 (bottom)
Utah State Historic Preservation Office, page 305 (right)
Utah State Historical Society, pages 48 (right), 56, 57, 269, 271 (top), 303 (top)
Wasatch Wildlife Watch, pages 287 (top), 299 (top)
www.RiverRestoration.com, pages 60, 61

Essayist
Brian Tonetti, pages 36, 58, 59, 60
Lewis Kogan, pages 7, 35, 51
Sarah Jack Hinners, page 69 (top)

iNaturalist
BJ Nichols, page 127
Dawn Renee Farkas Prasad, pages 16 (left), 215, 224
Heather McEntire, page 300 (left)
Jeff Langford, pages 21 (bottom), 78, 79, 86–89, 91, 92 (right), 94, 243 (top right)
Matthew Mulvey, PhD, pages 90, 109, 119, 131, 162 (left), 239, 251, 256 (bottom), 290 (bottom), 291 (left), 295 (bottom)
Rebecca Ray, pages 9 (bottom left), 121, 122, 129, 134 (right), 137 (left)

NHMU
Alec Lyons and Colby Bryson, page 48 (left)
Alyson Wilkins, page 305 (right)
Amelia Carter, pages 21 (top), 50, 66, 68, 174 (left), 179, 180 (top), 183 (left), 184 (right), 185, 187 (top), 191 (bottom), 203, 205, 209, 210, 217, 268, 270, 272, 274–276, 277 (top, bottom left), 285 (top), 313, 314, 315 (bottom)
Bryn Dentinger, pages 110 (right), 111, 112, 113, 117
Dawn Renee Farkas Prasad, pages 10, 192, 199, 221, 246 (right), 247 (left), 254, 255 (top), 256 (top), 261, 264 (left), 265 (top)
Ellen Eiriksson, pages 75, 282 (left)
Kirstin Roper, pages 9 (bottom right), 11 (top left, bottom), 15, 18, 25 (top), 27, 31, 32, 37, 38, 42, 65, 72, 74, 107, 176, 180 (bottom), 181, 184 (left), 219, 220, 233–236, 238, 240 (left), 242, 243 (left, right bottom), 247 (right), 248, 255 (bottom), 257, 259, 260, 279, 286 (left), 289, 290 (top), 291 (right),

294, 295 (top), 296, 298, 299 (bottom), 302, 303 (bottom), 304, 306, 308, 310, 311, 317, 319 (top), 320, 323 (top), 324, 325 (top), 326, 328–331, 346
Lisa Thompson, pages 64, 194 (left), 204, 225, 240 (right), 244 (right), 262, 264 (right), 265 (bottom), 266, 287 (bottom), 300 (right), 309
Mark Johnston, pages 277 (bottom right), 347
NHMU photographers, pages 46, 281, 282 (right)
Tim Lee, page 293

Shutterstock
512r, page 155
Ahturner, page 170 (bottom)
Annette Shaff, pages 28, 29
Apugach, pages 189 (top), 213
Arctic Flamingo, page 187 (right)
asturfauna, page 145
Bartow Photography, page 43 (left)
Beekeepx, page 182
BGSmith, page 154
Birdiegal, page 101
Borislav Borisov, page 81 (right)
Brandon Blinkenberg, page 125
Brian E Kushner, page 315 (top)
Checubus, page 41
Christian Buch, page 195
COULANGES, page 223 (right)
coxy58, page 158
CrackerClips Stock Media, page 123
Craig Chaddock, page 124 (right)
Danita Delimont, page 142 (top)
ddisq/Predrag Sepelj, page 43 (right)
Diana Lukyanova, page 177 (right)
Dimitry Taranets, page 198
Dotspencer, page 52
Dr.MYM, page 133 (bottom)
Eivor Kuchta, page 105
Elliotte Rusty Harold, page 23
Erik Agar, page 214
Fercast, page 102
Florian Teodor, page 126
fluidmediafactory, page 83
Gennady Grechishkin, page 143
Gerald A. DeBoer, page 49 (top)
Gerald Peplow, page 144
Govorov Evgeny, page 194 (right)
GTW, page 147 (right)
GypsyPictureShow, page 138
iliuta goean, page 170 (top)
Iwciagr, page 110 (middle)
Jack Bell Photography, page 149

SPECIAL THANKS

Special thanks to core book team members Casey Clifford, Amelia Carter, and Dawn Renee Farkas Prasad. Casey created the illustrated maps for the field trips and the cover illustrations and attended countless image selection meetings. Amelia arranged the meetings. She also tracked down, organized, and obtained permissions for hundreds of images. She took many photographs as well. Dawn helped Amelia navigate the vast NHMU exhibit photos archive and shot many photographs for the project.

Thanks to the many others at the Natural History Museum of Utah who supported this project in a myriad of ways.

INDEX

ABOUT THE EDITOR AND NHMU

Lisa Thompson is an exhibit developer and interpretive planner at the Natural History Museum of Utah, where she developed the "Nature All Around Us" exhibit. She is fascinated by how culture shapes the way we define nature and passionate about helping people connect to nature in their everyday lives.

The **Natural History Museum of Utah** is one of the leading scientific research and cultural institutions in the country. Established in 1963, the museum's ten permanent exhibitions are anchored by its state-of-the-art collections and research facilities containing more than 1.6 million objects. These collections are used in studies on geological, biological, and cultural diversity and the histories of living systems and human cultures within the Utah region. The museum hosts approximately 300,000 general visitors a year and broadens the reach of its mission through a variety of science-based outreach programs to communities and schools throughout Utah.